SOCIAL WORKERS IN POLITICAL OFFICE

Research in Social Work

Series Editors: **Anna Gupta**,
Royal Holloway, University of London,
UK, and **John Gal**, Hebrew University
of Jerusalem, Israel

Published together with the European Social Work Research Association (ESWRA), this series examines current, progressive and innovative research applications of familiar ideas and models in international social work research.

Also available in the series:

Social Work and Social Innovation
edited by **Jean Pierre Wilken**, **Anne Parpan-Blaser**, **Sarah Prosser**,
Suzan van der Pas and **Erik Jansen**

Living on the Edge
edited by **Samuel Keller**, **Inger Oterholm**,
Veronika Paulsen and **Adrian van Breda**

Migration and Social Work
edited by **Emilio José Gómez-Ciriano**, **Elena Cabiati**
and **Sofia Dedotsi**

When Social Workers Impact Policy and Don't Just Implement It
by **John Gal** and **Idit Weiss-Gal**

The Origins of Social Care and Social Work
by **Mark Henrickson**

Social Work Research Using Arts-Based Methods
edited by **Ephrat Huss** and **Eltje Bos**

Critical Gerontology for Social Workers
edited by **Sandra Torres** and **Sarah Donnelly**

Involving Service Users in Social Work Education, Research and Policy
edited by **Kristel Driessens** and **Vicky Lyssens-Danneboom**

Adoption from Care
edited by **Tarja Pösö**, **Marit Skivenes** and **June Thoburn**

Interprofessional Collaboration and Service User Participation
edited by **Kirsi Juhila**, **Tanja Dall**, **Christopher Hall** and **Juliet Koprowska**

The Settlement House Movement Revisited
edited by **John Gal**, **Stefan Köngeter** and **Sarah Vicary**

Social Work and the Making of Social Policy
edited by **Ute Klammer**, **Simone Leiber** and **Sigrid Leitner**

Find out more at:
policy.bristoluniversitypress.co.uk/
research-in-social-work

SOCIAL WORKERS IN POLITICAL OFFICE

A Comparative Perspective on Recruitment, Career Patterns and Social Advocacy

Edited by
Tobias Kindler, Sigrid Leitner,
Eva Maria Löffler and Klaus Stolz

First published in Great Britain in 2025 by

Policy Press, an imprint of
Bristol University Press
University of Bristol
1–9 Old Park Hill
Bristol
BS2 8BB
UK
t: +44 (0)117 374 6645
e: bup-info@bristol.ac.uk

Details of international sales and distribution partners are available at policy.bristoluniversitypress.co.uk

© Tobias Kindler, Sigrid Leitner, Eva Maria Löffler and Klaus Stolz 2025

The digital PDF and ePub versions of this title are available open access and distributed under the terms of the Creative Commons Attribution-NonCommercial-NoDerivatives 4.0 International licence (https://creativecommons.org/licenses/by-nc-nd/4.0/) which permits reproduction and distribution for non-commercial use without further permission provided the original work is attributed.

The open access funding of this book was provided by the Swiss National Science Foundation (grant 235372).

DOI: 10.51952/9781447373506

British Library Cataloguing in Publication Data
A catalogue record for this book is available from the British Library

ISBN 978-1-4473-7348-3 paperback
ISBN 978-1-4473-7349-0 ePub
ISBN 978-1-4473-7350-6 OA Pdf

The right of Tobias Kindler, Sigrid Leitner, Eva Maria Löffler and Klaus Stolz to be identified as editors of this work has been asserted by them in accordance with the Copyright, Designs and Patents Act 1988.

All rights reserved: no part of this publication may be reproduced, stored in a retrieval system, or transmitted in any form or by any means, electronic, mechanical, photocopying, recording, or otherwise without the prior permission of Bristol University Press.

Every reasonable effort has been made to obtain permission to reproduce copyrighted material. If, however, anyone knows of an oversight, please contact the publisher.

The statements and opinions contained within this publication are solely those of the editors and contributors and not of the University of Bristol or Bristol University Press. The University of Bristol and Bristol University Press disclaim responsibility for any injury to persons or property resulting from any material published in this publication.

Bristol University Press and Policy Press work to counter discrimination on grounds of gender, race, disability, age and sexuality.

Cover design: Bristol University Press
Front cover image: iStock/koto_feja

Contents

List of figures and tables		vi
Notes on contributors		viii
Acknowledgements		xii
1	Social workers in political office: conceptual framework and research agenda *Klaus Stolz and Sigrid Leitner*	1
2	Austria: social workers with political responsibility at the national level *Iris Kohlfürst*	12
3	Canada: social workers in the House of Commons *Anne-Marie McLaughlin*	30
4	Czechia: social workers as members of the Czech parliament *Agnieszka Zogata-Kusz and Tatiana Matulayová*	47
5	Finland: taking political office to a new level? *Christian Kroll, Sanni Salonen and Helena Blomberg*	64
6	Germany: between civic engagement and social advocacy *Eva Maria Löffler*	80
7	Israel: a limited presence on the national level *John Gal, Idit Weiss-Gal and Noa Binder-Eilat*	96
8	Italy: social workers in political office as a municipal phenomenon *Martina Francesconi and Riccardo Guidi*	112
9	Portugal: delayed political engagement and short terms of office *Francisco Branco*	129
10	Switzerland: strong representation of social workers in the cantonal and federal parliaments *Tobias Kindler*	150
11	United Kingdom: social workers in Westminster – party or profession? *Christin Reuter and Joanne Warner*	166
12	United States: opportunities and barriers for social work members of Congress *Shannon R. Lane and Allysha Bryant*	183
13	Comparative considerations on social workers in political office *Klaus Stolz, Sigrid Leitner and Tobias Kindler*	203
Index		216

List of figures and tables

Figures

5.1	Factors influencing the candidacy of county councillors and deputy councillors with a social worker background (%)	72
5.2	Views of social worker county councillors and deputy county councillors on the importance of social advocacy and opportunities to implement it in county councils (%)	75
9.1	Recruitment drivers for MPs	138
11.1	Number of SWMPs per election, 1992–2019	171
11.2	Number of SWMPs in comparison to MPs from other occupations, 1992–2015	173

Tables

2.1	Social workers in the Austrian parliament, 21st–27th legislative periods	20
2.2	Characteristics of social workers in the Austrian parliament and government, 21st–27th legislative periods	22
3.1	Social work practice experience of SWPs	37
3.2	SWPs' prior political experience	38
4.1	Characteristics of the social workers who have been members of the Parliament of the Czech Republic since 2006	53
4.2	MPs holding higher education degrees in selected helping professions, 2024	56
5.1	Social workers in the Finnish parliament	70
6.1	Social workers in national parliament, election periods 1–20	86
7.1	Social workers in the Knesset, terms 1–25	102
7.2	Gender, party affiliation, ethnicity and terms of office of social workers in the Knesset	104
7.3	Social welfare-related parliamentary activities of social workers in the Knesset	108
8.1	Basic characteristics of the interviewed SWHEOs at local level	118
9.1	Social workers elected to office in the Assembleia Nacional, 1934–74	134
9.2	Social workers elected to office in national and regional parliaments, legislative mandate VI to XIV, 1974–2028	135
9.3	Occupational groups in national parliament, legislative mandate XV, 2022–24	136
9.4	Sample of social workers elected to office at the municipal level, by position, 1990–93 to 2022–25	137

10.1	Characteristics of social workers in elected political office in the cantonal and national parliaments	156
10.2	Political and professional background of social workers in elected political office in the cantonal and national parliaments	159
11.1	Number and share of English constituencies represented by SWMPs and non-social worker Labour MPs, by constituency deprivation	172
11.2	Membership in social advocacy ministries and committees, 1992–2022	177
12.1	Social work members of Congress, 65th to 118th Congress	190
12.2	Social welfare-related legislation in the 118th Congress	197
13.1	Comparison of main characteristics of social work members of national parliaments	206

Notes on contributors

Noa Binder-Eilat is a social worker and a PhD student at Tel Aviv University, Israel. Her research focuses on political social work and social workers' policy engagement and policy practice in the political arena.

Helena Blomberg is Professor of Social Work at the Faculty of Social Sciences at the University of Helsinki, Finland. Her research interests include social workers' well-being, political engagement and attitudes towards welfare policies, as well as policy changes and agenda-setting power in the welfare state.

Francisco Branco is retired Associate Professor at the Catholic University of Portugal. He has a PhD in social work (specialising in social policy and social movements). He has taught on the history of social work and on social research and social policy. He is currently a lecturer on the inter-university PhD programme in social work at the Catholic University of Portugal and the University of Coimbra. His research focuses on poverty and public policies, especially citizenship, minimum social policies and child welfare. His research also looks at social work as a profession, the history of social work and political practice in social work.

Allysha Bryant is a political social worker and native New Yorker focused on dismantling structural injustices. She has served as council aide for District 33 of the New York City Council and was chosen as a doctoral policy fellow by the Council on Social Work Education in the United States. Currently, Allysha is Associate Director at Presbyterian Senior Services and leads NY Connects – Brooklyn, a resource hub for older adults and individuals with disabilities. She is pursuing a PhD in social welfare at Wurzweiler School of Social Work, and her research focuses on increasing political participation among marginalised groups.

Martina Francesconi holds a bachelor's degree in social work and social studies and a master's degree in sociology. She is currently working (through a research grant) at the Scuola Superiore Sant'Anna in Pisa Italy, where she conducts research on renewable energy communities and the involvement of third sector organisations. She also works for the Fondazione per la Coesione Sociale in Lucca, Italy, which focuses on projects for vulnerable people, particularly individuals with disabilities.

John Gal is Professor at The Paul Baerwald School of Social Work and Social Welfare at The Hebrew University of Jerusalem, Israel, and its former dean. He currently heads the welfare programme at the Taub Center for Social Policy Studies. His research focuses on social policy, social workers' policy engagement and the history of social work.

Riccardo Guidi is Associate Professor of Sociology at the University of Florence, Italy, where he teaches courses on social service organisations, policy practice for helping professions, and social policy. He is also co-convenor (with Idit Weiss-Gal and John Gal) of the Special Interest Group on Research on Social Work and Policy Engagement within the European Social Work Research Association. His research focuses primarily on social workers' policy engagement, social work professional organisations, welfare partnerships, volunteering and social participation.

Tobias Kindler is Research Associate at the IFSAR Institute of Social Work and Social Spaces at the Eastern Switzerland University of Applied Sciences and a PhD candidate at The Hebrew University of Jerusalem. His research focuses on social workers' policy engagement and policy practice.

Iris Kohlfürst is Professor at the University of Applied Sciences Upper Austria, involved in the bachelor's and master's social work programmes. Her teaching and research focus on ethics, theories and methods of social work, and political participation in social work. She is currently a board member of the Austrian Society for Social Work (ogsa).

Christian Kroll is Senior Lecturer in social work and social policy at the Swedish School of Social Science, University of Helsinki, Finland, and a reader in social work at Lund University, Sweden. His research interests include the legitimisation and legitimacy of welfare state reforms and attitude formation among the public, welfare state clients and professionals in a comparative perspective.

Shannon R. Lane is Professor-in-Residence at the University of Connecticut School of Social Work and the Director of the Nancy A. Humphreys Institute for Political Social Work. Her research focuses on political social work, social policy, macro practice, social work education and political justice.

Sigrid Leitner is Professor of Social Policy at the University of Applied Sciences Cologne, Germany. She is an expert in (comparative) research on gender effects of social policy and on varieties of familialism. Her recent research focuses on the policy engagement of social workers and social work organisations as well as the interest representation of vulnerable social groups.

Eva Maria Löffler is a social worker (MA), a postdoc at Cologne University of Applied Sciences and Professor of Social Work at International University Hamburg, Germany. Her research and teaching focus on the relationship between social work and social policy and the professional actions of social workers.

Tatiana Matulayová is Associate Professor at the Silesian University in Opava, Czech Republic. Her academic focus lies in the professionalisation of social work and innovative approaches to social work education.

Anne-Marie McLaughlin is Associate Dean of graduate programmes at the Faculty of Social Work, University of Calgary, Canada. Her practice background is in community mental health and child welfare in rural and northern communities. Her research interests are in professional social work practice, practice regulation and the translation of professional values into practice.

Christin Reuter is a researcher and PhD student in the Department of English Studies at Chemnitz University of Technology, Germany. Her research interests include British political culture, parliamentarianism, political careers and British party politics.

Sanni Salonen is a university teacher and a PhD student at the University of Turku, Finland. Her research focuses on social work students' and social workers' policy engagement and on child protection, particularly foster care and aftercare.

Klaus Stolz is a political scientist and professor of British and American social and cultural studies at Chemnitz University of Technology, Germany. He studied at the University of Freiburg, Germany, and the University of Edinburgh, United Kingdom, and taught at universities in Mannheim, Göttingen and Freiburg in Germany before moving to Chemnitz. He works in the field of comparative politics. His research interests include territorial politics, regionalism, nationalism, political careers and political professionalisation as well as all aspects of British politics.

Joanne Warner is Emerita Reader in Social Work at the University of Kent, United Kingdom. Her research interests include the politics of risk in social work, social work legitimacy and democratisation.

Idit Weiss-Gal is Professor at the Bob Shapell School of Social Work at Tel Aviv University, Israel, where she recently served as head. Her fields of research and teaching are social workers' policy engagement and the social work profession.

Agnieszka Zogata-Kusz is Assistant Professor in the Department of Christian Social Work at Palacký University Olomouc, Czech Republic. With a doctorate in political science, she focuses her research and teaching on macro practice in social work, particularly social workers' policy engagement. She also explores broader questions of civil society's policy engagement and migration and integration policies, occasionally linking them to policy practice.

Acknowledgements

This book project was based on an authors' workshop at Cologne University of Applied Sciences. The editors thank the Ministry of Culture and Science of the State of North Rhine-Westphalia for funding the workshop. In addition, the editors wish to acknowledge open access funding provided by the Swiss National Science Foundation (grant 235372).

1

Social workers in political office: conceptual framework and research agenda

Klaus Stolz and Sigrid Leitner

When Britain installed its welfare state in the wake of World War II, the British government was run by somebody who knew a thing or two about social policy and social services. The establishment of the free-to-all National Health Service, the expansion of the social insurance system (providing benefits for unemployment, sickness, maternity and retirement), the introduction of family allowance and the inception of a massive social housing programme were all overseen by Prime Minister Clement Attlee, the leader of the Labour Party at that time, who was also a former social worker and social work lecturer (Reeves and McIvor, 2014; Dickens, 2018). How did Attlee make the transition from social worker to elected professional politician? How important was his social work background and expertise for the formulation, advocacy and implementation of these social policy measures? Which other social policy programmes, in other times and national contexts, have benefited from elected politicians with a background in social work?

Social workers' impact on social policy is a burgeoning field of research at the interface of social work studies, social policy analysis and political science. The field is differentiated by various strands investigating not only the different 'stages, levels, modes and types of policy' but also the different 'routes that social workers choose to take in order to do so' (Gal and Weiss-Gal, 2023, p 29). Arguably, the most direct route into policy engagement for social workers is running for and eventually holding political office. This route entails participation in the authoritative decision-making process and thus provides social workers with the opportunity to directly influence decisions in favour of service users and the profession. Unlike other forms of social worker policy engagement, though, the route of holding elected office has only recently become the focus of academic scholarship (Weiss-Gal, 2017).

As this field of study is 'still in its infancy' (Gal and Weiss-Gal, 2023, p 29), empirical studies cover only a few countries: Canada (McLaughlin et al, 2019;

Greco, 2020), Germany (Leitner and Stolz, 2022; Löffler, 2023), Israel (Binder and Weiss-Gal, 2021), Switzerland (Amann and Kindler, 2021; 2022; Kindler and Amann, 2022; Demircali et al, 2023), the United Kingdom (Gwilym, 2017; Scourfield and Warner, 2022) and the United States (Lane, 2008; 2011; Lane and Humphreys, 2011; 2015; Meehan, 2018; 2019a; 2019b; 2021; Miller et al, 2021; Pence and Kaiser, 2022). Furthermore, these studies focus almost exclusively on factors that motivate social workers to run for and hold political office. Thus, we know that for social workers, the decision to engage in electoral politics is strongly influenced by social work education, social work practice (Gwilym, 2017; Greco, 2020; Binder and Weiss-Gal, 2021), gender (Lane and Humphreys, 2015; Meehan, 2018), age (Meehan, 2018), family background, biographical experiences (Gwilym, 2017; McLaughlin et al, 2019), social networks, psychological factors (Demircali et al, 2023) and membership of professional associations (Lane and Humphreys, 2011; Amann and Kindler, 2022; Binder and Weiss-Gal, 2021). What we know very little about, though, is to what extent social workers actually engage in this route, who does so, what facilitates and what hampers such an engagement, which offices are held and to what extent social workers use these offices for meaningful social advocacy that is in line with social work values and ethics.

This edited volume is a first attempt to systematically answer these questions for a number of liberal democracies. Based on a common conceptual framework, the country chapters draw together results of existing studies and analyse additional empirical data to provide readers with a country-specific image of social workers holding elected office. Thus, the volume fulfills the function of an academic handbook, a reference work with comprehensive information on single countries, contributing to a hitherto largely neglected field of study. This compendium is complemented by a final comparative chapter identifying major similarities and differences across countries and discussing potential explanations for the variations detected. Taking up major issues from our conceptual framework, this further advances the theoretical deliberations on social workers' policy engagement.

Conceptual framework

This section provides a first conceptual framework for the comparative study of social workers holding elected office. We start with a discussion on the definition, extent and structure of social work as a profession. This is followed by an account of our understanding of the institutional opportunity structures that social workers face when seeking elected office. Based on these structural features, we consider the political recruitment of social workers and their career patterns. Last but not least, we evaluate the chances for proactive social advocacy by social workers engaged in this distinct political pathway.

Social work as a profession

Any comparative study of social work and social workers has to start with a definition of the social work profession. As the educational and occupational pathways into social work differ considerably across countries, social workers in this project are defined as all those who have obtained an educational degree that identifies them as such. Social work education can be delivered by a range of further and higher education bodies, such as universities and colleges, which may be in the public, private and non-profit sectors. Some countries officially register examined social workers while others do not maintain a register. However, we expect the social work degree to be one that is formally recognised by the appropriate education authorities and regulators in each country.

Further variation exists with regard to the specific embedding of the social work profession into the national welfare state, including the social service sectors that social workers serve in, the employment structure (public/private), the relation between the profession of social work and other social professions, the working conditions (income, working time and so on) and the social status of social workers. These aspects might also be related to the general type of welfare regime a country belongs to. A large state-organised social service sector in the social democratic regime will impact the professionalisation of social work differently than the predominantly private sector services in the liberal regime or the reliance on family care in the service-lean conservative welfare regime. All these aspects of the occupational field provide a great variety of different qualifications, motives, incentives and opportunities to run (successfully) for elected office.

Institutional opportunity structures

From a neo-institutional perspective, political institutions and the careers of those who populate these institutions are intricately interrelated. In his classical account, Schlesinger (1966) depicts political institutions as opportunity structures conditioning individual career pathways and generating different collective career patterns in different countries. But how exactly does this work? According to Borchert (2011, pp 121–3), the career opportunities of a (would-be) politician in a given polity are defined by the three 'a's: the first, *availability*, captures the sheer number of existing political positions that are available and thus denotes a rather formal quality that does not vary across individual candidates or politicians; the second, *accessibility*, depicts the actual chance for candidates to obtain these positions; and the third, *attractiveness*, refers to the properties these positions come with (status, power, salary and so on). These latter two dimensions vary considerably across individual candidates as party, gender or even former occupation may alter individual chances for particular offices as well as individual assessments of them.

The political opportunity structure for social workers – that is, the framework defining incentives and chances for them to (successfully) run for political office – thus consists of a complex web of general and social work-specific institutional features. The most general of those institutions is the state structure, which depicts the different territorial levels of government – local, regional, national – the policy fields and the legislative competences they have and their constitutional position. Another important institutional feature is the system of government, including the relationship between executive and legislative branch (presidential versus parliamentary) and the internal structure of both branches (for example, the committee system). Further elements of this structure include the electoral system (majoritarian vs proportional representation), the party system and the concrete roles and functions political parties and interest groups fulfill (for a more detailed description of these structures, see Borchert, 2011, pp 123–8).

For a social worker standing for political office, these opportunity structures are further specified and complemented by the welfare regime that, according to Esping-Anderson's (1990) typology, has taken hold in each political system. Thus, liberal welfare regimes with high levels of social inequality might motivate social workers to engage more actively in elective politics due to a strong sense of responsibility to lobby for socially disadvantaged groups that usually do not have any other lobbying power. Social democratic regimes, though, might be more responsive to topics of social inequality, and here social workers may not feel such a strong pressure for political engagement. Finally, conservative regimes might rely on organised interests in the corporative processes of policy making, diminishing the role of individual social workers and requiring collective interest groups, like the big welfare associations in Germany, to take action. Gal and Weiss-Gal (2023, p 45) state that the manner in which the welfare state affects the policy engagement of social workers is not clear-cut, although (scarce) existing data suggests that policy engagement is more likely in developed welfare states.

With regard to the conventional opportunity structures, we might expect to see more social workers in parliament where parties of the Left (advocating proactive social policy) are stronger. We might also expect them in greater numbers at the level of government that deals with social work policy (for example, fields like housing, child and youth welfare and so on), which very often is the local or regional rather than the national/federal level. Fully professionalised political offices might be very attractive for social workers in positions below management level, while those in management and leadership positions might find it easier to get access to more influential political positions within the social work profession, and they might also be more willing to return to their former job after holding a political office.

Political recruitment

Political recruitment in liberal democracies has changed significantly over time. This is particularly the case for the educational and occupational background of parliamentarians. In the longue durée, we have witnessed a change from parliamentary bodies filled with noblemen and representatives of high social status to a more class-based form of parliamentary representation, including direct representation of disadvantaged classes. A further shift, though, has seen a development towards the highly educated middle class. In Europe, the era of state intervention and welfare state expansion has elevated the service sector and especially the public sector to become the most privileged recruiting ground (Cotta and Best, 2000, pp 497–504). For this time period, the profession of social work may be seen as another politics-facilitating occupation, alongside occupations such as those related to the law, teaching and journalism (King, 1981, pp 260–1). More recent studies have depicted a diversification of this recruitment pattern in liberal democracies (Best and Vogel, 2014, pp 65–8) with a decline of law and teaching backgrounds and an increase of representatives from the academic fields of economics, public administration, humanities and the social sciences (Gaxie, 2017, p 499).

A systematic estimation of the current role of social work as a recruitment pool for elected politicians would have to include several comparative perspectives. More than the absolute number of former social workers in a political body, it is their share in relation to the overall number of representatives as well as in relation to other occupational groups that provides some meaningful insight. Shifting from a political recruitment to an occupational opportunities perspective, we might, of course also ask what share of all social workers actually engage in elected politics. Finally, comparison across time helps to assess the current numbers and to discern possible trends.

Thus, apart from the extent of social workers' engagement, a more comprehensive picture would further identify patterns of recruitment and representation with regard to the types of social workers who are more or less prone to engage actively in electoral politics. Potentially relevant variables might be the individual's field of social work, their occupational position and whether they are working in the public or private sector.

Political career patterns

Political career patterns vary considerably across countries. In most liberal democracies, though, politics has become a profession with a more or less clearly defined career ladder to be pursued. Entry into politics works via a kind of apprenticeship in unpaid party and/or local government offices or via paid staff positions. These positions facilitate access to more powerful and prestigious, and usually better remunerated, parliamentary mandates or government offices at the regional and national levels (sometimes even local government offers professional political career opportunities). At this stage, politicians normally leave their former occupation (in our case, social work) to pursue a full-time and long-term career in professional politics. On an individual level, political professionalisation entails three major aspects: time commitment, remuneration and a long-term interest in career maintenance and advancement (see Borchert, 2003, pp 8–9).

Professional political careers might entail a great number of posts at different territorial levels (local, regional, national) and in different institutions (party, parliament, government). They might link these positions in different forms, producing patterns of frequent multidirectional movements, clear unidirectional pathways or even long-term static careers in a single position or institution (see Stolz, 2003). After life in full-time politics, politicians usually retire, often maintaining some voluntary or honorary political positions. In some cases, they are rewarded for their service to party and/ or country with another representative/administrative 'retirement position' that may even come with a full salary.

A comprehensive study of social workers in elected office would have to identify their particular forms of individual professionalisation and their political career pathways, focusing on their potential deviations from the general pattern in each country and the potential reasons for these deviations. Social workers may or may not be found disproportionally in non- or semi-professionalised political positions; they may or may not direct their careers towards a particular level of government (local, regional, national) or particular professional positions (such as a government position with a social policy remit). Social workers may pursue longer or shorter political careers. They may keep their social work job for short or long periods concurrently with a political mandate, or they may return to their former (social work) occupation after leaving a fully paid political position. The more the political careers of social workers resemble general career patterns, the less we may expect the individuals to maintain social work-specific values and interests.

Social advocacy

According to the global definition of social work (International Federation of Social Workers and International Association of Schools of Social Work, 2014), social advocacy is one of the main aims of the profession. In line with a common understanding of the concept, the study of social workers' advocacy is often reduced to their lobbying – that is, extra-parliamentary – activities. However, advocacy may also be understood as an essential part of political representation (Urbinati, 2000). From this perspective, holding political office could be a powerful instrument through which social workers pursue their social advocacy mission. To what extent those who run for office are actually motivated by this aim and to what extent they are successful in pursuing it once they hold political office, of course, remain open empirical questions. Following Max Weber (1958, p 84), we might speculate that once social workers start to live not only 'for' but also 'of' politics, they may also strive 'to make politics a permanent source of income'. In replacing social work with politics, though, their former occupational background might become increasingly irrelevant. In their new professional opportunity structure, the interests of their former clients have to compete not only with the public interests and party interests but also with individual career interests.

A comprehensive analysis of the substantive representation of vulnerable groups (that is, social advocacy) by (former) social workers is a very complex and difficult task. In this first account, we approach the question via two different sets of proxy indicators. First, we might explore their involvement in parliamentary committees, their executive positions (for example, as state or federal ministers and as city mayors) and their contributions to parliamentary papers, questions and debates. Are former social workers members of commissions and committees dealing with social policy issues? Do they initiate and support social policy reforms? Do they resist cuts in social spending or even attempt to improve public spending on social benefits? A second crucial aspect is the linkage politicians maintain with their former social work profession. Do politicians continue to practise social work concurrent to their mandate, and do they maintain close connections with former colleagues and social work organisations? A potential estrangement from the field of social work may be indicated by the lack of such close contacts and the failure to return to the field after their political term ends. Again, social workers' willingness and their chance to pursue social advocacy in the realm of elected politics may be seen to vary considerably across countries.

Structure of the book

Holding political office is a highly important form of policy engagement in all countries that permit free and open elections – that is, in all liberal democracies. As we cannot cover all of them in this book, we opted for a structured comparison of selected case studies offering variation across a wide range of potentially relevant institutional features. One of the most meaningful categorisations of countries in this respect remains Esping-Anderson's (1990) three worlds of welfare capitalism. To reflect this (potential) variation, we have assembled cases of liberal welfare regimes (Canada, the United Kingdom, the United States), conservative welfare regimes (Austria, Germany, Switzerland) and social democratic welfare regimes (Finland), and we have even included three cases of the disputed subcategory of Southern European regimes (Israel, Italy, Portugal) and one post-communist regime (Czech Republic). In addition, our case selection provides considerable variation with regard to what scholars of political careers generally perceive as the major features of the institutional opportunity structures for career politicians (Borchert, 2003). Our sample includes federal (Austria, Canada, Germany, Switzerland and the United States) and unitary (Czech Republic, Finland, Israel, Italy and Portugal) states, countries with proportional (Austria, Czech Republic, Finland, Germany, Israel and Switzerland) and plurality (Canada, Italy, the United Kingdom and the United States) electoral systems as well as parliamentary (Austria, Canada, Czech Republic, Finland, Germany, Israel, Italy, Portugal and the United Kingdom) and presidential (Switzerland and the United States) systems of government. Despite this wide range of institutional variation, we lay no claim on universality, as our case selection excludes large geographic areas (for example, Africa, Asia and Latin America) as well as important distinctions in terms of political economy (for example, the Global South).

As none of these features seems to ultimately determine the way social workers get into elected office, pursue political careers in these offices and behave as elected politicians, we have arranged country chapters in alphabetical order. Each country case study follows the template presented earlier, providing sections on: (1) Social work as a profession; (2) Institutional opportunity structures; (3) Political recruitment; (4) Political career patterns; and (5) Social advocacy. The closing chapter sketches out major similarities and differences between the country cases, identifies prominent patterns, discusses potential explanations for the detected variations and, based on these insights, considers ideas for further research.

References

Amann, K. and Kindler, T. (eds) (2021) *Sozialarbeitende in der Politik. Biografien, Projekte und Strategien parteipolitisch engagierter Fachpersonen der Sozialen Arbeit*, Frank & Timme.

Amann, K. and Kindler, T. (2022) 'Social workers in politics – a qualitative analysis of factors influencing social workers' decision to run for political office', *European Journal of Social Work*, 25(4): 655–67.

Best, H. and Vogel, L. (2014) 'The sociology of legislators and legislatures', in S. Martin, T. Saalfeld and K. Strom (eds) *The Oxford Handbook of Legislative Studies*, Oxford University Press, pp 59–81.

Binder, N. and Weiss-Gal, I. (2021) 'Social workers as local politicians in Israel', *British Journal of Social Work*, 52(5): 2797–813.

Borchert, J. (2003) 'Professional politicians: Towards a comparative perspective', in J. Borchert and J. Zeiss (eds) *The Political Class in Advanced Democracies*, Oxford University Press, pp 1–25.

Borchert, J. (2011) 'Individual ambition and institutional opportunity: A conceptual approach to political careers in multi-level systems', *Regional and Federal Studies*, 21(2): 117–40.

Cotta, M. and Best, H. (2000) 'Between professionalization and democratization: A synoptic view on the making of the European representative', in H. Best and M. Cotta (eds) *Parliamentary Representatives in Europe 1848–2000: Legislative Recruitment and Careers in Eleven European Countries*, Oxford University Press, pp 493–526.

Demircali, S., Kindler, T. and Amann, K. (2023) 'Social workers' intention to hold elected political office: A quantitative study based on the theory of planned behavior', *European Journal of Social Work*, 27(5): 977–87.

Dickens, J. (2018) 'Clement Attlee and the social service idea: Modern messages for social work in England', *British Journal of Social Work*, 48(1): 5–20.

Esping-Andersen, G. (1990) *The Three Worlds of Welfare Capitalism*, Princeton University Press.

Gal, J. and Weiss-Gal, I. (2023) *When Social Workers Impact Policy and Don't Just Implement It*, Policy Press.

Gaxie, D. (2017) 'Political and social background of political elites', in H. Best and J. Higley (eds) *The Palgrave Handbook of Political Elites*, Palgrave Macmillan, pp 498–506.

Greco, C. (2020) *'I've Got to Run Again': Experiences of Social Workers Seeking Municipal Office in Ontario*, Master's thesis, Wilfried Laurier University, Theses and Dissertations (Comprehensive), 2306, Available from: https://scholars.wlu.ca/etd/2306

Gwilym, H. (2017) 'The political identity of social workers in neoliberal times', *Critical and Radical Social Work*, 5(1): 59–74.

International Federation of Social Workers and International Association of Schools of Social Work (2014) 'Global definition of social work', Available from: www.ifsw.org/what-is-social-work/global-definition-of-social-work

Kindler, T. and Amann, K. (2022) 'Strategies of social workers' policy engagement—a qualitative analysis among Swiss social workers holding elected office', *Journal of Policy Practice and Research*, 3(4): 302–15.

King, A. (1981) 'The rise of the career politician – and its consequences', *British Journal of Political Science*, 11(3): 249–85.

Lane, S.R. (2008) *Electing the Right People: A Survey of Elected Social Workers and Candidates*, Doctoral dissertation, University of Connecticut, Digital Commons@UConn, Available from: https://digitalcommons.lib.uconn.edu/dissertations/AAI3351337

Lane, S.R. (2011) 'Political content in social work education as reported by elected social workers', *Journal of Social Work Education*, 47(1): 53–72.

Lane, S.R. and Humphreys, N.A. (2011) 'Social workers in politics: A national survey of social work candidates and elected officials', *Journal of Policy Practice*, 10(3): 225–44.

Lane, S.R. and Humphreys, N.A. (2015) 'Gender and social workers' political activity', *Affilia: Journal of Women and Social Work*, 30(2): 232–45.

Leitner, S. and Stolz, K. (2022) 'German social workers as professional politicians: Career paths and social advocacy', *European Journal of Social Work*, advance online publication, doi: 10.1080/13691457.2022.2117138

Löffler, E.M. (2023) 'Aus der Sozialen Arbeit in die Politik. Der professionelle und politische Werdegang von Sozialarbeiter:innen in der Landes- und Bundespolitik', *Soziale Arbeit*, 5(72): 176–83.

McLaughlin, A.M., Rothery, M. and Kuiken, J. (2019) 'Pathways to political engagement: Interviews with social workers in elected office', *Canadian Social Work Review*, 36(1): 25–43.

Meehan, P. (2018) '"I think I can … Maybe I can … I can't": Social work women and local elected office', *Social Work*, 63(2):145–52.

Meehan, P. (2019a) *Making Change Where It Counts: Social Work and Elected Office*, Doctoral dissertation, University of Michigan, Deep Blue Documents, Available from: https://hdl.handle.net/2027.42/151544

Meehan, P. (2019b) 'Political primacy and MSW students' interest in running for office: What difference does it make?', *Advances in Social Work*, 19(2): 276–89.

Meehan, P. (2021) 'Water into wine: Using social policy courses to make MSW students interested in politics', *Journal of Social Work Education*, 57(2): 357–71.

Miller, D.B., Jennings, E. and Angelo, J. (2021) 'Social workers as elected officials: Advocacy at the doorstep', *Journal of Social Work Education*, 57(3): 455–63.

Pence, E.K. and Kaiser, M.L. (2022) 'Elected office as a social work career trajectory: Insights from political social workers', *Journal of Social Work Education*, advance online publication, doi: 10.1080/10437797.2021.2019639

Reeves, R. and McIvor, M. (2014) 'Clement Attlee and the foundations of the British welfare state', *Renewal*, 22(3–4): 42–59.

Schlesinger, J.A. (1966) *Ambition and Politics: Political Careers in the United States*, Rand McNally.

Scourfield, J. and Warner, J. (2022) 'Knowing where the shoe pinches: Three Labour ministers reflect on their experiences in social work and politics', *Critical and Radical Social Work*, 10(3): 484–90.

Stolz, K. (2003) 'Moving up, moving down: Political careers across territorial levels', *European Journal of Political Research*, 42(2): 223–48.

Urbinati, N. (2000) Representation as advocacy: A study of democratic deliberation, *Political Theory*, 28(6): 758–86.

Weber, M. (1958 [1919]) 'Politics as a vocation', in H.H. Gerth and C. Wright Mills (eds) *From Max Weber*, Oxford University Press, pp 77–128.

Weiss-Gal, I. (2017) 'Social workers' policy engagement: A review of the literature', *International Journal of Social Welfare*, 26(3): 285–98.

2

Austria: social workers with political responsibility at the national level

Iris Kohlfürst

Connecting social work practice with policy engagement has a long tradition in the Austrian social work profession. The professionalisation of social work in Austria was pioneered by Ilse Arlt (1876–1960), who developed a theory of welfare and established that the prevailing policies are primarily responsible for the satisfaction of basic human needs. In addition, she regarded the welfare schools she founded as research institutions for fundamental research, particularly in the field of poverty, which she considered to be of great importance for the development of social policy (Frey, 2023). The notion of social work as a human rights profession with a political mandate has recently been reaffirmed in Austria. This is evidenced by the document *Ethical Principles of Social Work: A Framework for Social Work and Social Pedagogy* – published in 2024 by two Austrian social work professional organisations representing practice (the Austrian Professional Association of Social Work – obds) and science (the Austrian Society for Social Work – ogsa) – which explicitly mentions the political dimension of social work (obds and ogsa, 2024). To illustrate, the document stipulates that social workers should discern unfavourable sociopolitical developments and initiate and endorse political processes in a manner that enables active involvement in public sector planning processes (obds and ogsa, 2024).

One way social workers can engage in the political sphere is to hold a political office at the local, state or national level. The most prominent Austrian example of this is Johannes Rauch, a social worker who served as Federal Minister for Social Affairs, Health, Care and Consumer Protection from 2022 to 2025. This chapter outlines the avenues for holding political office at the national level, the proportion of social workers who assume such positions, their identifiable career patterns and the extent to which social work objectives are pursued in their political activities. A multi-method research approach was used to obtain comprehensive data (Flick, 2011). In addition to online document analysis, six social workers were interviewed in spring 2024 using a self-developed guide (Lamnek and Krell, 2016), and the content was analysed (Kuckartz, 2018). At the time, the interviewees were holding or had previously held political office at national, state or local levels.

They were chosen to ensure a diverse range of experiences (covering 4 to 15 years in office), with two interviewees selected from each of the three levels. Their time spent in social work practice ranged from 12 to 25 years. The results obtained through both research approaches were summarised thematically for the purpose of this chapter.

Social work as a profession

To understand the situation in Austria, it is important to distinguish between the terms social work and social pedagogy. Social work (as in *Sozialarbeit* – one word) has its historical roots in caring for the poor, while social pedagogy (*Sozialpädagogik*) has its origins in pedagogical context (Scheipl, 2003; Spitzer, 2010; obds, nd). The term *Soziale Arbeit* (two words; also translates as 'social work') unites the two strands and can therefore be seen as an umbrella term (Schilling and Klus, 2018). This semantic differentiation is not reflected in the English language. In this chapter, the term social work refers to both strands; where necessary, the terms social work/social pedagogy are distinguished.

In contrast to other helping professions, such as psychology or nursing, there is no comprehensive professional law in the context of social work. Prior to spring 2024, social work/social pedagogy was not a protected profession. Consequently, regardless of their qualifications, anyone working in the social sector could call themselves a social worker/social pedagogue. In March 2024, the Austrian parliament enacted the Social Work Designation Act (Sozialarbeits-Bezeichnungsgesetz, 2024), which establishes the qualifications required to hold the title of a social worker or social pedagogue. Qualification as a social worker according to this law is possible at nine universities of applied sciences and two private universities in Austria as part of a corresponding bachelor's or master's degree programme. Previously, the two-year and then three-year training programmes were offered at the former academies of social work (Fleischer and Trenkwalder-Egger, 2023; Hefel and Kohlfürst, 2023). From March 2027, graduates who have only completed a master's degree in social work (that is, without a bachelor's degree in social work) will have to provide proof of 60 European Credit Transfer and Accumulation System credits from the basic social work programme to be able to call themselves a social worker. To be able to call oneself a social pedagogue under the Social Work Designation Act, it is necessary to complete an appropriate training or study programme at the colleges of social pedagogy, pedagogical colleges, universities (Spitzer, 2011) or universities of applied sciences. There is not yet a binding core curriculum that regulates the necessary training content in relation to social work (Hefel and Kohlfürst, 2023); representatives of universities of applied sciences, universities and social work professional associations are currently working on a joint document (ogsa, nd). For the purposes of this chapter, social workers are understood as professionals who have completed the relevant training in accordance with the law and are, therefore, entitled to use the title.

In Austria, several professional organisations of social work with varying foci and target groups can be identified (Kulke et al, forthcoming). In some cases, a distinction is made between social work and social pedagogy. In terms of membership, the largest organisation is the obds (with around 1,100 members at the time of writing), which represents the interests of both social workers and social pedagogues. Its focus is on professional policy aspects of social work in Austria, including the legal protection of social workers, quality assurance and the fulfilment of the objectives of social work. The ogsa has a more academic focus and aims to promote the discipline and profession of social work through the further development of theory, research and teaching. Other organisations include the Professional Association for Academic Social Pedagogy (ÖFAS), the Austrian Social Pedagogy Network, the Professional Association of Austrian Social Pedagogues (BÖS), the Professional Association of Educational Scientists (BEB), the Austrian Committee for Social Work, the Austrian Society for Research and Development in Education (ÖFEB) – Social Pedagogy section, and the Austrian Society for Sociology – Social Work section. Membership in all these organisations is voluntary.

The precise number of social workers is not officially recorded; it was estimated in 2023 that 42,883 social workers in Austria had completed the training required under the Social Work Designation Act (obds, 2023). In terms of the gender distribution of all employees in the health and social sector, 78.2 per cent are women (Statistik Austria, nd-a). However, it is unclear what share of these employees are currently engaged in social work activities. Based on the total workforce of 4,482,900 individuals who were not self-employed in 2023 (Statistik Austria, 2024), it can be estimated that approximately 1 per cent of all employees are social workers. Social Economy Austria (Sozialwirtschaft Österreich – SWÖ) is an association of Austrian social and health care companies that has attracted numerous organisations from the social work sector as members. The objective of the SWÖ is to guarantee standardised working conditions for the private social care and health care sector (SWÖ, nd). In 2006, a collective agreement was established for the first time with the objective of regulating various aspects of employment, including normal working hours, overtime and remuneration. As reported in 2024, the standard working week for full-time employees is 37 hours, with the gross annual salary ranging from just under EUR 44,000 to EUR 65,400 (SWÖ, 2024). In comparison, the median gross annual income of full-time employees amounted to EUR 47,855 in 2022 (Statistik Austria, nd-b). Employers in child and youth welfare are mainly public bodies; in addition, there are numerous organisations of varying sizes that are financed by state subsidies (Halfar, 2011) and offer social work services in areas such as health, family, social affairs, justice, education and schools, integration and equality, and the labour market.

Institutional opportunity structures

To delineate the institutional opportunities for holding political office, it is necessary to first describe the basic features of the political system in Austria. The Austrian constitution differentiates five principles that shape the country's political structure: (1) the democratic principle – the decision-making process is based on popular sovereignty; (2) the republican principle – the state is a public matter; (3) the rule of law principle – state administration may only be exercised on the basis of the law; (4) the federal principle – there is division of political power between the national government and the nine federal states; and (5) the principle of separation of powers – state functions must be organisationally separate. Furthermore, the Austrian state has additional objectives, including everlasting neutrality. Austria has been a member of the European Union (EU) since 1995 (Ucakar et al, 2017).

Austria is a parliamentary democracy (Parlament Österreich, nd-a), with general elections held at regular intervals to represent the people at local, state, national and EU levels. At 1 January 2024, the population of Austria was approximately 9,160,000, with almost 20 per cent of this number holding non-Austrian citizenship (Migration.gv.at, nd) and thus being excluded from Austrian elections at national and state levels. Instruments of direct democracy are the petition for referendum, the plebiscite and the referendum (Ucakar et al, 2017).

At national level, two chambers – the National Council (Nationalrat) and the Federal Council (Bundesrat) – form the Austrian parliament. The National Council is elected directly by the people. A legislative period typically lasts five years. In the event of the National Council dissolving itself or receiving a vote of no confidence, a new election may be held prematurely. The main task of the National Council is to discuss, scrutinise, draft and pass laws (Parlament Österreich, nd-b). The work of parliamentary committees plays a key role in this, as most of the items on the agenda are discussed there before being voted on in the plenary sessions. Although the number and thematic focus of the committees are stipulated by the constitution, they primarily mirror the ministerial structure and are newly elected in each legislative period.[1] Their composition reflects the strength of the parliamentary party groups, called 'clubs', in the plenary sessions. The clubs send their policy area specialists and experts to the committees (Parlament Österreich, nd-c). The Federal Council consists of 60 members and represents the participation of the federal states in national legislation. The term of office of the mandataries is, therefore, dependent on the legislative period of the respective parliaments at state level (*Landtage*). The Federal Council has relatively weak participation rights; its right to object to legislative decisions of the National Council generally only leads to postponement (Parlament Österreich, nd-d).

The Austrian national government (the chancellor, the vice-chancellor and a varying number of ministers) is not directly elected but appointed by the Austrian president (after nomination by the chancellor); most members of parliament resign their mandate when they take up a government post. It is also possible to take up a government post without a parliamentary mandate, although this is exceptional (Parlament Österreich, nd-e). The Austrian president, directly elected by the people, is the head of state and in addition to representative duties has the formal power to appoint or dismiss the government, reject proposed ministers or dissolve the National Council (Parlament Österreich, nd-f).

Austrian democracy is a party democracy – parties are considered the most important political actors and, as institutions, promote or end political careers (Jenny, 2023). Membership of or affiliation to a political party is a requirement for obtaining a mandate in the parliament; conversely, members of parliament are bound to the respective party in terms of their activities and voting behaviour (*Klubzwang*). During a legislative period, a member of parliament may give up or lose their party membership; in this case, the person remains in the National Council or Federal Council, but has a free mandate.

The following parties were represented in the 27th legislative period (2019–24): the Austrian People's Party (ÖVP; 71 mandates or 38.8 per cent); the Social Democratic Party of Austria (SPÖ; 40 mandates or 21.9 per cent); the Freedom Party of Austria (FPÖ; 30 mandates or 16.4 per cent); The Greens – The Green Alternative (Die Grüne; 26 mandates or 14.2 per cent); and NEOS – The New Austria and Liberal Forum (15 mandates or 8.2 per cent). One person, a former member of the FPÖ, has a free mandate (0.5 per cent). In this period, the ÖVP and the Greens were responsible for government, based on a coalition agreement (Parlament Österreich, nd-b). Generally, the lines of political conflict do not run between parliament and the government, but rather between the actors of the governing parties (in the 27th legislative period, this is members of parliament and members of the government of the ÖVP and the Greens) and the parliamentarians of the opposition parties (the SPÖ, the FPÖ and NEOS; Praprotnik, 2023). Austrian politics is characterised by what is known as 'social partnership', in which the main economic interest groups of employers and employees cooperate with each other and with the government to contribute to economic growth and social peace (Sozialpartner, nd).

Political offices for social workers are possible in two contexts. On the one hand, there are functions that are not directly legitimised by public elections, such as participation in political parties or social partnership organisations and membership of government at state or national levels. On the other hand, it is possible to take on a political office that is legitimised by an election. The formal prerequisite for this is the right to stand for election, which Austrian citizens receive from the age of 18. Similar possibilities also exist at EU level. Non-Austrian EU citizens whose main place of residence is in Austria may stand as a candidate in local elections, but not in state or national elections. According to Borchert (2011), in addition to this basic *availability*, the *accessibility* and *attractiveness* of political offices are crucial factors in taking up a career – this is discussed in more detail later.

Regarding accessibility, the interviewed social workers were asked to give their personal assessment of the ease of access to political office at national level. They reported that it seemed easy in some cases, but it was more challenging in others. First, the individual had to find a party they could identify with. Then, there is competition and sometimes very hierarchical structures with a seniority principle to be negotiated, accompanied by uncertainty about (re-)election.

Regarding attractiveness, participants were asked to name possible challenges in taking up a political office. They described the political system as toxic, as it is about power, competition and the mechanisms that go with it. Only political majorities are decisive, and the focus is on individual interests rather than on the common good. In terms of participation in government, participants expressed that the nature of the compromises that have to be made can be questionable. And in the role of opposition, policy change can be suggested, but if it is not supported by the government, there are limited opportunities for change. A great deal of pragmatism and realism is therefore required, recognising that not everything can be improved. It was also noted that the culture of dialogue has changed in the last years, with the climate becoming more aggressive and 'black and white' thinking prevailing. In addition, being in the public eye and being held accountable – something which is intensified by social media – was described as a challenge. Individuals may have to endure blame for failed projects that were unsuccessful because of resistance from coalition partners. The lack of opportunities to work in politics at a higher level on a part-time basis and, even more, the expectation to be constantly available were also seen as challenging. The lack of cross-party formats for learning political competences was also noted. One interviewee observed that regardless of party affiliation, individual health suffers. While politicians start out fresh and fit, over time they develop weight problems, sleep disorders and symptoms of stress. Furthermore, some reported that it is not desirable to take on a political office at national level as this involves many processes of negotiation with interest groups/lobbyists and less direct interaction with citizens. One interviewee saw local politics as being closer to the style of social work.

To determine the factors that contribute to success in taking up a political office, the interviewees were asked about their motivations and circumstances leading to their initial engagement in politics. All of them demonstrated a fundamental interest in politics, with some already having been politically active at school or university or in social movements. Nearly all interviewees confirmed that they had been approached by individuals already engaged in the political field. It seems crucial to receive a personal request or invitation to become more involved in politics. The desire to expand one's network or, in the case of a relocation, to navigate a new living environment, the opportunity to pursue a significant career shift, personal curiosity and the chance to explore new opportunities were key motivators for becoming engaged in politics. One social worker mentioned that it was an honour to have been entrusted with their respective role. Furthermore, one participant had been recognised previously for their professional expertise as a social worker and hoped to contribute to policy development. The desire to align personal values and ideas about politics with the professional role was also mentioned as a motivation to take on a political career. The interviewees expressed a desire to play an active role in shaping evidence-based policy, contributing new ideas, campaigning against injustice and improving people's living conditions.

Political recruitment

In the 27th legislative period (2019–24), there were two social workers in political office at national level. These were Stefan Schennach, member of the Federal Council (Parlament Österreich, nd-g), and Johannes Rauch, who, as mentioned earlier, held the position of Federal Minister for Social Affairs, Health, Care and Consumer Protection from March 2022 to March 2025 (Parlament Österreich, nd-h). An analysis of the National Council shows the following composition regarding the professional background of political functionaries: of the 183 mandates, 35 members (19.1 per cent) had a background in law professions, 25 members (15.3 per cent) had a business background and 20 members (11.0 per cent) came from the agricultural sector (Parlament Österreich, nd-i). No member of the National Council had a background in social work. Based on the social workers making up a 1 per cent share of the total working population in Austria, as noted earlier, social workers are (1) over-represented in the government (6.7 per cent, with one chancellor and 14 ministers); (2) under-represented in the National Council (0 per cent, with 183 members of parliament; here, it is estimated that about two members of parliament are from the social work sector); and (3) over-represented in the Federal Council (1.6 per cent, with 60 members of parliament). If the personnel changes over the course of the entire legislative period are taken into account, the figures slightly change: social workers were (1) over-represented in the government (4.3 per cent out of a total of now 23 people who held a position as chancellor and/or minister); (2) under-represented in the National Council (still 0 per cent out of a total of now 215 people); and (3) slightly under-represented in the Federal Council (0.9 per cent out of a total of now 114 people).

Due to the small number of social workers in political office at the national level in the 27th legislative period, the six legislative periods before that were also analysed to determine the extent to which social workers have served in national political office. Table 2.1 gives an overview of these seven legislative periods with the corresponding government coalition and the actual number of social workers in the Austrian parliament as well as their names, gender and party affiliations. Apart from Johannes Rauch, no social workers were active in the respective governments.

As shown in Table 2.1, a total of 11 social workers were involved in politics at national level in the 25-year period from 1999 to 2024. Table 2.2 characterises these 11 people in more detail using various variables. As Efgani Dönmez held positions in both the Federal Council and the National Council, he is counted twice, resulting in a total of 12 cases.

A comparison of the seven social workers in the National Council with all members of the National Council in the 27th legislative period shows that in terms of gender distribution, women were over-represented in the group of social workers: just under 40 per cent of all members of the National Council were female (Parlament Österreich, nd-j), but 86 per cent of the social workers in the National Council were female. The percentage for the National Council reflects the similarly high percentage of women working in the social sector (78.2 per cent; Statistik Austria, nd-a). Further differences were identified in terms of party political orientation in that the social workers active in the National Council were more likely to belong to the Left-wing spectrum.

Political career patterns

Political parties structure the career patterns of politicians (Detterbeck, 2011) in that the respective institutional circumstances, party traditions and the status of the party (in opposition or government) are decisive for political careers. Based on biographical information on professional background, public offices and party positions, a recent study analysed 1,158 members of parliament in the period 1945–2019 who belonged to the SPÖ or the ÖVP. The career profiles were relatively stable: before being nominated for the National Council, the politicians held office at local or state level and/or were active in political parties, trade unions and/or other social partnership organisations. This so-called 'ox tour', or

Table 2.1: Social workers in the Austrian parliament, 21st–27th legislative periods

Legislative period	Number of social workers	Name (gender), party
21st (October 1999–December 2002) Coalition: ÖVP/FPÖ		
National Council	1	• Ludmilla Parfuss (f), SPÖ
Federal Council	1	• Stefan Schennach (m), Grüne
22nd (December 2002–October 2006) Coalition: ÖVP/FPÖ		
National Council	2	• Barbara Riener (f), ÖVP • Heidemarie Rest-Hinterseer (f), Grüne
Federal Council	3	• Stefan Schennach (m), Grüne • Waltraut Hladny (f), SPÖ • Gabriele Mörk (f), SPÖ
23rd (October 2006–October 2008) Coalition: SPÖ/ÖVP		
National Council	1	• Barbara Riener (f), ÖVP
Federal Council	4	• Stefan Schennach (m), Grüne/free mandate • Waltraut Hladny (f), SPÖ • Gabriele Mörk (f), SPÖ • Efgani Dönmez (m), Grüne/free mandate
24th (October 2008–October 2013) Coalition: SPÖ/ÖVP		
National Council	3	• Daniela Musiol (f), Grüne • Tanja Windbüchler-Souschill (f), Grüne • Barbara Riener (f), ÖVP
Federal Council	3	• Stefan Schennach (m), SPÖ • Efgani Dönmez (m), Grüne • Waltraud Hladny (f), SPÖ
25th (October 2013–November 2017) Coalition: SPÖ/ÖVP		
National Council	2	• Daniela Musiol (f), Grüne • Tanja Windbüchler-Souschill (f), Grüne
Federal Council	2	• Stefan Schennach (m), SPÖ • Efgani Dönmez (m), Grüne/free mandate

Table 2.1: Social workers in the Austrian parliament, 21st–27th legislative periods (continued)

Legislative period	Number of social workers	Name (gender), party
26th (November 2017–October 2019) Coalition: ÖVP/FPÖ		
National Council	2	• Efgani Dönmez (m), ÖVP/free mandate • Birgit Silvia Sandler (f), SPÖ
Federal Council	1	• Stefan Schennach (m), SPÖ
27th (October 2019–October 2024) Coalition: ÖVP/Grüne		
National Council	0	
Federal Council	1	• Stefan Schennach (m), SPÖ

Note: Christine Lapp (21st–24th legislative periods) is not included as her degree in Social Economy and Social Work does not meet the legal requirements of the Social Work Act 2024 for identification as a social worker.

climbing up through various positions, enables a party-specific political socialisation (Korom, 2022), even if there are subtle differentiations in internal party careers. Although most members of regional or national parliaments remain at their respective level, it can be observed that politicians are more likely to move from the regional to the national level than vice versa (Pilet et al, 2014).

Before discussing the political careers of social workers represented in the National Council and the Federal Council, the career of social worker Johannes Rauch is described in detail (Vorarlberg, nd). Born in the state of Vorarlberg in Austria in 1959, Rauch completed his training as a social worker in 1987 at the Academy for Social Work in Bregenz and worked for several years in the fields of social psychiatry, unemployment assistance and debt counselling (1986–97), lastly as managing director of a work initiative, before entering politics full time in 2004. His professional identification with social work has continued, and Rauch has maintained his membership of the obds. His political activities began in 1985 when he became a member of the Green Party; he co-founded the Green Forum Rankweil (a city with about 11,000 residents in Vorarlberg) and was its chair for a period. From 1990 to 2010, Rauch was active in local politics, and from 1995 he was also involved in state politics. After becoming a member of the board of the Vorarlberg Greens, he was their spokesperson from 1997 to 2021. From 2000 to 2014, Rauch was a member of the state parliament, and from 2004 to October 2014, he was chair of the Green parliamentary group. From October 2014 to the beginning of March 2022, Rauch was member of the state government

Table 2.2: Characteristics of social workers in the Austrian parliament and government, 21st–27th legislative periods

Variable	National Council (n = 7)	Federal Council (n = 4)	Government (n = 1)	Total (n = 12)
Gender				
Female	6 (86%)	2 (50%)	–	8 (67%)
Male	1 (14%)	2 (50%)	1 (100%)	4 (33%)
Age at the beginning of the first legislative period served				
21–30	–	–	–	–
31–40	3 (43%)	1 (25%)	–	4 (33%)
41–50	3 (43%)	2 (50%)	–	5 (42%)
51–60	1 (14%)	1 (25%)	–	2 (17%)
> 60	–	–	1 (100%)	1 (8%)
Party at the beginning of the first legislative period served				
SPÖ	2 (28.5%)	2 (50%)	–	4 (33%)
ÖVP	2 (28.5%)	–	–	2 (17%)
Grüne	3 (43%)	2 (50%)	1 (100%)	6 (50%)
Duration of political terms				
1–5 years	3 (43%)	2 (50%)	1 (100%)	6 (50%)
6–10 years	3 (43%)	1 (25%)	–	4 (33%)
11–15 years	1 (14%)	–	–	1 (8%)
> 15 years	–	1 (25%)	–	1 (8%)

in Vorarlberg and responsible for the following areas: development cooperation, national and international aid, aid to Eastern Europe, IT, environmental and climate protection, public transport and mobility management, mechanical and electrical engineering, waste management, bicycle infrastructure, energy autonomy and energy-related environmental and climate protection. Rauch was active in national politics first during 2008 to 2013, as a member of the national board of the Greens. His second period of involvement in national politics began on 8 March 2022, when he was nominated as Federal Minister for Social Affairs, Health, Care and Consumer Protection.

When reconstructing the career patterns of the 11 social workers who took up a position at national level between 1999 and 2024, the following similarities can be identified: all social workers in the National Council, the Federal Council and the government worked in a social work field for several years after completing their training. Those social workers who took up a position in the National Council ended their social work activities for this time, while some of the mandataries of the Federal Council continued to work in social work. All have in common that they were already politically active at local or state level or in a political party before taking up political office at national level. No social worker directly entered politics at the highest level. Of the nine who no longer hold a political mandate at national level, five are not politically active, while four took up another political office after leaving the National Council or the Federal Council (for example, as a local councillor, deputy mayor or member of a state parliament). Regarding their professional career, two returned to social work, one is employed by a municipality in a managerial position, one works in the economic sector, one is self-employed and two are retired. For two social workers still active in politics, no further information on their professional activities can be found.

Social advocacy

This section discusses the extent to which social workers align their political actions with the goals of social work and use their political office to engage in social advocacy. This is based on the assumption that the personal background of office-holders influences political decisions. For example, in a comparative analysis, Elsässer and Schäfer (2023) found that the sociodemographic composition of parliaments has an impact on the substantive representation of different social groups. Since it is mainly politicians with academic qualifications in highly respected professions who make decisions, there is a risk that these are more likely to be 'in line with the preferences of better-off citizens' (Elsässer and Schäfer, 2023, p 480). In terms of gender background, the authors also found a link between the representation of women in parliaments and the restructuring of the welfare state (Elsässer and Schäfer, 2018). The composition of parliaments is therefore relevant for the social policy spending profiles.

In the 27th legislative period, Rauch was the third Minister for Social Affairs, Health, Care and Consumer Protection; his two predecessors were a teacher and a medical doctor (Parlament Österreich, nd-k; nd-l). As described earlier, Rauch continued to identify and position himself as a social worker. He referred to this in various contexts, including interviews (ORFSound, 2024), and his membership of the obds was publicly known (Vorarlberg, nd). During his time in office, this was reflected in his involvement in several projects in the social sector, such as the implementation of the Social Work Designation Act, his statement in favour of free and accessible abortion (ORF, 2024) and his involvement in the fight against poverty through, for example, the Housing Umbrella (Wohnschirm, nd), the valorisation of social benefits (Bundesministerium Soziales, Gesundheit, Pflege und Konsumentenschutz, nd) and advocacy for basic child protection (ORFSound, 2024).

Because of the importance of the National Council in terms of political power, as outlined earlier, only the social workers represented there were analysed in terms of their political activities. To assess the implementation of social advocacy, spokesperson roles and the content of their political activities were analysed to determine whether they are related to social work according to its global definition. Of the seven social workers represented in the National Council, four held a spokesperson role during their respective term of office, and three of these were related to social work: spokesperson for migration/integration; spokesperson for constitutional and democratic policy and family policy; and spokesperson for foreign policy, development policy and civil service.

The analysis of political activities, including independent motions for resolutions, independent motions, dependent motions for resolutions, motions for debates, written questions, amendments, oral questions, motions to set deadlines for reports and petitions, shows that the social workers in the National Council carried out a total of 648 activities during their term of office, 461 (71 per cent) of which were related to social work. The following categories can be differentiated: (1) promoting democracy – that is, supporting postal voting, citizens' initiatives, proper handling of public funds, voting rights for foreigners, transparency; (2) implementing human rights nationally or internationally – that is, minimising discrimination and implementing children's rights, gender equality, peace efforts and accessibility; (3) promoting services for the community – that is, supporting community service, the voluntary social/ecological year, memorial/peace/social/voluntary service; (4) ensuring implementation of health measures – that is, supporting assumption of costs for medical treatment, free condoms, protection against tobacco, filling of vaccination gaps and healthy food; (5) being active in the area of children/young people/family – that is, supporting protection of young people, reduction of child poverty, implementation of the kindergarten year, family allowance, parental leave allowance and so on; and (6) being active in other issues, such as dealing with the begging ban, care leave, pension law and child-friendly road traffic regulations. Two social workers were jointly responsible for almost 498 activities (of which 392 were social work related), while the remaining activities were shared between five social workers. It is noticeable that it was mainly those members of parliament belonging to parties that were not part of the governing coalition who carried out these political activities.

In interviews, the social workers were also asked about the influence of their professional identity on their political behaviour. All respondents stated that their professional background had a major influence on their political understanding and actions. For example, they expressed that their professional knowledge of the realities of people's lives made it easier for them to understand reports of social grievances, to act quickly and to implement administrative guidelines successfully. They also stated that their ethical attitude influenced their understanding of their political role, characterised by representing those who are weaker, addressing distribution of power, promoting democratisation and changing the social framework accordingly. Finally, they said that the methodological skills of social work are helpful in everyday political life – knowing how to conduct discussions makes it easier to deal with conflict, influences behaviour regarding leadership and in meetings, and makes it possible to understand people and perceive their needs. In addition, their professional socialisation allows them to consider different points of view and to present issues in an understandable way.

Conclusion

The political mission of social work is anchored in the professional identity of Austrian social workers. There are opportunities to take on a political office at national level within the National Council and the Federal Council or as part of the Austrian government. In the 21st–27th legislative periods (1999–2024), 11 social workers (8 women and 3 men, mainly belonging to the Greens or the SPÖ) held political office at national level. Compared with their share of the total labour force, social workers were under-represented in the National Council and the Federal Council and over-represented in the national government in the 27th legislative period. Political careers are determined by the party and classic career patterns can be reconstructed. This applies for the 11 social workers, who started in political office at local and state levels before holding an office at national level. The professional identity of the social workers in the National Council influenced their political understanding, which was reflected in the thematic focus of their political activities. It seems to be essential for social workers in political office to implement the values of social work in terms of social justice and the realisation of human rights.

Note
[1] In the 27th government, there was a total of 39 committees, such as the Committee on Labour and Social Affairs, the Committee on Youth and Family Affairs, the Committee on Finance, the Committee on Health and the Committee on Human Rights. There were also four committees of inquiry as instruments of political control. A detailed list of all committees is available at: www.parlament.gv.at/recherchieren/ausschuesse.

References

Borchert, J. (2011) 'Individual ambition and institutional opportunity: A conceptual approach to political careers in multi-level systems', *Regional & Federal Studies*, 21(2): 117–40.

Bundesministerium Soziales, Gesundheit, Pflege und Konsumentenschutz (nd) 'Valorisierung der Sozialleistungen', *Bundesministerium Soziales, Gesundheit, Pflege und Konsumentenschutz*, Available from: www.sozialministerium.at/Themen/Soziales/Soziale-Themen/Valorisierung-Sozialleistungen.html [Accessed 22 September 2024].

Detterbeck, K. (2011) 'Party careers in federal systems: Vertical linkages within Austrian, German, Canadian and Australian parties', *Regional and Federal Studies*, 21(2): 245–70.

Elsässer, L. and Schäfer, A. (2018) 'Die politische Repräsentation von Frauen und der Umbau des Sozialstaats', *Polit Vierteljahresschr*, 59: 659–80.

Elsässer, L. and Schäfer, A. (2023) 'Political inequality in rich democracies', *Annual Review of Political Science*, 26: 469–87.

Fleischer, E. and Trenkwalder-Egger, A. (2023) 'Unterbrochene Traditionen – Verspätete Professionalisierung', *soziales_kapital*, 27: 6–24.

Flick, U. (2011) *Triangulation. Eine Einführung 3, aktualisierte Auflage*, VS Verlag für Sozialwissenschaften.

Frey, C. (2023) 'Arlt, Ilse', *socialnet*, Available from: www.socialnet.de/lexikon/475 [Accessed 15 September 2024].

Halfar, B. (2011) 'Finanzierung Sozialer Arbeit', in H. Otto and H. Thiersch (eds) *Handbuch Soziale Arbeit. Grundlagen der Sozialarbeit und Sozialpädagogik. 4, völlig neu bearbeitete Auflage*, Ernst Reinhardt, pp 407–14.

Hefel, J.M. and Kohlfürst, I. (2023) 'Die Rolle der ogsa im österreichischen Akademisierungsprozess der Sozialen Arbeit', *soziales_kapital*, 27: 25–43.

Jenny, M. (2023) 'Politische Parteien und Parteiensystem', in K. Praprotnik and F. Perlot (eds) *Das Politische System Österreichs. Basiswissen und Forschungseinblicke*, Böhlau, pp 101–28.

Korom, P. (2022) 'Half a century of little change within the Austrian legislative elite. A prosopographical study of ÖVP and SPÖ members of parliament (1945–2019)', Zenodo, doi: 10.5281/zenodo.6389997.

Kuckartz, U. (2018) *Qualitative Inhaltsanalyse: Methoden, Praxis, Computerunterstützung*, Beltz Juventa.

Kulke, D., Kohlfürst, I. and Kindler, T. (forthcoming) 'Social work professional organisations in Austria, Germany and Switzerland', in R. Guidi (ed) *Social Work Professional Organisations: An International Comparative Perspective*, Policy Press.

Lamnek, S. and Krell, C. (2016) *Qualitative Sozialforschung: mit Online-Materialien. 6, vollständig überarbeitete Auflage*, Beltz.

Migration.gv.at (nd) 'Geographie und Bevölkerung', *Migration.gv.at*, Available from: www.migration.gv.at/de/leben-und-arbeiten-in-oesterreich/oesterreich-stellt-sich-vor/geografie-und-bevoelkerung [Accessed 15 September 2024].

obds (Österreichischer Berufsverband der Sozialen Arbeit) (2023) *Schätzungen zur Anzahl der Sozialarbeiter*innen und Sozialpädagog*innen in Österreich*, *obds*, obds, Available from: https://obds.at/wp-content/uploads/2023/02/Schaetzungen-zur-Zahl-der-Absolvent_innen_obds_2023_final.pdf [Accessed 4 July 2024].

obds (Österreichischer Berufsverband der Sozialen Arbeit) (nd) 'Was ist Soziale Arbeit?', *obds*, Available from: https://obds.at/was-ist-soziale-arbeit/ [Accessed 18 July 2025].

obds (Österreichischer Berufsverband der Sozialen Arbeit) and ogsa (Österreichische Gesellschaft für Soziale Arbeit) (2024) *Ethische Grundsätze der Sozialen Arbeit. Ein Rahmen für Sozialarbeit und Sozialpädagogik in Österreich*, obds and ogsa, Available from: https://obds.at/dokumente/entwurf-ethische-grundsaetze-in-der-sozialen-arbeit-ein-rahmen-fuer-sozialarbeit-und-sozialpaedagogik-in-oesterreich [Accessed 15 September 2024].

ogsa (Österreichische Gesellschaft für Soziale Arbeit) (nd) 'Kerncurriculum Bachelor Soziale Arbeit', *ogsa*, Available from: www.ogsa.at/kerncurriculum/#:~:text=Das%20Kerncurriculum%20dient%20prim%C3%A4r%20einer,Anforderungen%20einen%20offenen%20Gestaltungsrahmen%20erm%C3%B6glichen [Accessed 4 July 2024].

ORF (2024) 'Rauch will Abtreibung aus Strafgesetzbuch streichen', *ORF*, Available from: https://vorarlberg.orf.at/stories/3261021 [Accessed 22 September 2024].

ORFSound (2024) 'Neues bei Neustädter. Minister Rauch zieht Bilanz', *ORFSound*, Available from: https://sound.orf.at/podcast/vbg/neues-bei-neustaedter/minister-rauch-zieht-bilanz [Accessed 22 September 2024].

Parlament Österreich (nd-a) 'Demokratie in Österreich', *Parlament Österreich*, Available from: www.parlament.gv.at/verstehen/demokratie-wahlen/demokratie-in-at [Accessed 15 September 2024].

Parlament Österreich (nd-b) 'Nationalrat', *Parlament Österreich*, Available from: www.parlament.gv.at/verstehen/nationalrat/#:~:text=Der%20Nationalrat%20hat%20zahlreiche%20Aufgaben,dem%20Bundesrat%20%E2%80%93%20kann%20Bundesgesetze%20beschlie%C3%9Fen [Accessed 15 September 2024].

Parlament Österreich (nd-c) 'Ausschüsse', *Parlament Österreich*, Available from: www.parlament.gv.at/verstehen/nationalrat/ausschuesse/index.html [Accessed 15 September 2024].

Parlament Österreich (nd-d) 'Aufgaben', *Parlament Österreich*, Available from: www.parlament.gv.at/verstehen/bundesrat/aufgaben [Accessed 15 September 2024].

Parlament Österreich (nd-e) 'Bundesregierung', *Parlament Österreich*, Available from: www.parlament.gv.at/verstehen/politisches-system/bundesregierung [Accessed 15 September 2024].

Parlament Österreich (nd-f) 'Bundespräsident:in', *Parlament Österreich*, Available from: www.parlament.gv.at/verstehen/politisches-system/bundespraesident [Accessed 15 September 2024].

Parlament Österreich (nd-g) 'Bundesrat', *Parlament Österreich*, Available from: www.parlament.gv.at/recherchieren/personen/bundesrat [Accessed 24 September 2024].

Parlament Österreich (nd-h) 'Johannes Rauch', *Parlament Österreich*, Available from: https://www.parlament.gv.at/person/21029 [Accessed 18 June 2025].

Parlament Österreich (nd-i) 'Nationalrat', *Parlament Österreich*, Available from: www.parlament.gv.at/recherchieren/personen/nationalrat [Accessed 15 September 2024].

Parlament Österreich (nd-j) 'Frauenanteil im Nationalrat', *Parlament Österreich*, Available from: www.parlament.gv.at/recherchieren/statistiken/personen-statistiken/frauen/NR [Accessed 22 September 2024].

Parlament Österreich (nd-k) 'Rudolf Anschober', *Parlament Österreich*, Available from: www.parlament.gv.at/person/24 [Accessed 22 September 2024].

Parlament Österreich (nd-l) 'Dr. Wolfgang Mückstein', *Parlament Österreich*, Available from: www.parlament.gv.at/person/19043 [Accessed 22 September 2024].

Pilet, J., Tronconi, F., Oñate, P. and Verzichelli, L. (2014) 'Career patterns in multilevel systems', in K. Deschouwer and S. Depauw (eds) *Representing the People: A Survey among Members of Statewide and Substate Parliaments*, Oxford Academic, pp 209–26.

Praprotnik, K. (2023) 'Das Parlament: Nationalrat und Bundesrat', in K. Praprotnik and F. Perlot (eds) *Das Politische System Österreichs. Basiswissen und Forschungseinblicke*, Böhlau, pp 157–85.

Scheipl, J. (2003) 'Soziale Arbeit in Österreich – ein Torso?', in K. Lauermann and G. Knapp (eds) *Sozialpädagogik in Österreich*, Hermagoras/Mohorjeva, pp 10–42.

Schilling, J. and Klus, S. (2018) *Soziale Arbeit. Geschichte – Theorie – Profession* (7th edn), Ernst Reinhardt.

Sozialpartner (nd) 'Die österreichische Sozialpartnerschaft', Available from: www.sozialpartner.at [Accessed 15 September 2024].

Spitzer, H. (2010) 'Soziale Arbeit in Österreich', *Neue Praxis*, 40(3): 321–30.

Spitzer, H. (2011) 'Aktuelle Entwicklungen und Herausforderungen Sozialer Arbeit in Österreich', in H. Spitzer, H. Höllmüller and B. Hönig (eds) *Soziallandschaften: Perspektiven Sozialer Arbeit als Profession und Disziplin*, VS, pp 55–68.

Statistik Austria (2024) 'Anzahl der Erwerbstätigen in Österreich nach Branchen im Jahr 2023', *Statista*, Available from: https://de.statista.com/statistik/daten/studie/607428/umfrage/erwerbstaetige-in-oesterreich-nach-branchen [Accessed 15 September 2024].

Statistik Austria (nd-a) 'Unselbständig Erwerbstätige (ILO) nach Vollzeit/Teilzeit, Wirtschaftszweig und Geschlecht – Jahresdurchschnitt 2023', *Statistik Austria*, Available from: www.statistik.at/statistiken/bevoelkerung-und-soziales/gender-statistiken/erwerbstaetigkeit [Accessed 22 September 2024].

Statistik Austria (nd-b) 'Jährliche Personeneinkommen', *Statistik Austria*, Available from: www.statistik.at/statistiken/bevoelkerung-und-soziales/einkommen-und-soziale-lage/jaehrliche-personeneinkommen [Accessed 22 September 2024].

SWÖ (Sozialwirtschaft Österreich) (2024) *Kollektivvertrag der Sozialwirtschaft Österreichs*, SWÖ, Available from: www.swoe.at/folder/1289/SW%C3%96_KV_2024_Webversion.pdf [Accessed 15 September 2024].

SWÖ (Sozialwirtschaft Österreich) (nd) 'Satzung des SWÖ-KV 2022', *SWÖ*, Available from: www.swoe.at/1001,4040,0,2.html [Accessed 15 September 2024].

Ucakar, K., Gschiegl, S. and Jenny, M. (2017) *Das politische System Österreichs und die EU*, Facultas.

Vorarlberg (nd) 'Rauch Johannes', *Vorarlberg*, Available from: https://vorarlberg.at/web/landtag/-/rauch-johannes [Accessed 22 September 2024].

Wohnschirm (nd) 'WOHNSCHIRM: Für sichere Wohnverhältnisse', *Wohnschirm*, Available from: https://wohnschirm.at [Accessed 22 September 2024].

3

Canada: social workers in the House of Commons

Anne-Marie McLaughlin

Canadian social workers seeking to promote social justice and transform society to one that upholds the rights of all to 'fair and equitable access to services, resources and opportunities' (CASW, 2024) could consider a macro approach to practice with direct impact on policy – namely, a career in politics. In this chapter, I examine how the profession of social work in Canada aligns with a political career and how the Canadian political environment provides opportunities and challenges for aspiring social work politicians. I also examine the career paths of Canadian social workers elected to the federal House of Commons and review some of their noteworthy contributions.

Social work as a profession

In Canada, social work is a regulated profession. The aim of regulation is the protection of the public against incompetent or unethical practice. Regulation of the profession occurs through national educational standards as well as through provincial and territorial regulatory bodies with delegated legislative authority. Both the educational institutions and the regulatory bodies perform gatekeeping functions within the profession (Yan et al, 2021). In addition, many Canadian social workers voluntarily belong to a non-regulatory national body, the CASW. This national body, supported by the provincial associations, advocates for the profession and acts as a voice for social justice by producing policy and position papers on matters of social importance. There are approximately 22,000 members across Canada (figure for 2024; CASW, nd).

National education standards are set by an independent accreditation body for educational institutions, the Canadian Association for Social Work Education (CASWE). The CASWE sets educational policy and standards for both the bachelor's (BSW) and the master's (MSW) of social work degrees. The aim is to ensure consistency and equivalence across Canadian schools of social work, to distinguish BSW education from MSW education and to advocate for and support high-quality social work education. Provincial regulatory bodies, made up of social workers as well as members of the public, stipulate eligibility for practice, set practice standards, and enforce standards through continuing education requirements and disciplinary measures. Power to enforce regulations comes from enacted provincial legislation, which delegates authority to the provincial regulatory body.

As Canada is composed of ten provinces and three territories, there is variation in the standards of the profession. Currently, in most provinces and territories, to practise as a social worker, qualified individuals must be registered with their provincial regulatory body and have at a minimum a BSW from an accredited institution. Alberta and the Northwest Territories are outliers as they register social workers educated as diploma holders at the community college level; Nunavut and the Yukon do not currently require social workers to register.

Within the Canadian workforce of around 20 million (Statistics Canada, 2024), there are approximately 70,000 registered social workers (Canadian Council of Social Work Regulators, 2017), accounting roughly for only 0.35 per cent of the total Canadian workforce. In contrast, membership in the national association, the CASW, is approximately 22,000. Regulation in most jurisdictions in Canada is mandatory, while membership in the association is voluntary. In terms of gender composition, 77 per cent of registered social workers identify as female and 23 per cent as male; in the overall Canadian workforce, women make up only 47 per cent and men 53 per cent (Statistics Canada, 2024).

However, not every social worker who is educated and practising is regulated. For example, in the province of British Columbia, some social workers are exempt from regulation and registration: those employed by the Ministry of Child, Family and Community Services and those who work for an Indian band, a tribal council or a treaty First Nation (Social Workers Act 2008). Additionally, many practitioners were grandparented into the profession during the 1980s and 1990s when mandatory registration legislation became more common. Grandparenting allowed those who were practising as social workers but without the requisite education to register, be regulated and remain working.

The last comprehensive survey of the social work profession in Canada was conducted in 2000 (Stephenson et al, 2001). At the time, social workers made up over 30 per cent of the total social service sector workforce, which included those employed in hospitals, community health centres, mental health clinics, schools, advocacy organisations, government departments, social services agencies, child welfare settings, family services agencies, correctional facilities, social housing organisations, family courts, school boards and consultation agencies, employee assistance and private counselling programmes (Statistics Canada, 2021; Canadian Institute for Health Information, 2023). Recently, the CASW drew attention to a growing demand for social workers in Canada, particularly child welfare workers. In their survey of 3,258 social workers, 75 per cent reported that caseloads were unmanageable, 72 per cent reported insufficient time with clients, and 45 per cent of those who left the professions stated that they did so due to burn-out (CASW, 2018). Respondents also expressed concerns that systemic factors were pushing de-professionalisation in child welfare practice.

A national study investigating working conditions and career satisfaction among 5,393 Canadian social workers found that, although social work salaries (ranging from CAD 50,000 to CAD 65,000) were above the median income of Canadians, wages were significantly below those of other professionals (Bejan et al, 2014). According to Statistics Canada (2024), the median income in 2024 for nurses was CAD 80,000 and for psychologists, CAD 102,000. Increasing numbers of social work practitioners are moving into clinical and private practice, where salaries can be much higher (Kourgiantakis et al, 2023). Post COVID-19 pandemic impacts on the profession have also been pronounced, with an increase in social workers retiring, many struggling with the rapid transition to telehealth (Ashcroft et al, 2022) and higher levels of mental health concerns (Alaggia et al, 2024). Additional challenges faced by Canadian social workers are increasing requirements for overtime, larger caseloads, inadequate supervision and concerns about a decline in the quality of services (Bejan et al, 2014; McKenzie, 2016). These reports reveal complex and challenging work environments with inadequate support and supervision as well as low wages relative to other professions, but a social work workforce committed to quality client care (Baines et al, 2009).

Institutional opportunity structures

Frustration with the status quo and the lack of ability to influence policy and contribute to the development of a fair and just society are reasons why social workers run for political office (McLaughlin et al, 2019). But how attractive is a political career and what opportunities exist for social workers in Canada to make politics a viable career at the federal level? Borchert (2011) indicates that political career paths are influenced by personal characteristics, such as ambition, but also tied to institutionalised opportunity structures – that is, the *availability*, *accessibility* and *attractiveness* of the political office.

Social workers seeking election to a political office in Canada must choose between three levels of government: federal, provincial/territorial and municipal. The federal government is responsible for national and international issues such as national defence, public safety, criminal law, fisheries, Indigenous relations, immigration and foreign affairs, and currency, while provincial governments are responsible for regional issues such as education, social services and health care delivery, and natural resources. Municipal governments, not usually supported by party structures, receive their power from provincial governments rather than the Constitution and are responsible for local issues such as public transit, policing, land use planning, recycling/waste removal and libraries.

In terms of seat availability, the fewest available seats are at the federal level with 343 members of Parliament (MPs) representing the Canadian population of around 40 million (Parliament of Canada, nd-a); at the provincial level, there are approximately 750 available seats. Provincial seat allocation varies by population, with, for example, the province of Québec (population 9 million plus) having 125 seats in its National Assembly, while the province of Prince Edward Island (population 177,000 plus) has only 27 seats in its Legislative Assembly. Likewise, the number of available electoral seats at the municipal level varies with population size; the largest municipalities with populations in excess of 1 million (for example, Toronto, Montreal, Calgary) have as many as 65 elected members. Smaller municipalities may have only a mayor and three or four councillors. There are over 5,000 municipalities in Canada (Statistics Canada, 2017), making this level of government the most readily available to interested social workers pursuing elected office.

Canada's decentralised federation with shared power between levels of government was founded on respect for the economic, cultural and linguistic differences of its constituents. However, tension between federal, provincial and municipal levels of government often test collaborative aspirations, and regional divides persist (Cameron and Simeon, 2002). Boundaries between levels of government are not impermeable – for example, although health care is largely a provincial matter, the federal government leverages its spending power to set national standards for health care (Atkinson et al, 2013).

Canada has been classified as a liberal welfare state (Beland et al, 2020) and has a complex mix of federal and provincial social security programmes. Provincial and territorial governments have considerable autonomy in most labour and social policy areas, setting eligibility requirements and benefit levels, while the federal government has jurisdiction over redistributive programmes such as Employment Insurance, the Canada Pension Plan and the Guaranteed Income Supplement. In addition, the federal government administers, funds and has responsibility to provide on-reserve social programmes for First Nations communities (Koebel and Pohler, 2019). While Canadians support the redistributive aspects of the welfare state and provision of universal programmes such as family benefits, health care and old-age pensions (Beland et al, 2020), regional and provincial inequities exist. For example, the province of Québec has more robust welfare provisions and higher social spending than most other provinces (Haddow, 2014; Daigneault, 2021).

In terms of attractiveness, at both the provincial and federal level, changes have occurred that make a Canadian political career increasingly attractive. Through the process of professionalisation, Canadian legislatures have instituted more generous compensation, including better pension benefits and supplemental payments to certain positions and appointments. They have also increased staffing and provided funds for constituency and caucus work as well as research and library staff. In addition, there has been a standardisation of legislatures' sessions or sitting days as well as structural changes such as all-party committees that set budgets and policy for legislatures (Moncrief, 1994; Docherty, 2003). For many social workers with political ambition, compensation may contribute to the attractiveness of a political career.

The Canadian federal parliamentary system is based on the British Westminster model. Parliament, the legislative arm of government, is a bicameral system with the House of Commons, known as the lower house, and the Senate, or the upper house. The House of Commons is made up of elected members from across Canada, each from individual constituencies. Seats in the House of Commons are distributed across Canada in proportion to the population (Elections Canada, 2023) . Candidates must win the nomination of their political party before they can run in the federal election; the candidate who wins the most votes wins the seat. Elected members sit in the House according to the party they belong to. The Senate, or 'chamber of "sober second thought"' (Lawlor and Crandall, 2013), consists of members appointed by the governor general, on the advice of the prime minister, to represent Canada's regional interests. New legislation must pass the Senate before it becomes law.

Elections at the federal level use the 'first past the post', or single-member plurality, system (Lundberg, 2007). Although there are multiple parties registered with Elections Canada (the body responsible for running federal elections), as of 2025 only five parties have elected members in the federal parliament: the Liberal, Conservative and New Democratic parties as well as the Green Party and Bloc Québécois (a regional party that promotes Québec's interests and only runs candidates in the province of Québec). More noteworthy is the fact that only two parties have ever formed the federal government in Canada: the Liberals and the Conservatives. At different times in Canada's history, the Liberals and the Conservatives have both represented centrist political ideologies, though more polarisation has been seen in recent years (Cochrane, 2015; Merkley, 2022). The 2003 merger of the Reform Party (renamed Canadian Alliance) and the Progressive Conservative Party created the Right-leaning Conservative Party of Canada, signalling a clearer Left–Right divide in Canadian politics (Lucardie, 2007).

The Conservative Party of Canada values social conservatism, free markets and small government. The New Democratic Party (NDP) is Left of centre, socially progressive, labour-friendly and supportive of government intervention. The Liberal Party remains more centrist (Cochrane, 2015), but is frequently characterised as centre-Left (Merkley,

2022). The Green Party, an environmentally progressive party, was established in 1983, but has so far failed to gain support from a significant portion of the electorate and struggles for recognition. Bloc Québécois is a regional sovereigntist party that ascended in the 1993 general election but has lost ground more recently. Although social workers are not obligated to support any particular party, there is some indication that many align with the more socially progressive values of parties on the Left or centre-Left (McLaughlin et al, 2019).

Political recruitment

Using the Parlinfo Canadian parliamentary database (Parliament of Canada, nd-b), corroborated with biographical information collected from individual MPs' websites, social media profiles and media reports, a total of 27 parliamentarians elected to the federal House of Commons were identified as social workers or having post-secondary social work education.

Considering there have been 5,258 elected MPs since confederation (1867), the number of social workers ever elected seems rather low. However, this assessment has to be qualified. First of all, the share of social workers in parliament (0.5 per cent) is still higher than the share of social workers in the current Canadian workforce (0.35 per cent). Second, as fewer than 400 women have ever been elected to the House of Commons, the low share of social workers, a dominantly female profession, is hardly surprising. Of those 400 elected women, 15 were social workers – a relatively high share of 3.75 per cent.

In our sample, there were slightly more women social work parliamentarians (SWPs) (15 or 55 per cent) than men SWPs (12 or 45 per cent). Over the last two federal elections (2021, 2025) women have made up less than one third (30 per cent) of all Canadian federal parliamentarians, while constituting 51 per cent of the total population (Raney, 2020; Bonikowska, 2022). In the federal election held in September 2021, six of the seven social workers elected (85.7 per cent) were female.

Notably the nursing profession has had less representation, with only 14 (0.26 per cent) of parliamentarians identifying as a nurse. Those identifying as teachers (n = 370) make up 7 per cent of parliamentarians elected since 1867, while those trained in law (n = 1,083) make up over 20 per cent.

The majority of SWPs held either a BSW (n = 11, 40.7 per cent) or an MSW (n = 8, 29.6 per cent). One (3.7 per cent) held a diploma in social work. The remainder either had degrees from outside Canada (n = 2, 7.4 per cent) or degrees from adjacent fields (n = 2, 7.4 per cent) or their education could not be specified (n = 3, 11.1 per cent). In terms of party affiliation, 20 (74.1 per cent) belonged to parties considered to be Left or centre-Left on the political spectrum: the Liberal Party of Canada (n = 13, 48.2 per cent), the NDP (and its precursor, the Co-operative Commonwealth Federation; n = 7, 25.9 per cent). The remaining 7 (25.9 per cent) belonged to Right-leaning parties: the Conservative Party of Canada (n = 5, 18.5 per cent) and Bloc Québécois (n = 2, 7.4 per cent). Almost two thirds were 50 years of age or younger at the time they were first elected to federal politics (n = 17, 63 per cent), and the mean age when first elected was 46 (range: 29–63). This is younger than the average age of legislators in general, which, in 2016, was 56.8 years (Bonikowska, 2022).

More recently, the number and significance of SWPs seems to have increased. The House of Commons elected in 2021 contained seven SWPs (2.1 per cent). These seven sitting parliamentarians represent the highest ever number of social workers elected to federal office in one sitting (the highest number previously was in 2015, when five social workers were elected). The Liberals held 156 (46.2 per cent) seats out of 338. SWPs held five seats and made up 3.2 per cent of the Liberal Party faction in the House of Commons. Of the select group of MPs chosen to be in the government's cabinet (n = 40), three (7.5 per cent) were SWPs.

Political career patterns

Pre-parliamentary careers

Many of the SWPs in our sample of 27 had long careers as practising social workers prior to entering politics: 12 (44.4 per cent) worked in the profession for more than 10 years, and 33 per cent of these SWPs worked for more than 16 years in the profession. Three of the SWPs in our sample (11.1 per cent) had less than five years' experience as practising social workers before moving into political office; one was trained in social work but never held a social work position.

As depicted in Table 3.1, our SWPs were most likely to have had micro or direct practice experience prior to entering politics (n = 11, 40.7 per cent), including in medical and psychiatric social work, youth work and case work with child welfare. The next largest share (n = 9, 33.3 per cent) were engaged in macro social work, which included employment as executive director of a child protection agency and other family-serving organisations, administrator of hospital-based social services and other executive positions in the human services. Mezzo-level work formed a smaller group (n = 5, 18.5 per cent) and included those providing community service and development, social planning and supervisory activities. For two SWPs, their social work employment histories could not be specified.

Parliamentary careers

Political career path models, such as the springboard model, suggest that those with ambition typically progress up a political career ladder (Stolz, 2003)

Table 3.1: Social work practice experience of SWPs

Type of social work practice	Total n = 27
Micro practice (individual client service, child welfare, mental health, counselling)	11
Mezzo practice (community development, group work, community organising, supervising, planning)	5
Macro practice (policy, organisational management, administration, teaching)	9
Unspecified	2

from local to national office, gaining increasing prestige and remuneration. This hierarchical and unidirectional process is not the norm in Canada (Borchert, 2011). In fact, in Canada political career paths are described as unattractive in part because clear progressive pathways are nearly non-existent (Docherty, 2011; Weber et al, 2024). A Canadian federal political career is typically short and unreliable, with as many as two thirds of the members of the House of Commons replaced each election (Docherty, 2003). Further, with power concentrated with the prime minister and the cabinet, most federally elected parliamentarians serve extensive time on the backbenches and have few opportunities to impact policy or initiate change.

The length of tenure for SWPs is not significantly different from the tenure of parliamentarians in general, which has been found to be 9.1 years on average (Pow, 2015). In our sample of 20 SWPs whose terms in federal parliament has ended (seven were still serving at the time of writing), 5 (25 per cent) served for less than four years, 6 (30 per cent) served for 5–8 years, 4 (20 per cent) served for 9–12 years, 3 (15 per cent) served for 13–16 years and 2 (10 per cent) served for more than 16 years. The average length of tenure for an SWP in the House of Commons was 9.5 years. This equates to approximately two terms, as federal elections tend to run on a four-year cycle. The longest-serving SWP, Walter Dinsdale (Conservative), served from 1951 for 31 years until his death in office in 1982.

The Canadian political career path has also been described as bifurcated in that those with ambition choose between provincial or national politics. Barriers exist, making movement between levels of government difficult (Borchert, 2011). For example, the move between provincial and federal levels is difficult due to a lack of integration in party organisation (Webb, 2015; Pow, 2018). Although two political parties (the Liberals and the Conservatives) have dominated politics at both the federal and provincial levels, a disconnect exists between these multilevel parties as they do not consistently share infrastructure – such as party voting lists – fundraising processes or even ideology. As a result, the movement from provincial to federal politics does not provide dependable opportunities.

That is not to say movement does not happen, and in our database of 27 federally elected SWPs, a significant number (n = 6, 22.2 per cent) also had experience in provincial politics. For example, Alexa McDonough, the provincial party leader for the NDP in Nova Scotia from 1980 to 1994, and the first woman to lead a political party in that province, ran for and won the federal leadership and was elected in 1997. Likewise, Dave Barrett was first elected to the provincial legislature in British Columbia in 1965 and later led the NDP, serving as premier in the province (1972–75), then successfully made the leap to federal politics in 1988 as a member of the NDP (Hawthorn, 2018).

Activities that represent political experience include having been elected to a provincial or municipal legislature, school board or special interest group, as well as being involved in political party staff work. Table 3.2 shows a breakdown of those in our sample of 27 who had prior political experience: 6 members (22.2 per cent) had been elected to provincial government, 5 (18.5 per cent) had been elected to municipal legislatures, 2 had been elected to school board positions and 2 had been elected as president of special interest groups (both 7.4 per cent) and 4 had political staffing experience (14.8 per cent). Three of the SWPs (11.1 per cent) had more than one type of political experience prior to their election to the federal parliament. Overall, 16 (59.3 per cent) of SWPs had prior political experience, while 11 (40.7 per cent) had no prior political experience.

Dodeigne (2018) suggests that regional political arenas should be considered an end in themselves rather than a springboard to the national level. Stolz (2003) argues that a regional culture (in Canada, the provincial/territorial culture) and strong regional identity is incentive for remaining at the regional political level. Provincial political careers may be more attractive for some due to less demanding travel schedules and less time away from home. Also, the opportunities for career advancement, such as through a position in cabinet, are seen as greater at the provincial level. Cabinet positions bring with them increased ability to impact policy, but also additional compensation through cabinet appointments and committee work. Additionally, for the politically

Table 3.2: SWPs' prior political experience

Type of prior political experience	N (%)
Provincial government	6 (22.0%)
Municipal legislature	5 (18.5%)
School board	2 (7.4%)
Elected president of a special interest group	2 (7.4%)
Political staffing	4 (15.0%)

ambitious, a member of the provincial legislature holding a cabinet seat is more likely to be re-elected (Docherty, 2011).

In a foundational Canadian study examining Canadian federal parliamentary career paths, Barrie and Gibbins (1989) report on 3,803 elected members from 1867 to 1984. They found that 14 per cent of parliamentarians had prior provincial experience and 26 per cent had municipal experience, while 59 per cent were considered amateurs with no prior political experience. More recently, Pow (2018) examined data on over 1,000 Canadian MPs serving between 1993 and 2015. He found that 8 per cent could be classified as having politics as their primary career, while 45 per cent had some degree of prior electoral experience, demonstrating there may be an in increasing number of federal politicians having prior electoral experience. However, a significant share (47 per cent) of newly elected MPs in Pow's study were political amateurs.

Our sample reflects Docherty's (2011) findings that there is no singular Canadian political career path. However, our SWPs had significantly more political experience than those in Pow's (2018) sample. While many could be seen as political neophytes with no prior political experience, 60 per cent had some experience. Interestingly, Docherty pointed out in 2011 that politicians at the federal level were more likely to have had experience at the municipal level (27 per cent) than at the provincial level (10 per cent). Our own sample indicates a more even split between experience at the provincial (22 per cent) and municipal (18 per cent) levels. Adding election to school boards (n = 2) to the municipal category (n = 5), as others have done, 26 per cent of our SWPs had municipal experience.

Although no single career path can describe the experience of our social work sample, Lucienne Robillard exemplifies a significant proportion of our sample who not only had vast political experience prior to being elected to the federal government, but also had significant and varied pre-parliamentary social work experience. Lucienne Robillard obtained her MSW at age 22 and practised clinical social work in a large urban hospital. Her career progressed quickly as she worked in community social services, managing social programmes and community relations, eventually moving into health care administration in hospital-based social services. She was named Public Curator of Québec, responsible to protect the rights of vulnerable adults, and she was elected President of the Association of Social Service Practitioners in the health sector of Québec and later President of the Administrative Commission for Mental Health Services. She was elected to the Québec National Assembly in 1989 and held a variety of cabinet posts at the provincial level, including Minister of Health and Social Services. She ran and was elected to the federal parliament in 1995, serving for nearly 13 years. During that time, she held a number of important portfolios, including Minister of Labour,

Minister of Citizenship and Immigration and President of the Treasury Board, and in 2006 she was named deputy leader of the Liberal Party (National Assembly of Québec, 2024). She resigned her seat in 2008 but continued to work for the Liberal Party of Canada.

Post-parliamentary careers

The SWPs in our sample had the opportunity to influence public policy at the highest level while in office, but what about their policy impacts following their political tenure? Were they able to continue to advance social policy for social change? One of the apparent characteristics of our Canadian SWPs is their commitment to public service – more so than their commitment to one specific public issue or social cause. Many in our sample of SWPs were dedicated to the idea of public service, human rights, democracy and social justice.

Audrey McLaughlin (NDP MP, 1987–97) is one such example. She was the first woman to lead a national political party in Canada and remained an influential social policy advocate following her tenure as a federal politician. Subsequently, in 1997, she was elected President of Socialist International Women, whose main concerns are peace, human rights and democracy. In 2000, she travelled to Kosovo to work with women candidates in that region's first democratic election, continuing her lifelong efforts to encourage inclusiveness in public affairs. From 2005 to 2006, she was appointed by the prime minister to serve on the National Roundtable on the Economy and Environment, whose mission was to generate and promote innovative ways to advance Canada's environmental and economic interests. More recently, McLaughlin was Chair of Grandmothers to Grandmothers – Yukon (part of the Stephen Lewis Foundation), connecting grandmothers in Africa to those in other countries, raising funds and raising awareness; this reflected McLaughlin's belief that one should act both globally and locally (Government of Canada, 2021; Pioneer Women of the Yukon, nd).

Eugène Rhéaume (Conservative MP, 1963–66) continued to influence policy after leaving elected office through his work with Indigenous people and communities. In particular, he worked for the recognition of Métis people in the Canadian Constitution (Mackay, 2013). He was a vocal advocate for improving housing for Indigenous people and chaired a national task force examining the issues. This work helped initiate programmes resulting in the construction and repair of well over 25,000 homes (Meili, 2013). He was also instrumental in the formation of the Native Council of Canada, an organisation dedicated to promoting Indigenous rights, especially Métis and non-status rights, and, as it was later, the Congress of Aboriginal Peoples. His advocacy work led to appointments with the Royal Commission on

Labrador, the Royal Commission on Electoral Reform and the Canadian Human Rights Commission.

Other SWPs accepted seats on various boards, many of which were related to social issues of personal importance. Alexa McDonough (NDP MP, 1997–2008), for example, accepted a seat with the Alzheimer's Society Board of Directors. She had a family history of Alzheimer's and was dedicated to this cause. Bonnie Brown (Liberal Party MP, 1993–2008) followed her political career with volunteer work for Advancement of Women Halton – a group she was instrumental in founding – which is dedicated to gender equality and brings together local women's organisations to lobby on issues including democracy, childcare, pay equity and, more recently, missing and murdered Indigenous women and girls. Margaret Mitchell (NDP MP, 1979–93) followed her tenure in the House of Commons as the first Chair of the BC Advisory Council on Human Rights. While most SWPs entered macro-level positions following their career in federal Parliament, one, Louise Hardy (NDP MP 1997–2000), pursued a clinical practice career.

Social advocacy

Docherty (2003) suggests that the possibility to influence public policy and legislation in the Canadian federal parliament can best be realised through an appointment to cabinet. Impressively, social workers in the House of Commons have held some high-profile and influential parliamentary and governmental positions. Overall, of the 27 elected SWPs, 8 (29.6 per cent) have been appointed as parliamentary secretaries (a junior role sometimes seen as a stepping stone to a cabinet appointment), 6 (22.2 per cent) have held cabinet posts, 5 (18.5 per cent) have held the position of whip/deputy whip, 3 (11.1 per cent) have been leader of their party and 2 (7.4 per cent) have been named caucus chair, leaving only 3 (11.1 per cent) to the backbenches. In parliament at the time of writing, three social workers held cabinet positions: the Honourable Diane Lebouthillier, Minister of Fisheries, Oceans and the Canadian Coast Guard; the Honourable Ginette Petitpas Taylor, Minister of Veterans Affairs and Associate Minister of National Defence; the Honourable Dan Vandal, Minister Responsible for Prairies Economic Development Canada, Minister Responsible for the Canadian Northern Economic Development Agency and Minster of Northern Affairs. These portfolios may not represent traditional areas of focus for social work, but – according to recent SWPs – they may benefit from a social work lens and the skill set that social workers bring (McLaughlin et al, 2019).

It is difficult to speak definitively about the social advocacy impacts of elected SWPs at the federal level. Cabinet ministers are not independent actors in the Canadian system and are constrained by centralised party policy and the goals of the prime minister. Policy direction is commonly set out in mandate letters delivered to incoming ministers (Ie, 2023). Examining the legislative impacts of SWPs in the last two sittings of the House of Commons, we can see that the number of bills brought forward or sponsored by SWPs was minimal: four in total with only one receiving Royal Assent (Bill C-13). The bills, while important, were not directly related to traditional social advocacy issues. Some dealt with changes to regulations, such as Bill C-13, sponsored by the Honourable Ginette Petitpas Taylor, which enacts the use of French in federally regulated private business. Petitpas Taylor was at that time the Official Languages Minister. In an interview about her job, Petitpas Taylor spoke of the importance of promoting the use of the French language but she also advocated for the recognition of Indigenous languages and the importance of preserving and supporting identity and culture. She also spoke of her government's commitment to reconciliation with Indigenous people and preserving and promoting language as part of that (Canadian Press, 2021). What the social worker brings to their office is an in-depth understanding of social and cultural issues that impact individual and collective wellbeing, plus an ability to frame discussions from this holistic person-in-environment perspective.

Conclusion

For those social workers who seek to influence policy and contribute to a just society, a move into the political arena comes with opportunities and challenges. A seat at the federal cabinet table is seen as the apex of a political career, and we have seen in this study that social workers have held an outsized role in federal positions of influence. A contributing factor may be the profession's structural lens and social justice value base, which provide a critical analysis of social issues (McLaughlin et al, 2019). Not surprisingly, SWPs elected to the federal House of Commons have been predominantly female and enter politics at a younger age than their counterparts. Further, in comparison to parliamentarians in general, SWPs tend to have more political experience prior to their mandate, split nearly evenly between provincial and municipal. Finally, the values of the profession and the pursuit of social justice appear to be animating elements of their post-political careers. In fact, for many of our SWPs, politics could be seen as an instrumental and influential aspect of their lifelong social work practice.

References

Alaggia, R., O'Connor, C., Fuller-Thomson, E. and West, K. (2024) 'Troubled times: Canadian social workers' early adversities, mental health, and resilience during the COVID-19 pandemic', *International Social Work*, 67(1): 99–118.

Ashcroft, R., Sur, D., Greenblatt, A. and Donahue, P. (2022) 'The impact of the COVID-19 pandemic on social workers at the frontline: A survey of Canadian social workers', *British Journal of Social Work*, 52(3): 1724–46.

Atkinson, M.M., Béland, D. and Marchildon, G.P. (2013) *Governance and Public Policy in Canada: A View from the Provinces* (1st edn), University of Toronto Press.

Baines, D., Davis, J.M. and Saini, M. (2009) 'Wages, working conditions, and restructuring in Ontario's social work profession', *Canadian Social Work Review*, 26(1): 59–72.

Barrie, D. and Gibbins, R. (1989) 'Parliamentary careers in the Canadian federal state', *Canadian Journal of Political Science*, 22(1): 137–45.

Bejan, R., Craig, S.L. and Saini, M. (2014) 'I love my job but.... A portrait of Canadian social workers' occupational conditions', *Canadian Social Work*, 16(1): 21–45.

Béland, D., Marchildon, G.P. and Prince, M.J. (2020) 'Understanding universality within a liberal welfare regime: The case of universal social programs in Canada', *Social Inclusion*, 8(1): 124–32.

Bonikowska, A. (2022) 'Who are Canada's legislators? Characteristics and gender gaps among members of legislative bodies', *Economic and Social Reports*, 2(9): 1–17.

Borchert, J. (2011) 'Individual ambition and institutional opportunity: A conceptual approach to political careers in multi-level systems', *Regional and Federal Studies*, 21(2): 117–40.

Cameron, D. and Simeon, R. (2002) 'Intergovernmental relations in Canada: The emergence of collaborative federalism', *Publius: The Journal of Federalism*, 32(2): 49–72.

Canadian Council of Social Work Regulators (2017) 'Publications & resources', *Canadian Council of Social Work Regulators*, Available from: https://ccswr-ccorts.ca/publications-resources [Accessed 17 September 2024].

Canadian Institute for Health Information (2023) 'Social workers', *Canadian Institute for Health Information*, Available from: www.cihi.ca/en/social-workers [Accessed 17 September 2024].

Canadian Press (2021) 'Promoting French and preserving Indigenous languages a priority: Petitpas Taylor', *LethbridgeNewsNOW*, 22 November, Available from: https://lethbridgenewsnow.com/2021/11/22/promoting-french-and-preserving-indigenous-languages-a-priority-petitpas-taylor [Accessed 17 September 2024].

CASW (Canadian Association of Social Workers) (nd) 'About CASW', *CASW*, Available from: www.casw-acts.ca/en/about-us/about-casw [Accessed 17 September 2024].

CASW (2018) 'Understanding social work and child welfare: Canadian survey and interviews with child welfare experts', Available from: https://www.casw-acts.ca/sites/default/files/attachments/CASW_Child_Welfare_Report_-_2018.pdf [Accessed 26 June 2025].

Cochrane, C. (2015) *Left and Right: The Small World of Political Ideas*, Queens University Press.

Daigneault, P.M., Birch, L., Béland, D. and Bélanger, S.D. (2021) 'Taking subnational and regional welfare states seriously: Insights from the Quebec case', *Journal of European Social Policy*, 31(2): 239–49.

Docherty, D. (2003) 'Political careers between executive hopes and constituency work', in J. Borchert and J. Zeiss (eds) *The Political Class in Advanced Democracies: A Comparative Handbook*, Oxford University Press, pp 67–83.

Docherty, D. (2011) 'The Canadian political career structure: From stability to free agency', *Regional and Federal Studies*, 21(2): 185–203.

Dodeigne, J. (2018) 'Who governs? The disputed effects of regionalism on legislative career orientation in multilevel systems', *West European Politics*, 41(3): 728–53.

Elections Canada (2023) 'House of Commons seat allocation by province 2022–2032', *Elections Canada*, Available from: www.elections.ca/content.aspx?section=res&dir=cir/red/allo&document=index&lang=e [Accessed 17 September 2024].

Government of Canada (2021) 'Audrey McLaughlin', *Government of Canada*, Available from: www.canada.ca/en/women-gender-equality/commemorations-celebrations/women-impact/politics/audrey-mclaughlin.html [Accessed 17 September 2024].

Haddow, R. (2014) 'Power resources and the Canadian welfare state: Unions, partisanship and interprovincial differences in inequality and poverty reduction', *Canadian Journal of Political Science*, 47(4): 717–39.

Hawthorn, T. (2018) 'Dave Barrett: the man who changed a province', *The Tyee*, 3 February, Available from: https://thetyee.ca/News/2018/02/03/Dave-Barrett-Obit [Accessed 17 September 2024].

Ie, K.W. (2023) 'Ministerial mandate letters and co-ordination in the Canadian executive', *Canadian Journal of Political Science*, 56(4): 811–31.

Koebel, K. and Pohler, D. (2019) 'Expanding the Canada workers benefit to design a guaranteed basic income', *Canadian Public Policy*, 45(3): 283–309.

Kourgiantakis, T., Ashcroft, R., Mohamud, F., Benedict, A., Lee, E., Craig, S. et al (2023) 'Clinical social work practice in Canada: A critical examination of regulation', *Research on Social Work Practice*, 33(1): 15–28.

Lawlor, A. and Crandall, E. (2013) 'Committee performance in the Senate of Canada: Some sobering analysis for the chamber of "sober second thought"', *Commonwealth & Comparative Politics*, 51(4): 549–68.

Lucardie, P. (2007) 'Pristine purity: New political parties in Canada', *American Review of Canadian Studies*, 37(3): 283–300.

Lundberg, T.C. (2007) 'Electoral system reviews in New Zealand, Britain and Canada: A critical comparison', *Government and Opposition*, 42(4): 471–90.

Mackay, S. (2013) 'Idolizing Riel, MP Gene Rheaume helped Métis find a place', *Globe and Mail*, 10 December, Available from: www.theglobeandmail.com/news/politics/idolizing-riel-mp-gene-rheaume-helped-metis-find-a-place/article15865381 [Accessed 17 September 2024].

McKenzie, C. (2016) 'Burnout north of 60: Supporting social workers in Nunavut, Canada', *Critical Social Work*, 17(2): 21–41.

McLaughlin, A.M., Rothery, M. and Kuiken, J. (2019) 'Pathways to political engagement: Interviews with social workers in elected office', *Canadian Social Work Review*, 36(1): 25–44.

Meili, D. (2013) 'Go, Gene, go: Métis leader worked to level the playing field for Indigenous peoples', *Windspeaker*, 13 November, Available from: https://windspeaker.com/news/footprints/go-gene-go-metis-leader-worked-level-playing-field-indigenous-peoples [Accessed 17 September 2024].

Merkley, E. (2022) 'Polarization eh? Ideological divergence and partisan sorting in the Canadian mass public', *Public Opinion Quarterly*, 86(4): 932–43.

Moncrief, G.F. (1994) 'Professionalization and careerism in Canadian provincial assemblies: Comparison to U.S. state legislatures', *Legislative Studies Quarterly*, 19(1): 33–48.

National Assembly of Québec (2024) 'Lucienne Robillard', *National Assembly of Québec*, Available from: www.assnat.qc.ca/en/deputes/robillard-lucienne-5135/biographie.html [Accessed 17 September 2024].

Parliament of Canada (nd-a) 'Members of Parliament', *Parliament of Canada*, https://learn.parl.ca/understanding-comprendre/en/people-in-parliament/members-of-parliament [Accessed 17 September 2024].

Parliament of Canada (nd-b) 'Parlinfo', *Parliament of Canada*, Available from: https://lop.parl.ca/sites [Accessed 5 June 2025].

Pioneer Women of the Yukon (nd) 'Change-makers: Honorable Audrey McLaughlin', *Pioneer Women of the Yukon*, Available from: https://yukontrailblazers.ca/changemakers/honorable-audrey-mclaughlin [Accessed 17 September 2024].

Pow, J.T. (2015) *Leave It to the Amateurs: A Career Development Explanation of Political Inexperience among Members of the Canadian Parliament*, Master's thesis, University of British Columbia, Vancouver, UBC Theses and Dissertations, Available from: https://open.library.ubc.ca/collections/ubctheses/24/items/1.0166641 [Accessed 31 May 2025].

Pow, J.T. (2018) 'Amateurs versus professionals: Explaining the political (in)experience of Canadian Members of Parliament', *Parliamentary Affairs*, 71(3): 633–55.

Raney, T. (2020) 'Canada's legislature: A (gendered) parliament for the people', in M. Tremblay and J. Everitt (eds) *The Palgrave Handbook of Gender, Sexuality, and Canadian Politics*, Palgrave Macmillan, pp 167–86.

Statistics Canada (2017) 'Municipalities in Canada with the largest and fastest-growing populations between 2011 and 2016', *Statistics Canada*, 8 February, Available from: www12.statcan.gc.ca/census-recensement/2016/as-sa/98-200-x/2016001/98-200-x2016001-eng.cfm [Accessed 17 September 2024].

Statistics Canada (2021) 'National Occupational Classification (NOC) 2021 (Version 1.0): 41300 – social workers', *Statistics Canada*, Available from: www23.statcan.gc.ca/imdb/p3VD.pl?Function=getVD&TVD=1322554&CVD=1322870&CPV=41300&CST=01052021&MLV=5&CLV=5#shr-pg0 [Accessed 17 September 2024].

Statistics Canada (2024) 'Labour Force Survey, February 2024', *The Daily*, Available from: https://www150.statcan.gc.ca/n1/daily-quotidien/240308/dq240308a-eng.htm [Accessed 6 October, 2024].

Stephenson, M., Rondeau, G., Michaud, J.C. and Fiddler, S. (2001) *In Critical Demand: Social Work in Canada*, Grant Thornton.

Stolz, K. (2003) 'Moving up, moving down: Political careers across territorial levels', *European Journal of Political Research*, 42(2): 223–48.

Webb, H. (2015) 'Changing house: The law affecting a move between elected offices', *Canadian Parliamentary Review*, 38(1): 23–8.

Weber, A., Bodet, M.A., Gelineau, F. and Blais, A. (2024) 'An election too far: Why do MPs leave politics before an election?', *Party Politics*, 30(3): 493–504.

Yan, M.C., Lee, J. and Ko Ling Chan, E. (2021) 'Mechanisms of gatekeeping in the social work profession: Lessons learned from Canada, Hong Kong and South Korea', *British Journal of Social Work*, 51(8): 3283–300.

4

Czechia: social workers as members of the Czech parliament

Agnieszka Zogata-Kusz and Tatiana Matulayová

In Czechia, policy engagement of social workers has only recently become the topic of academic consideration. It has been present sporadically in research (for example, Kodymová, 2011; Janebová et al, 2015; Zogata-Kusz et al, 2022). As for the study programmes preparing future social workers for practice, the issue of affecting political and policy processes has never been a regular part of them. Social work has instead been presented as an instrument of social policy, and social workers have mostly been presented as being objects of social policy rather than as actively trying to influence unjust or ineffective systems that have negative impacts on social work and service users. We might consider such a situation as one of the factors adversely affecting social workers' policy engagement, including engagement in politics as politicians. In this chapter, we discuss factors affecting the number of social workers in political office and their political career paths, as well as their social advocacy in parliament.

Social work as a profession

The social work profession in the Czech territory has evolved dynamically and inconsistently over the 20th century (Matoušek and Havrdová, 2021). In recent years, there has been ongoing discussion, in the context of the professionalisation of social work, about the need for a separate professional law. Despite promises from various ministries over the past decade, no such law has been enacted, reflecting the profession's limited power (Weiss-Gal and Wellbourne, 2008). At the time of writing, social work practice is regulated by various laws, with the Social Services Act being the key one. We can say that with its adoption in 2006, social work became a regulated profession. Specific laws set qualification requirements for an occupation in social work, including tertiary education not only in social work but also in fields such as social pedagogy, special education and law.

Tertiary education for social workers is offered by higher vocational schools (European Qualifications Framework Level 6) and universities. The Association of Educators in Social Work sets minimum educational standards, collaborating with the Ministry of Labour and Social Affairs and the Ministry of Education, which consider these standards for programme accreditation. The Ministry of Education ensures the quality of tertiary education, while universities need the consent of the Ministry of Labour and Social Affairs for social work programmes to meet regulatory standards. Historically, minimum standards have focused on direct practice. As a result, bachelor's programmes in social work emphasise service provision over policy engagement (Zogata-Kusz and Baláž, 2022) and Czech social work graduates are not sufficiently prepared for the clash of powers as potential policy actors (Baláž, 2023). Although practitioners often call for policy changes, they frequently do not see themselves as agents of change (Zogata-Kusz et al, 2022).

In Czechia, as of 2021 there are over 22,000 social workers, which represents 0.43 per cent of the 5.2 million employed individuals (ČSÚ, 2024a). The profession is highly feminised. Despite there being no reliable statistics on the number of female social workers, the partial data indicates that women make up over 90 per cent of the profession (for example, Zajacová, 2023, p 63). As of the end of 2021, the areas of social work with the largest numbers of employees are social services, with 13,378 social workers, and public administration, with 9,037 social workers (Zajacová, 2023, p 79). Nevertheless, there is neither unified guidelines for reporting the number of social workers, nor a public registry of social workers. Social workers in Czechia do not have a strong professional organisation to represent them. The existing professional associations have only a few hundred members altogether.

The gross salaries of social workers in Czechia depend on their level of education and the length of their experience in the field. These salaries range from CZK 15,470 (EUR 610) to CZK 50,020 (EUR 1,974) per month, as outlined in Government Regulation 341/2017 Coll. In 2022, the average gross salary across the national economy was CZK 39,306 (EUR 14,72; Ministry of Labour and Social Affairs – MPSV, 2022). These numbers only confirm long-standing perceptions that social work is considered an undervalued and underpaid profession. This is largely due to the chronic underfunding of the social services sector as well as disparities in compensation between the public administration and non-profit sectors. The chronic underfunding of the social services sector not only results in low wages but also creates unstable employment conditions, such as temporary job contracts, and uncertainty regarding fair wage increases compared to other sectors (Trlifajová and Hurrle, 2018).

Nonetheless, social workers in Czechia are aware of the societal challenges that justify the need for the profession (Vojtíšek and Matulayová, 2023). The pressures created by neoliberal democracy, the market economy and major crises (among other factors) increase the demands on social workers to be active in public discourse, get involved in social advocacy and influence policy processes. Social workers are aware of their role in advocating for the rights and legally protected interests of service users. However, whether they are willing and able to increase their engagement in influencing policy remains an unanswered question (Vojtíšek and Matulayová, 2023), and so far we know little about social workers in political office. In the next section, we focus on the institutional opportunity structures and point out the factors related to the political system itself that may affect social workers' willingness and ability to hold political office at the national level.

Institutional opportunity structures

Political career opportunities for Czech social workers exist at four governance levels: national, regional and local as well as the European Union level. Here, we concentrate on the national level and examine social work members of parliament (SWMPs). Keeping in mind opportunity structure factors, and especially institutional factors (Gal and Weiss-Gal, 2023), we refer to Borchert's (2011) three 'a's and describe the *availability*, *accessibility* and *attractiveness* of political office in the Czech national parliament.

Availability

The Czech Republic is a unitary parliamentary republic, with the president serving as the head of state. Executive authority lies with the government, headed by the prime minister, accountable to the Chamber of Deputies. The Chamber of Deputies serves as the lower chamber of the parliament, the state's legislative authority, with the Senate as the upper chamber.

When one thinks about the structures enabling social workers to pursue elected position at the national level, attention naturally gravitates towards parliament. The Chamber of Deputies, consisting of 200 mandates for deputies serving four-year terms, is the central body. The mandates are distributed according to a proportional electoral system and relate to the number of votes cast in the 14 multi-member districts. The electoral districts coincide with self-governing regions. Candidates must be at least 21 years old. The law determines the maximum number of candidates per list, and this ranges from 14 to 36, depending on the district's population size. In 2021, the number of deputies elected in each district ranged from 5 to 23 (Czech Statistical Office – ČSÚ, 2021b). To secure mandates, a political grouping must surpass an electoral threshold of 5 per cent of valid votes. Since 2021, the thresholds for coalitions have stood at 8 per cent for coalitions of two and 11 per cent for three or more political groupings (Act of Law 247/1995 Coll, on elections to the Parliament of the Czech Republic §49).

The Senate of the Czech Republic consists of 81 members serving six-year terms, elected in a majoritarian electoral system. To ensure stability, one third of the Senate is elected every two years. Candidates are required to be at least 40 years old. In a two-round majority system, each of 81 constituencies elects one candidate. Besides candidates from political parties, movements and coalitions, independent candidates can run for a senatorial mandate under specific conditions.

Parliamentary bodies are special forums where the policy process can be affected. These are mainly committees, which are regular working bodies, and commissions, which are specific working bodies for control, special topics or tasks. Each chamber has its own committees and commissions. We may consider those parliamentary bodies focusing on social issues as especially attractive for social workers and other specialists experienced in the social area. One of the committees regularly established in the Chamber of Deputies is the Social Policy Committee. In the ninth parliamentary term (starting in 2021), it established subcommittees on: Information Technology, Benefit Systems and Issues of the Employment Office; Socially Excluded Areas and the Integration of People after Serving a Sentence; Social Health Boundaries; and Social Services and Persons with Disabilities. As for commissions, examples include the Permanent Commission for Family and Equal Opportunities (Chamber of Deputies – PSP, 2024a). The Senate bodies function in a similar way. For instance, in the 14th electoral term, there is the Permanent Commission for Labour and the Committee for Social Policy with the Subcommittee for the Family (Senát Parlamentu České republiky, 2024).

The Chamber of Deputies and the Senate vote on which committees and commissions will be established and how many members they will have. Whether or not social workers become members of the specific committees and commissions depends, however, on the parliamentary factions in each chamber. A potential barrier to advancing social issues may be represented by the general rule that a deputy can sit on a maximum of two committees and a senator can sit on one committee. Nonetheless, deputies who are not committee members may participate in the meetings and discussions, which may be an opportunity to raise one's voice despite being a non-member (Law no 90/1995 on the Rules of Procedure of the Chamber of Deputies; Law no 107/1999 on the Senate Rules of Procedure).

As well as engagement in the parliamentary working bodies, institutional opportunities to have a voice on social issues exist in other fundamental parliamentary activities, such as proposing bills, submitting written amendments, delivering speeches in the chamber and raising oral interpellations. Furthermore, beyond their legislative duties, deputies and senators may engage in social advocacy by organising conferences and seminars at parliament to address legislative issues, thus providing platforms for dialogue with experts. This may add gravity to a given issue and open up further possibilities for solving related problems.

Accessibility

Social workers entering national politics have to join a political grouping (that is, a party or movement), either as members or as independent candidates, to secure a spot on the candidate list. An alternative in elections for the Senate is gathering 1,000 signatures from voters in the given electoral district. Real accessibility of positions in parliament depends heavily on party nomination strategies, so this is a key factor influencing social workers' political careers. Moreover, access to mandates is limited by competition. In the 2021 elections, 5,243 candidates from 22 groupings vied for 200 mandates, and only four political groupings secured mandates (ČSÚ, 2021b).

The party nomination strategy determines if and where a political group positions its representatives on the candidate list. There are no institutional restrictions on the nomination process, except for certain democratic principles, barring discrimination based on factors such as gender or religion (Outlý and Prouza, 2013). There are no quotas for ethnic minorities or women in elections to the Chamber of Deputies, nor limits on holding multiple offices. Consequently, the positioning of the candidates on the list is entirely at the discretion of the political grouping. By placing candidates in top realistic (that is, guaranteeing election) positions, groupings can significantly influence election outcomes. Among the factors increasing a candidate's chances of securing a realistic spot on a parliamentary list are: prior political engagement, demonstrated party loyalty, political experience, campaign leadership, media proficiency, residence in a regional or district capital, an age between 41 and 50, higher education, experience in a party/political staff role and, to some extent, being male (Dvořák and Pink, 2023). Involvement in a political party's activities – even as a volunteer – increases a social worker's chances of becoming the party's candidate.

However, in the Czech proportional electoral system with flexible candidate lists, voters have several preferential votes, allowing them to affect the results by selecting candidates from various parts of the list. In the Chamber of Deputies, voters can influence the order using four preferential votes, with candidates needing at least 5 per cent of such votes for their list to advance. The election of candidates from unrealistic positions is rare, as voters typically favour those in the top spots on the list (Kneblová, 2014). Social workers, particularly those who work in communities and are widely known, have a great chance of gaining preferential votes.

Attractiveness

The attractiveness of having a mandate as a deputy is high, as is evident from the ratio of candidates to mandates. In the 2021 elections, on average, 26 candidates vied for each seat (ČSÚ, 2021b). When assessing the attractiveness of a position on the basis of financial remuneration, parliamentary mandates rank highly. As per Act No 236/1995, a member of the Chamber of Deputies received CZK 94,775 per month in 2024 (PSP, 2024b), significantly exceeding the average gross monthly nominal wage. In the case of social workers, salaries are significantly lower. Additional responsibilities boost remuneration; for instance, a subcommittee deputy chairperson receives over CZK 105,000, and a parliamentary chamber chairperson earns over CZK 267,000. Furthermore, deputies receive expenses for representational duties, meals and transportation (PSP, 2024b). This means that they are able to *live off politics*, following Weber (1919 [2009]). The legislation, however, allows deputies and senators to pursue external employment (for example, as a community social worker) within specific limits outlined in the Act on Conflict of Interests.

If one assesses the position's attractiveness on the basis of prestige, joining parliament in Czechia is not attractive. Political professions, notably membership of the Chamber of Deputies, have had low prestige for quite some time. As Ryšavý points out, this is partly due to the media's focus on corruption cases involving specific politicians (Ryšavý, 2016, p 65). Overall, while the position of members of parliament offers significant social and financial advantages, its attractiveness from the perspective of prestige is heavily affected by the negative general image of politics. Keeping all this in mind, in the next section we analyse the number and roles of social workers in the Czech parliament.

Political recruitment

To examine the number, roles and political careers of Czech social workers in national politics, we conducted exploratory research, as this is the first study on Czech social workers as national politicians.[1] We identified individuals on the basis of their social work education, though not all of them had practical experience in social work. Because of the absence of comprehensive parliamentary registers in Czechia, we investigated the educational backgrounds of deputies and senators and their political careers using their personal, party or other websites. We then examined the websites of the Chamber of Deputies and the Senate to analyse the parliamentary careers and activities of the social workers we identified. Additionally, we conducted a semi-structured interview with Pavla Golasowská, a SWMP who has both education and experience in social work.

From 2006 up to the parliament that started in 2021, there have been seven members of the Chamber of Deputies and one senator who graduated from social work programmes. Additionally, two senators previously worked as social workers but did not graduate from social work programmes and so were not included in our sample. This small group was diverse as regards their sociodemographic and other characteristics (see Table 4.1). There were

Table 4.1: Characteristics of the social workers who have been members of the Parliament of the Czech Republic since 2006

	Name (gender), year of birth	Highest social work qualification	Social work experience	Municipal council mandate	Regional council mandate	Tenure as an MP	Political grouping affiliation
The Chamber of Deputies	Pavla Golasowská (F), 1964	BSW	Family social worker for 9 years	A town with approximately 34,000 inhabitants, 2010– Deputy mayor, 2022–	–	2014–17 (as a substitute) 2017–21 2021–	KDU-ČSL (Christian democrats) – a member since 2009
	Igor Hendrych (M), 1967	PhD	–	A town with approximately 55,000 inhabitants, 2018– Deputy mayor, 2018–22	2016–	2021–	ANO 2011 movement (a centrist populist party) – a member since 2014
	Karel Sládeček (M), 1963	MSW	–	A city with approximately 285,000 inhabitants, 2010–13	2016–20	2021–	SPD (Freedom and Democracy Party; a Right-wing populist and Eurosceptic party) – a member since 2020 Previously a member of a local political movement and a non-parliamentary political party
	Jan Čechlovský (M), 1974	MSW	Social prevention worker for 6 years Project manager for 2 years	A town with approximately 23,000 inhabitants, 2002– Deputy mayor, 2004–06 and 2012–14 Mayor, 2006–10	–	2010–13	ODS (Civic Democratic Party) – a member since 2001

(continued)

Table 4.1: Characteristics of the social workers who have been members of the Parliament of the Czech Republic since 2006 (continued)

	Name (gender), year of birth	Highest social work qualification	Social work experience	Municipal council mandate	Regional council mandate	Tenure as an MP	Political grouping affiliation
	Jiří Koubek (M), 1976	BSW	–	The capital, Prague, 2018–22; The municipal district of Prague-Libuš, 2010–Mayor, 2010–22	–	2013–17	TOP 09 (liberal conservatives) – a member since 2010
	Yvona Kubjátová (F), 1969	MSW	Child protection worker for 10 years	A city with approximately 102,000 thousand inhabitants, 2002–14	2008–20 Deputy governor, 2008–16	April–June 2010 (as a substitute)	ČSSD (Czech Social Democratic Party) – a member since 1998
	Jiří Valenta (M), 1965	BSW	–	A city with approximately 186,000 inhabitants, 2006–14	2012–16 and 2020–	2013–17	KSČM (Communist Party of Bohemia and Moravia) – a member since 2004
The Senate	Miroslav Adámek (M), 1973	MSW	Child protection/drug prevention worker for 11 years; Director of a social services organisation for 14 years	A town with approximately 25,000 inhabitants, 2022–Mayor, 2022–	–	2018–	An independent, in the Senate for the ANO 2011 movement (a populist centrist party)

Note: BSW = bachelor's degree in social work; MSW = master's degree in social work two women, which is not a small proportion when compared to the overall share of women in the Chamber of Deputies, which in the last elections (in 2021) reached only 25 per cent (ČSÚ, 2021b). However, given the level of feminisation of the profession, there was a huge imbalance in favour of men. The youngest social worker entering the Chamber of Deputies was 36 and the oldest was 58 when they were elected. The average age of the first election to parliament was 45.3 (personal email correspondence with V. Sklenář, Department of Informatics, Office of the Chamber of Deputies, 22 November 2024), which is similar to the average age of 46 for all parliamentarians. All SWMPs come from middle-size or large municipalities (with a minimum of 23,000 inhabitants). Interestingly, each represents a different political grouping – communists, social democrats, Christian democrats, civic democrats, liberal conservatives, a centrist populist movement and a far-right party; the senator is from a centrist populist movement. Simplifying party allegiance patterns, we might say that two SWMPs are affiliated with right-wing parties, two belong to centrist parties, two are aligned with parties on the left of the political spectrum and two represent a catch-all party (sometimes positioned in the Czech political spectrum as centrist with a tendency towards populism). Their small number and strong heterogeneity suggest there may not be a *typical* profile of Czech SWMPs.

It is interesting to compare SWMPs with MPs who hold higher education degrees in selected other helping professions and to examine what percentage of the workforce they represent. Although such a comparison is subject to methodological limitations (comparing the share of people with a particular educational qualification to the share of people in a particular occupation), we proceeded as this allows for rough estimates of the relative share of social workers in parliament. Moreover, this methodological distortion applies uniformly across all groups.

When analysing the composition of parliament, we found that among helping professions, teachers are clearly predominant. During the 2013–17 term, as many as 30 teachers held seats in the Chamber of Deputies alone. Over the two terms following that, this number decreased, and as of 2024, there were 20 in the Chamber of Deputies and 12 in the Senate, constituting 11.38 per cent of all the 281 MPs. In 2023, there were approximately 176,000 teachers in Czechia (ČSÚ, 2024a), including academic pedagogues, which equates to 3.38 per cent of the workforce. As for medical doctors, their representation has ranged between 9 and 22 over the last five terms. For example, in 2022, out of 63,000 medical doctors and dentists (1.21 per cent of the workforce; ČSÚ, 2024b), 17 served as deputies and 15 as senators, representing 11.38 per cent of parliament as of 2024. Regarding lawyers – more specifically, advocates, as their numbers are easier to determine – out of 13,063 advocates in 2024 (0.25 per cent of the workforce; Czech Advocate

Table 4.2: MPs holding higher education degrees in selected helping professions, 2024

Profession	Prevalence in Czechia*	Current representation in parliament**
Social workers	22,415 (0.43%)	4 (1.42%)
Teachers	176,000 (3.38%)	32 (11.38%)
Medical doctors	63,000 (1.21%)	32 (11.38%)
Advocates	13,000 (0.25%)	8 (4.27%)
Psychologists	10,000 (0.19%)	0 (0.00%)

Notes: * Percentages are of the total workforce (n = 5.2 million); ** percentages are of the total MPs in parliament (n = 281)

Chamber, cited in Kábelová, 2024), none were in the Chamber of Deputies, while 8 served in the Senate, constituting 4.27 per cent of all MPs as of 2024.

Other helping professions requiring higher education are represented rarely. For example, over five parliamentary terms, there was only one psychologist (serving for a single term) out of approximately 10,000 psychologists in Czechia (Unie psychologických asociací ČR, z.s., 2022).

As of 2024, 4 out of 281 MPs were social workers (see Table 4.1), constituting 1.42 per cent of all MPs. When comparing this share with social workers' share in the overall Czech workforce of approximately 0.43 per cent, it becomes evident that social workers are over-represented in parliament. However, as discussed and as Table 4.2 shows, other helping professions are even more over-represented.

In the next section, we reflect on the career paths of Czech MPs and the factors influencing them, comparing the patterns with those of SWMPs.

Political career patterns

The Czech multilevel political system, characterised by lack of strict separation between governance levels, supports various political career paths. Bernard and Čermák (2021), drawing on Borchert and Stolz's (2011) concept of political opportunities, found that ascending career paths are common. Typically, politicians move from municipal roles directly to the Chamber of Deputies or, more frequently, to the Senate. The proportion of 'parachutists', or those who start in parliament without prior local or regional experience, is relatively low – around one third in the Senate and slightly higher in the Chamber of Deputies. Descending career paths, where national-level politicians take up regional or municipal roles, are rare (Bernard and Čermák, 2021).

Given the high number of municipal councillors (over 60,000), it is only for a small percentage of them that their position in local government functions as a stepping stone for advancing to the Chamber of Deputies or the Senate. Bernard and Čermák (2021) identify three key factors affecting upward political mobility: the type of political party, the size of the municipality and gender. Candidates from newer political parties and those from larger municipalities, such as Prague, have better chances of moving to national positions. Gender also plays a significant role, with women being clearly under-represented in national politics (Gelnarová, 2010; Sztwiertnia and Hellová, 2012; Vohlídalová et al, 2016; ČSÚ, 2021b). Men are about twice as likely as women to advance to higher levels, while women often remain at the municipal level. The gender gap is bigger at the national level than at the local level (Bernard and Čermák, 2021). We may expect that at least the size of the municipality and gender are factors that negatively affect social workers' engagement in national politics, given that as many as 54 per cent of Czechia's 6,258 municipalities have populations of less than 500 inhabitants (ČSÚ, 2021a) and that the Czech social work field is a heavily feminised profession.

Although the number of SWMPs is too small for quantitative analysis, we can observe that they tend to follow the general trend of ascending career paths. As shown in Table 4.1, almost all social work members of the Chamber of Deputies joined their political factions, most of which were already well established, before starting their political careers. One had been a member of some other – non-parliamentary – political parties. Only the senator was independent and did not belong to the political movement he represented. All but one of the SWMPs began their political career at the local level as a member of the municipal council in a city or big town, and SWMPs have been in politics permanently for between 15 and 20 years. Some SWMPs had the experience of being a mayor or deputy mayor. The one exception is the political career of the only social work senator: Miroslav Adámek. A former youth officer at the town hall and director of a non-profit organisation providing social services, he began his political career directly at the national level as a senator. During his electoral term in the Senate, he ran successfully for a position in a municipal council and even became its mayor. It is worth noting that it was only at that time that he gave up his position as director in the non-profit organisation.

SWMPs stayed in the Chamber of Deputies for 1.28 legislative periods on average, which is less than the average for all deputies for the last five terms (that is, from 2006 up to the parliament that started in 2021), which stands at 1.72 (personal email correspondence with V. Sklenář, Department of Informatics, Office of the Chamber of Deputies, 22 November 2024). Mandate accumulation, in which politicians hold multiple positions across different levels, is another notable feature of the Czech political system. All but one of the SWMPs accumulated mandates at various levels of governance at some point. The representative of the communist party (Jiří Valenta) even accumulated mandates at all three levels between 2012 and 2014. Mandate accumulation is possible because most municipal and regional council mandates are non-professional and less time-consuming, allowing politicians to balance multiple roles. Mayors and other professional local politicians frequently become members of parliament, and this was the case for three SWMPs (see Table 4.1).

Political experience and previous mandate accumulation were vital factors that enabled those social workers who finished their careers at the national level to continue in politics at lower levels. A specific case is represented by Yvona Kubjátová, a long-term employee of her city's social and health department and the head of local and regional-level departments dealing with social services. She was active in politics mainly at the local and regional levels. She entered the Chamber of Deputies in 2010, though only for the two last months of the tenure, as a substitute. She did not run for office in the next parliamentary elections, preferring to focus on the lower levels of governance.

Other than Kubjátová, no other former SWMP has returned to being a social worker following their time in parliament. In addition to the two SWMPs who remained in full-time professional politics after leaving the national parliament, one moved to a position in the private business sector (others have still been in the parliament, with one simultaneously continuing his academic involvement in the field of social work).

To conclude, while, due to the small number of positions that SWMPs have occupied, we cannot talk about general patterns, we observe that the political career paths of social workers generally corresponded to those of other Czech politicians, with ascending political trajectories and holding multiple positions being common.

Social advocacy

Social workers holding an elected political position may pursue many political goals and advance a broad set of policies. Since social work education and practice may have made them more sensitive to unjust systems and aspects of the social environment that have a negative effect on service users, we expect that they would use their positions to engage in social advocacy and attempt to advocate for social justice.

However, when analysing the parliamentary engagement of the Czech SWMPs, we found that this is not always the case. As mentioned earlier, not all of the SWMPs had experience in social work practice or had even worked in social issues-related positions. However, those who did were indeed engaged in the work of parliamentary bodies dealing with social issues (for example, the Committee for Social Policy and the Permanent Commission on Family Issues and Equal Opportunities). They also submitted bills or written amendment proposals or gave speeches regarding social problems, although, naturally, not about social problems exclusively. Those who only had social work education without any practical experience in social work focused mostly on other issues.

Such a situation is not surprising given that policy engagement, as mentioned earlier, is not an integral part of social work education in Czechia, which is focused on work with individual service users (Zogata-Kusz and Baláž, 2022). Moreover, many social workers do not attempt to influence policies that affect their service users (Zogata-Kusz et al, 2022). Consequently, we may expect that people without experience from the field not only have less knowledge about the impact of social legislation on daily practice but also are less sensitive to this or not as prepared to get involved in changing it. Furthermore, in Czech culture, higher education degrees are seen as highly valuable on the labour market, though they do not always correspond to the personal interests of graduates (Český rozhlas Dvojka, 2018; Respekt, 2018).

To illustrate the social advocacy activities of Czech SWMPs, we present the case of Pavla Golasowská in more detail. She is a social worker and has served as a deputy for the Christian and Democratic Union-Czechoslovak People's Party (KDU-ČSL; part of the government formed in 2021) since 2014, when she replaced a deputy who was appointed as the ambassador to Germany. While active in social legislation (regarding, for example, state social support), her primary advocacy in social issues developed in her second term. In an interview in April 2024, Golasowská said that her main motivation for staying in the Chamber of Deputies was the need to champion issues such as hospice care and multi-year funding for social service organisations. Between 2017 and 2021, when her party was in opposition, Golasowská was a member of the Committee for Social Policy, the Subcommittee on Social Services and Persons with Disabilities and the Permanent Commission on Family Issues and Equal Opportunities . Analysis of the parliamentary website shows that, in that period, she submitted 53 written amendments, almost all concerning social issues (pension insurance, social services, benefits for persons with disabilities, childcare services, social and legal protection of children and so on). Golasowská co-proposed 49 bills, nearly half of them on social issues. She spoke at 35 sessions (out of 120), frequently demonstrating expertise in social work and acting as an advocate for disadvantaged people and quality social services. In the interview, she highlighted her key achievements, which included securing compensation for sterilised Romani women and amending a bill on abused children. In the latter case, Golasowská collaborated with a centre supporting children and families affected by domestic violence. In the term that started in 2021, because she belongs to the governmental party, she has been less visible in the parliament. At the same time, she also served as the deputy mayor for social prevention in her hometown, which has a population of nearly 35,000. Nevertheless, Golasowská has served on the Social Policy Committee, the Subcommittee on Social Health Boundaries and the Subcommittee on National Minorities. By May 2024, she had submitted two amendments on child protection and co-proposed four bills, including one on the protection of health from addictive substances and one on registered partnerships. Golasowská pointed out that many of her topics come from external organisations or individuals. She has maintained ties with social work through her former non-governmental organisation employer and community volunteer work, such as organising community breakfasts. Her advocacy has extended beyond legislation to raising awareness via conferences and round-tables. For example, at a bereaved mother's request, she organised an event on suicide to raise awareness, engage young people and support a foundation for funding therapies.

Conclusion

We envision social workers as agents of change, capable of promoting social justice and influencing public policy, including by serving as politicians at national level. Although the number of SWMPs has been modest over the five parliamentary terms from 2006, with eight SWMPs in total, social workers are in fact over-represented in parliament relative to their share of the workforce. Social workers' political careers resemble those of other politicians. To understand the representation of social workers in parliament, we focused on institutional and environmental factors. Regarding institutional factors, we particularly emphasise the importance of political party nomination strategies, especially those related to gender and residence, which can limit social workers' electoral opportunities. In terms of environmental factors, the professional discourse within social work poses additional limitations. Specifically, there is insufficient emphasis on macro practice and policy engagement in both practice and education. We believe that addressing these gaps could enhance social workers' motivation and ability to pursue political roles. As evidenced by a few examples, when social workers become active politicians, they often prioritise social issues and are capable of driving meaningful change in national parliament.

Note
[1] We thank our students Adéla Kadlčíková, Lucie Bendiková, Kristýna Warlová and Slavomír Glomb for their assistance with the data collection.

Funding
The work on the text was supported by the Internal Grant Agency of Palacký University Olomouc (grant IGA_CMTF_2024_009).

References

Baláž, R. (2023) 'Be ready for the clash of powers: Theorising power for teaching policy practice in social work', *European Journal of Social Work*, 26(4): 773–85.

Bernard, J. and Čermák, D. (2021) 'Vzestupné a sestupné politické dráhy českých poslanců a senátorů', *Acta Politologica*, 13(1): 22–42.

Borchert, J. (2011) 'Individual ambition and institutional opportunity: A conceptual approach to political careers in multi-level systems', *Regional and Federal Studies*, 21(2): 117–40.

Borchert, J. and Stolz, K. (2011) 'Introduction: Political careers in multi-level systems', *Regional and Federal Studies*, 21(2): 107–15.

Český rozhlas Dvojka (2018) 'Vladimíra Dvořáková: Pro mě není problém, že politik nemá vysokou školu, ale že podvádí', *Český rozhlas*, Available from: https://dvojka.rozhlas.cz/vladimira-dvorakova-pro-me-neni-problem-ze-politik-nema-vysokou-skolu-ale-ze-7578239 [Accessed 17 September 2024].

CSO [Czech Statistical Office] (2024) Labour Market in the Czech Republic - Time Series - 1993–2023. 201A Employed persons by areas and regions, Available from: https://csu.gov.cz/docs/107508/f159ac35-e3e6-6cb6-4941-21b78e9dcfa0/25013124042.xlsx?version=1.0

ČSÚ (Český statistický úřad) (2021a) *Malý lexikon obcí 2021*, Český statistický úřad.

ČSÚ (Český statistický úřad) (2021b) 'Volby do Poslanecké sněmovny Parlamentu České republiky konané ve dnech 8.10. – 9.10.2021', *ČSÚ*, Available from: https://volby.cz/pls/ps2021/ps?xjazyk=CZ [Accessed 17 September 2024].

ČSÚ (Český statistický úřad) (2024a) 'Pracovníci a mzdy ve vzdělávání', *ČSÚ*, Available from: https://csu.gov.cz/pracovnici-a-mzdy-ve-vzdelavani?pocet=10andstart=0andpodskupiny=233andrazeni=-datumVydani#data-a-casove-rady [Accessed 17 September 2024].

ČSÚ (Český statistický úřad) (2024b) 'Pracovníci a mzdy ve zdravotnictví', *ČSÚ*, Available from: https://csu.gov.cz/pracovnici-a-mzdy-ve-zdravotnictvi?pocet=10andstart=0andpodskupiny=263andrazeni=-datumVydani [Accessed 17 September 2024].

ČSÚ (Český statistický úřad) (nd) 'Výběrové šetření pracovních sil (VŠPS)', Available from: https://csu.gov.cz/vykazy/vyberove_setreni_pracovnich_sil [Accessed 17 September 2024].

Dvořák, P. and Pink, M. (2023) 'Party nomination strategies in flexible-list PR: Which candidate characteristics lead to realistic positions?', *East European Politics and Societies*, 37(4): 1448–71.

Gal, J. and Weiss-Gal, I. (2023) 'The policy engagement of social workers: A research overview', *European Social Work Research*, 1(1): 47–64.

Gelnarová, J. (2010) 'Reprezentace žen v politice z pohledu politické teorie aneb "Co všechno znamená, když se řekne, že ženy jsou v politice podreprezentovány?"', *Acta Politologica*, 2(2): 120–35.

Janebová, R., Hudečková, M., Zapadalová, R. and Musilová, J. (2015) 'Příběhy sociálních pracovnic a pracovníků, kteří nemlčeli – Způsoby řešení dilemat', *Czech and Slovak Social Work*, 15(2): 25–39.

Kábelová, A. (2024) 'Kolik je advokátů a kolik advokátek? Kde je koncipientů "0"?', *Advokátní Deník*, 29 October, Available from: https://advokatnide nik.cz/2024/10/29/kolik-je-advokatu-a-kolik-advokatek-kde-je-koncipie ntu-0/ [Accessed 17 September 2024].

Kneblova, E. (2014) 'Využívání preferenčních hlasů', in V. Havlik (ed) *Volby do Poslanecké sněmovny 2013*, Munipress, pp 239–58.

Kodymová, P. (2011) 'Reformní paradigma v praxi české sociální práce', in E. Marášová (ed) *Politiky a paradigmata sociální práce*, Univerzita Tomáše Bati ve Zlíně, Fakulta humanitních studií, pp 59–62.

Matoušek, O. and Havrdová, Z. (2021) 'Beginning anew: Social work education in the Czech Republic after the Velvet Revolution', in W. Lorenz, Z. Havrdová and O. Matoušek (eds) *European Social Work After 1989*, Springer, pp 17– 31.

MPSV (Ministerstvo práce a sociálních věcí) (2022) 'Sdělení Ministerstva práce a sociálních věcí o vyhlášení průměrné mzdy v národním hospodářství za první až třetí čtvrtletí roku 2022 pro účely zákoníku práce', 426/2022 Sb, *MPSP*, Available from: https://www.google.com/url?sa=t&source= web&rct=j&opi=89978449&url=https://www.mpsv.cz/cms/docume nts/38d01deb-e84b-74a0-bc67-ac29afe16757/426_2022.pdf&ved=2ahU KEwiDlpHq5YWOAxUa8LsIHb-RIU0QFnoECBoQAQ&usg=AOvV aw1-e9gNDwveSsxDyiVloTTK [Accessed 17 September 2024].

Outlý, J. and Prouza, J. (2013) *Navrhování a výběr kandidátů: politické strany v ČR a ve střední Evropě*, Civipolis.

PSP (Poslanecká sněmovna parlamentu České republiky) (2024a) 'Výbory, komise a delegace', *PSP*, Available from: www.psp.cz/sqw/organy.sqw? [Accessed 17 September 2024].

PSP (Poslanecká sněmovna parlamentu České republiky) (2024b) 'Časté dotazy', *PSP*, Available from: www.psp.cz/sqw/hp.sqw?k=675andz=3729 [Accessed 17 September 2024].

Respekt (2018) 'Titulománie', *Respekt*, Available from: www.respekt.cz/ vase-dopisy/titulomanie [Accessed 17 September 2024].

Ryšavý, D. (2016) 'Career politicians a dozen years after regionalisation of the Czech Republic (2000–13)', *The Journal of Legislative Studies*, 22(1): 54–82.

Senát Parlamentu České republiky (2024) 'Orgány Senátu a senátorské kluby', *Senát Parlamentu České Republiky*, Available from: www.senat.cz/ organy/index.php?ke_dni=13.9.2024andO=14andlng=cz [Accessed 17 September 2024].

Sztwiertnia, R. and Hellová, D. (2012) 'Ženy v lokální politice – případová studie obcí do tří tisíc obyvatel v Moravskoslezském kraji', *Politologický časopis*, 19(3): 260–75.

Trlifajovà, L. and Hurrle, J. (2018) 'Work must pay: Does it? Precarious employment and employment motivation for low-income households', *Journal of European Social Policy*, 29(3): 376–95).

Unie psychologických asociací ČR, z.s. (2022) 'Návrh zákona o psychologických a psychoterapeutických službách', *UPAČR*, Available from: https://upacr.cz/navrh-zakona-o-psychologickych-a-psychoterapeutickych-sluzbach/ [Accessed 17 September 2024].

Vohlídalová, M., Maříková, H., Čermáková, M. and Volejníčková, R. (2016) *Sólo pro soprán: O ženách v české politice*, Sociologický ústav AV ČR, v.v.i.

Vojtíšek, P. and Matulayová, T. (2023) 'Vize pro sociální práci', *Czech and Slovak Social Work*, 5: 72–86.

Weber, M. (1919 [2009]) 'Politika jako povolání', in M. Weber, *Metodologie, sociologie a politika*, selected and edited by Miloš Havelka, Oikoymenh, pp 243–93.

Weiss-Gal, I. and Welbourne, P. (2008) 'The professionalisation of social work: A cross-national exploration', *International Journal of Social Welfare*, 17: 281–90.

Zajacová, M. (2023) Sociální práce jako profese v České republice, Dissertation, Charles University Digital Repository, Available from: http://hdl.handle.net/20.500.11956/179227 [Accessed 17 September 2024].

Zogata-Kusz, A. and Baláž, R. (2022) 'For what do we educate future social workers? For service delivery or policy engagement?', Paper presented at the 20th Anniversary Conference of the European Network for Social Policy Analysis (ESPAnet): Social Policy Change between Path Dependency and Innovation, Vienna, 12–16 September.

Zogata-Kusz, A., Navrátil, P. and Matulayová, T. (2022) 'Politická praxe – výzva pro české vzdělavatele v sociální práci', *Czech and Slovak Social Work*, 2022(6): 56–68.

5

Finland: taking political office to a new level?

Christian Kroll, Sanni Salonen and Helena Blomberg

This chapter focuses on politicians with a social worker background in Finland, a country typically considered part of the Nordic welfare state model. It examines such politicians at both the national and county levels. First, the chapter provides a brief overview of members of Parliament (MPs) with a social worker background, noting that, historically, their number has been relatively limited. Furthermore, new empirical findings are presented concerning social workers elected to the new county-level councils in the newly established regional entities known as 'wellbeing services counties'. Introduced in 2023, these 21 counties are responsible for organising health, social and rescue services in Finland. The empirical findings are based on a survey conducted in spring 2024 on the political recruitment of social workers to county councils, their career paths and their social advocacy.

Social work as a profession

In international comparison, Nordic and, perhaps above all, Finnish social workers can be regarded as having a strong position both as part of the welfare system and as a profession with academic qualifications (Lorenz, 1994; Meeuwisse and Swärd, 2006). Finnish social workers are trained exclusively at research universities, where, since the 1990s, social work has been taught as a specialist subject on a par with other social science subjects. The master's degree in social sciences with a major in social work, which is required for legal registration as a social worker, aims to equip the graduate with both professional and more generic academic competences. The fact that, in Finland, the academic discipline of social work was historically a sub-programme within the subject of social policy is still reflected in the relatively strong emphasis in teaching curricula on structural explanations for, and policies against, social problems (Blomberg and Kroll, 2017).

The Finnish welfare system – one incarnation of the rather generous Nordic comprehensive and universal welfare state with an emphasis on public services (Anttonen and Sipilä, 1996) – could be regarded as recognising these special competences today. An example of this is the inclusion in the

Social Welfare Act 1301/2014 of the task for public sector social workers to conduct 'structural social work', with the dual objectives of influencing and actively participating in (local/county) political processes through the gathering of information and knowledge from field work and actively making suggestions to (local and, later on, county) decision makers about how to develop services on the basis of detected shortcomings.

Although social workers have extensive university education and a relatively strong position within the fairly comprehensive welfare state, there are structural limitations when it comes to the number of social workers that could reasonably be expected to hold political office in Finland. This stems from the fact that there are only some 8,200 registered social workers of working age in the country of 5.6 million inhabitants, a tiny percentage of the total of 2,373,934 individuals aged 18 to 64 in gainful employment in all sectors in 2023 (Statistics Finland, 2023a), of which a total of some 366,200 work in the social and health care sector (15.4 per cent of the total workers) (Finnish Institute for Health and Welfare, 2024).

The comparatively low number of social workers in Finland results from the introduction in the 1990s of universities of applied sciences and a dual tertiary education system that distinguishes between these universities and research universities. This created two distinct professions within social services: social service workers with bachelor's degrees from universities of applied sciences and social workers educated at research universities. Social service workers, who are more numerous and handle more 'practical' social services, are legally distinct from social workers. The latter have greater professional discretion and handle the most demanding tasks. This chapter focuses solely on social workers.

Due to the high level of education of Finnish social workers and their position and competences, they are often compared to medical doctors within the health care sector. Furthermore, social work is a strongly female-dominated profession – in 2022, only 6.8 per cent of licensed social workers employed in the public sector were men. The predominant age group among social workers in the public sector was 35–44 years, comprising 29 per cent of the workforce (Finnish Institute for Health and Welfare, 2024).

Institutional opportunity structures

In this section, we briefly consider some of the many aspects that have been found in previous research to be of potential importance for career patterns and political professionalisation in the Finnish political system and which could also be assumed to have a bearing on social workers who wish to engage in the political process proper. Many of these aspects, such as the electoral system, described later, have implications at the local, regional and national levels. Since the focus of our chapter is on the opportunities provided by the new county decision-making level regarding social and health services, the more specific opportunity structure for this decision-making level is also described later in this section.

Some of the general aspects derive from the electoral system (the general principles of which are the same for elections at all levels except for presidential elections), which is a combination of a proportional list system and mandatory candidate voting. While the total number of votes is decisive for the number of seats a party or equivalent receives in a given electoral district, the individual candidates who are elected (within the limits set by the total number of party votes) are those on the party list who receive the largest number of personal votes (Karvonen, 2011).

Traditionally, local and county party branches of (even major) political parties have few or no paid officials, requiring individual candidates to build their own support groups, often using personal economic resources (Ruostetsaari, 2003, p 110). This can limit opportunities for some potentially interested individuals, such as social workers, whose salaries have been lower than the salaries within many other professions requiring a higher university education (Local Government and County Employers, 2022; Statistics Finland, 2022a). However, at the local level, particularly in small rural municipalities where people often know each other and the number of votes needed to be elected is low, financial resources may not be a decisive factor.

Although the electoral system makes it possible to stand without being on the list of an established political party, the power and position of political parties in decision making in Finland are generally robust (see Ruostetsaari, 2003). Furthermore, while the electoral system, where every vote counts, usually seems eager to include many (even politically independent) candidates on lists, parties can still be assumed to be important for the political career opportunities of individual candidates in many ways. Structural, tactical and voter-related factors appear to contribute to an individual's chances of receiving votes. Karvonen (2011) found that party size, voting district magnitude, list alliances and incumbency influence the distribution of votes for candidates in parliamentary elections. The Finnish parliament has 200 members elected for four-year terms, with most former and current MPs representing established parties.

An additional perspective related to the recruitment of social workers as politicians has to do with the structural circumstances within the rather comprehensive Finnish welfare system. Finnish social workers, supported by the welfare system, have ample opportunities for political advocacy. Research also shows their commitment to social justice and their political engagement (af Ursin et al, 2023; Kallio et al, 2023). However, some studies indicate that they prefer to separate their professional identity from their personal political views, seeing social work as apolitical, which has implications regarding collaboration with political decision makers (for example, Kallio, 2021).

To the extent that social workers wish to engage politically, Finland's social and health reform of 2023 would seem to have added an important new level to the political opportunity structures of social workers. Previously, the Finnish welfare system followed the traditional Nordic model of organising public services, assigning to the municipal level the responsibility for, among others, health, social, educational and rescue services, which were funded by local taxes. However, due to worsening municipal economic conditions, urbanisation and an ageing population, service provision varied significantly between municipalities. To address these issues, the responsibility for organising health, social and rescue services was transferred to 21 new county entities – the wellbeing services counties mentioned earlier – each governed by an elected county council. Uniquely, this reform also amalgamated health, social and rescue services into one joint sector, despite concerns from social service representatives about the potential dominance of health care in decision making. A notable change in the reform is that these counties have no taxation rights and are financed through the state budget. Along with state-imposed caps on expense growth to reduce public spending, this has led to substantial service cuts and has also sparked intense political debate over the reform's implications and the responsibilities of the parties involved.

Voter turnout for the first wellbeing services county election, held in 2022, was low at 47.5 per cent, prompting a debate on democracy and ways to improve participation. Helimäki (2022) attributes this low turnout to the fact that the election was held just six months after the reform, which led to campaign issues and limited preparation time, meaning that mostly only those deeply interested in politics voted. Despite these challenges, the main traditional parties prevailed, and the impact on the electoral success of social work candidates remains unclear.

The county councils, taken together, comprise a total of 1,379 councillors (and an equal number of deputy councillors). New county councils have 59–79 members, larger than most municipal councils, which have 13–27 members (although municipal councils in larger cities have 43–79 members). Consequently, an individual councillor's impact may be less significant at the new county council level than it was at the municipal level, which was previously responsible for social and health services.

Still, early reports and our own statistics indicate that in the only election at the time of writing, the opportunity structure provided for health and social care professionals at county level seems to have been rather favourable. Candidates working in social and health services in general were heavily over-represented among candidates in the county council elections: while, as noted earlier, 15.4 per cent of employees in Finland work in social and health services, 24.3 per cent of the nominated candidates belonged to this group (Statistics Finland, 2022b). This is probably not surprising, given that most social and health professionals who were previously employed by municipalities were transferred to the wellbeing counties following the administrative reform. The over-representation of social care and health care professionals may indicate voters' desire to have experts in the field decide on their region's welfare services (Helimäki, 2022): a total of 30.1 per cent of elected councillors were social and health care professionals (compared to 24.3 per cent of those standing for election; Statistics Finland, 2022b).

Many of the candidates, both from the social and health service sector and beyond, were active politicians at both municipal and national levels, since it is possible to hold dual or even 'triple' mandates. Nearly 40 per cent of municipal politicians were nominated in county elections (Borg, 2023). Unlike MPs, county (and municipal) councillors are not paid employees, but hold regular jobs alongside their public office. County councillors receive meeting allowances, compensation for income loss, travel expenses and per diems, as outlined in the Act on Wellbeing Services Counties 2021/611, §87. Each county sets its own per diem amounts, and these varied from EUR 4,000 to EUR 19,000 per councillor annually in 2023 (Yle, 2024).

Overall, from the perspective of opportunity structures, it seems difficult to make any clear assumptions about what would affect political career patterns, especially for social workers. The fact that the wellbeing services county elections, central to this chapter, had been held only once at the time of writing greatly limits the ability to draw on previous research on this matter, making it a subject for the present inquiry instead. However, a county council established to regulate social (and health) services should, in principle, make it a highly attractive political office for social workers (more so than for many non-social workers). One would also expect that they might have preferential access through party recruitment and/or voter preferences because of their occupation.

Political recruitment

When starting our investigation into Finnish social workers holding political office at different levels, we initially relied on publicly available data on their backgrounds at the three administrative levels that exist today in Finland: national, county and local. There seems to be only one MP with a background in social work in the most recent (one-chamber, 200-seat) parliament (elected in 2023). Meanwhile, at county level, a total of 21 regular councillors and 24 deputy councillors (deputies to the regular councillors) with a social worker background were elected in the wellbeing services county elections in late 2022, out of a total of 1,379 councillors and an equal number of deputy councillors. Data on the educational or professional background of the nearly 9,000 elected municipal councillors is difficult to obtain. Based on these findings and considering that the county councils were established explicitly and exclusively to provide and regulate social, health and rescue services, which tentatively makes them an ideal arena for social worker politicians, we decided to concentrate mainly on the county level for more detailed empirical data collection. However, initially, we examine the situation at the level of MPs, including a retrospective view to the extent possible. Whereas the section on MPs in this chapter is based solely on secondary sources, for the county level we conducted a web survey of all those with a social worker background holding elected positions as councillors or deputy councillors in the wellbeing services counties.

Political recruitment at the national level

Since social work was not introduced as a study subject in Finland until after World War II, this also marks the beginning of our research period. In the national parliaments from 1948 to the parliament elected in 2023, there have been eight social worker MPs (see Table 5.1), five representing the Social Democratic Party, two the (conservative) National Coalition Party and one the Left Alliance. All of them were women. Three of them were in their mid-forties when elected for the first time, four were in in their mid-thirties, and one was aged 27. It seems that all but one had been working as a social worker at some point before being elected.

The fact that all MPs with a background in social work are women is not surprising given that social work is a highly female-dominated field in Finland. The overall representation of women in the Finnish parliament has strengthened throughout its history. When the parliament first convened in 1907, women made up 9.5 per cent of MPs, whereas in the 2023 parliamentary elections, 46 per cent of elected representatives were women (Parliament of Finland, nd).

MPs with a background in social work are elected at a lower-than-average age: the mean age at the time of their election is 39 years old, while the average age for MPs, based on statistics covering the years 1945–2023, is 48 years (Parliament of Finland, 2023). In recent decades, roughly 40 per cent of the MPs elected to the Finnish parliament have been new representatives, though in the 2023 parliamentary elections, only 30.5 per cent of the elected representatives were new MPs. This indicates that entering the parliament as a new member is challenging. Regarding educational background, the proportion of higher education graduates among parliamentarians has been on the rise, and in the 2023 elections, three quarters of the elected representatives had a higher education degree (Statistics Finland, 2023b), including the social worker MP.

Of the 2,424 candidates for the 200 seats in parliament in the 2023 elections, there were 16 social workers, of whom 1 was elected. This has

Table 5.1: Social workers in the Finnish parliament

Name	Gender	Age when first elected as MP	Party	Term of office
Helena Marttila	Female	39	Social Democratic Party	12 April 2023–
Heidi Viljanen	Female	39	Social Democratic Party	17 April 2019–4 April 2023
Anneli Kiljunen	Female	46	Social Democratic Party	19 March 2003–4 April 2023
Satu Taiveaho	Female	27	Social Democratic Party	19 March 2003–19 April 2011
Marjaana Koskinen	Female	33	Social Democratic Party	24 March 1995–19 April 2011
Terttu Huttu-Juntunen	Female	44	Left Alliance	24 March 1995–23 March 1999
Anneli Taina	Female	36	National Coalition Party	21 March 1987–23 March 1999
Margit Borg-Sundman	Female	46	National Coalition Party	22 July 1948–28 March 1954 22 July 1958–22 March 1970

been the average almost continuously since 1948, with at least one social worker MP in parliament, except for the periods from 1955 to 1957 and from 1971 to 1986, when there were none. However, since social worker MPs were usually elected for consecutive terms, there were at times two social worker MPs in parliament during the same term. Given the small number of social work professionals in Finland (noted earlier), one cannot necessarily talk about an 'under-representation' of social worker MPs.

Political recruitment in the wellbeing services counties

We turn next to the social workers who were elected to the first ever wellbeing services county councils. Information on the professional background of councillors (and deputy councillors) was gathered through the Finnish Broadcasting Company's (Yle) web-based 'Election machine', which contains the names of all candidates standing for election. This information was combined with information from the JulkiSuosikki register maintained by Valvira, the National Supervisory Authority for Welfare and Health, through which it is possible to identify registered social workers. The vast majority of trained social workers have listed themselves on the Valvira register. In principle, however, there may have been candidates with a qualification in social work who did not publicly declare this when standing for election or who had obtained their qualification before it became mandatory for (public) social workers to register with Valvira.

Based on our checks, a total of 111 persons officially registered as social workers stood in this election. Of these, 21 were elected as regular councillors and 24 as deputy councillors. Thus, according to our calculations, 1.5 per cent of all councillors were social workers (21 of 1,379), and the percentage for deputy councillors was similar. Considering that social work is a relatively niche profession in Finland, this share of councillors can be regarded as quite large. However, according to our analyses, medical doctors, for example, seem to have been even more over-represented, comprising 9.9 per cent of all elected councillors.

Only one of the county councillors/deputy councillors with a background in social work was under the age of 30. The average age of the elected social worker councillors was 46.5 years, which is slightly lower than the average age of all those elected to county councils (51.1 years) (Statistics Finland, 2022b). Only 12 per cent of the social worker candidates and 7 per cent of the elected county councillors/deputy councillors with a background in social work were men, which is not surprising since social work is a highly female-dominated field. In comparison, only slightly more than half (53.5 per cent) of all those elected to county councils in 2022 were women (Borg, 2023). Furthermore, in about half of the wellbeing services counties, there was at least one social worker councillor. All county councillors or deputy county councillors represented traditional parties, mostly the Social Democratic Party or the Centre Party.

We now turn to our survey data[1] consisting of responses from 21 county councillors/deputy councillors. To investigate in further detail the aspects facilitating political recruitment among social workers holding elected political office at the county council level, we used the Civic Voluntarism Model developed by Verba et al (1995) as a heuristic tool. The model has previously been used in research on policy engagement among social work students and professionals (for example, Gal and Weiss-Gal, 2015; Schwartz-Tayri, 2021; Kindler and Ostrander, 2022; Kim et al, 2023). According to the model, an individual's policy engagement can be explained by resources, psychological commitment and recruitment networks. Individuals with resources (time, money, expertise) and psychological commitment (interest and ideological fervour) are more likely to engage in social influence activities, especially if they are asked to participate. Membership in various recruitment networks can also facilitate political participation – for example, running for office.

Our results (Figure 5.1) show that there are several factors influencing (voluntary) political participation – in this case, the decision to stand for county elections. With reference to the Civic Voluntarism Model, we can conclude that *resources*, measured as the desire to use (self-perceived) social

Figure 5.1: Factors influencing the candidacy of county councillors and deputy councillors with a social worker background (%)

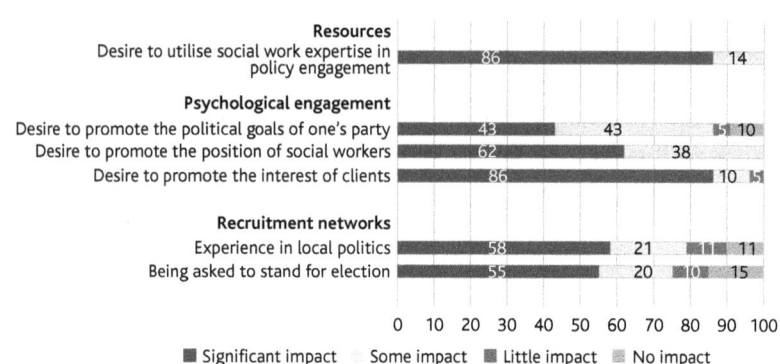

work expertise in policy engagement, was considered by a large majority of respondents to be a significant factor when choosing to stand for election. Different aspects of *psychological engagement* were also considered important, but to varying degrees. The desire to promote the interest of clients in social work was considered a significant factor by a large majority of respondents. The wish to promote the interests of social workers was also a significant factor according to a majority of the respondents. In contrast, the desire to promote the political goals set by one's party was significant for less than half of the respondents. *Recruitment networks*, measured as previous experience in local politics and being asked to stand for election, were significant for about half of respondents.

In sum, the two factors perceived as most important when choosing to stand for election at county level were the desire to utilise one's social work expertise in policy engagement and the desire to promote the interests of social work clients.

Political career patterns

Career paths at national level

Shifting the focus to career paths and back to the parliament level, MPs with a social worker background have been long-standing representatives, serving from two to five terms in parliament, with one exception (see Table 5.1). This is often the case in Finnish politics, which tends to be rather person-centred. It appears that while three of the MPs had been active as social workers before being elected, the remaining five MPs had held more senior positions, with most serving as social directors.

Furthermore, it can be concluded that at national level, most MPs with a social worker background obtained quite prominent positions within the parliamentary system during their political career (often, but not exclusively, in committees and other groups related to social and health care). Two even served as government ministers: the social democrat MP Terttu Huttu-Juntunen served as one of two concurrent Ministers of Social and Health Affairs. The conservative MP Anneli Taina served first as Minister of the Environment and then as Minister of Defence in the late 1990s (in the same government as Huttu-Juntunen). Thus, at one time, there were two ministers with a background in social work in the same broad coalition government led by the social democrat Prime Minister Paavo Lipponen. This government was called the 'six-pack', since it included six parties, ranging from the Left Alliance to the National Coalition Party. After leaving parliament, the career paths of social worker MPs have been quite diverse. Three MPs retired after their parliamentary career, while three returned to the field of social work, but in rather prominent leading positions within municipal social services or in positions as executives in social work-related organisations or associations. One social worker MP (who had also been a minister) continued to hold a very senior position in the state's regional administration, that of governor (in Finnish, *maaherra*/in Swedish *landshövding*) – this post has since been abolished. One of the MPs is serving in parliament. The average length of parliamentary terms for MPs with a background in social work is 12 years, which is longer than the average length for Finnish MPs overall, which is 8.5 years when examining the entire history of parliament. All MPs with a background in social work are women, and, on average, female MPs have a slightly longer total duration of terms in office compared to male MPs (Library of Parliament's Information Service, personal communication, 29 August 2024).

Career paths at county level

To obtain some more information on the career paths of county councillors with a background in social work, we posed several questions in our survey. We started by asking about the employment status of the councillors and deputy councillors. One third of respondents worked in a managerial position in the field of social welfare or social work within a wellbeing services county. However, a significant proportion (one quarter) of respondents were not employed in a position related to social work. Only three respondents worked with clients within their county. It must be noted that due to the response rate, we may have missed out on some councillors who worked with clients. However, all respondents had prior work experience as a social worker, and two thirds had worked as a social worker for at least ten years, while one respondent had less than two years of work experience in social work.

We also examined work experience in different subfields of client work. The majority of respondents indicated that they had worked with different client groups during their careers. Most had experience working with children and families and with young people. Only one respondent had no experience at all of client social work. Furthermore, about half of the respondents had also worked with the unemployed, while about two fifths had experience of working with clients within the criminal justice system, with immigrants and refugees, people with chronic illness, individuals with substance abuse problems or individuals with disabilities. Since Finnish social work is rather specialised and these services are not integrated, it seems that the respondents had moved between tasks and workplaces during their career, which is very common among Finnish social workers generally, as found in national surveys of social workers and social work students (for example, af Ursin et al, 2023).

Furthermore, about three quarters of respondents had been active in party politics before becoming a county councillor/deputy county councillor, and this had been for nine years on average. Overall, 77 per cent of those elected to county councils were serving as municipal councillors at the time of their election (Borg, 2023). A majority of our respondents (13 out of 21) had also been, or was still, a municipal councillor before being elected to county council, for ten years on average. Since the term for municipal/city councils is four years, county councillors/deputy councillors can be regarded as quite experienced municipal politicians. According to our results, quite a few respondents had also been engaged in civil society activities. About half of the respondents had been active in organisations or associations involved in social advocacy, for eight years on average. It is possible that respondents were still active in party politics, municipal politics or other organisations, but our data does not allow for such a detailed analysis.

In our survey, we were also interested in councillors' and deputy councillors' plans for a future political career. At the time of the field work, there was one year left before the next county elections, in 2025. We asked whether respondents were interested in standing in the upcoming county elections. Only one fifth of respondents considered it very likely that they would run as a candidate, while nearly half could not say whether or not they would stand.

In addition, over half of respondents expressed an interest in actively engaging in politics at the national level. This interest in national politics was also reflected in separate analyses concerning the 2023 parliamentary elections: of the 16 candidates that had a background in social work, 10 also ran in the county council elections in 2022.

Social advocacy

We now move on to survey findings concerning social advocacy among county councillors/deputy councillors with a social worker background. Figure 5.2 presents the results for two sets of questions, concerning how councillors perceive the importance of different types of policy advocacy

Figure 5.2: Views of social worker county councillors and deputy county councillors on the importance of social advocacy and opportunities to implement it in county councils (%)

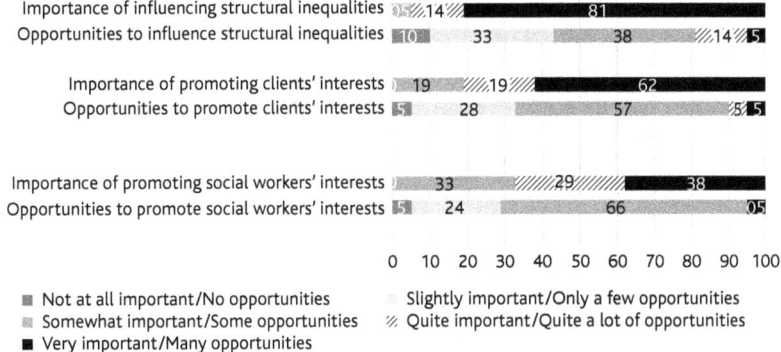

and how they perceive the opportunities they have to promote different types of issues in the county councils. A vast majority (81 per cent) of respondents stated that it is very important to try to influence structures that create inequality and disadvantage. Furthermore, 62 per cent stated it is very important to try to promote the interests of social work clients. Only 38 per cent stated it is very important to promote the interests of social workers.

Concerning respondents' perceived *opportunities* to promote these issues, the picture is different. Very small shares of the respondents reported that they have many or quite a lot of opportunities to influence structural conditions, the interests of social work clients and the interests of social workers. Instead, two thirds of respondents reported that they have *some* opportunities to promote the interests of social workers and almost six tenths stated they had some opportunities to promote the interests of social work clients, while less than half stated that they had some opportunities to influence structural factors that create inequality and disadvantage.

We also asked respondents to provide an example of how they have implemented social advocacy in their role as a county councillor or deputy county councillor. Several respondents indicated that they had addressed themes related to social work and social issues in their speeches at county council sessions and/or within the county council commissions they were members of. Specifically, they highlighted topics such as implementation of legislative changes related to child welfare aftercare and the role of health social work, which have emerged as prominent and contemporary issues in social work within the wellbeing services counties.

In addition to social issues that affect social work clients, several social workers mentioned that they had highlighted the position of social workers in their speeches and opinion pieces. For example, they discussed issues related to the attractiveness of the social sector as an employer and the workplace wellbeing of social workers.

Five respondents did not answer the question, and some of the respondents, all deputy county councillors, indicated that they felt that their capacity to engage in social advocacy was very limited due to their infrequent attendance at county council sessions. Nevertheless, one of these respondents reported making a concerted effort to address issues related to social work and social concerns during meetings of their party's council group.

Conclusion

By way of conclusion, we sum up some central findings concerning opportunity structures, recruitment, career patterns and social advocacy among Finnish social workers elected as politicians. A general conclusion that can be drawn based on our research on social worker MPs and county councillors is that the limited absolute number of social workers holding political office should not be regarded either as 'low' civic engagement by social workers in politics or as being a consequence of unfavourable opportunity structures. Considering the total number of professional social workers in Finland, they can, rather, be regarded as having succeeded fairly well in their efforts to attain political office (although not as well as medical doctors, for example). One reason for this could be related to their significant educational and professional status in the country. However, it could also be due to characteristics of the Finnish political system, where 'every vote counts' and where electoral districts are often small. The latter is especially true of (rural) municipal elections, where people often know each other personally, the number of votes required to be elected can be very low and financial resources might not be a decisive factor.

Of special interest here is the role of the new county-level political councils. The traditional parties dominated the first elections in 2022, and the party political background of the social worker councillors aligns with the Finnish/Nordic political climate, where support for the welfare model has traditionally been characteristic across large parts of the political spectrum. Our study, however, indicates that the creation of the county-level constituencies in Finnish politics give rise to a *recruitment* pattern characterised by a shift from the amateur to the career politician (see Borchert, 2003), both in general and as regards to social workers holding elected office. This is because many elected county councillors (with a social worker background) have prior experience in politics at different levels (when social workers are concerned, mainly at municipal level). Furthermore, many social worker councillors have extensive experience in leadership roles within or outside the public social service sector before being elected, often not engaging directly in client work. They also consider national political careers. This 'professionalisation of social worker politicians' might be a response to the need for the social sector to be heard in policy making, which is often dominated by health care professionals. It may also be the result of political changes favouring high-profile social workers from large cities.

Another tentative conclusion concerns the social worker councillors' views on the preconditions for *policy advocacy*. Our results indicate that social worker councillors view their policy advocacy impact as moderate and they are uncertain about running again in the next elections. This may be due to the larger, integrated organisational environment, combined with state government demands for substantial spending cuts. Additionally, the lack of clarity regarding decision-making power and varying degrees of discretion within councils concerning social services, guided by state-level information, may contribute to councillors' uncertainty. Respondents in this study seem to a large degree to have been established (local) politicians who were elected as representatives of established parties, indicating the importance of such political (recruitment) networks (see the earlier discussion on the Finnish party system). Nonetheless, our results show that almost all respondents seem to perceive themselves mainly as (social) policy advocates. Above all, they want to work to alleviate inequality by using their professional skills in political decision making. There is still a lack of objective data to ascertain the extent to which they have attempted to fulfil these aspirations.

Note

[1] To obtain more information on recruitment (as well as on career patterns and social advocacy, reported later in the chapter), in the spring of 2024 we collected survey data from registered social workers who had been elected as either a councillor or a deputy councillor. We contacted them via email addresses that were publicly available on the counties' websites. Two reminders were sent out. The survey was in Finnish, but participants were given the option to answer open-ended questions in their native language if this was not Finnish (Finland is bilingual Finnish/Swedish, and Sami is an official language in parts of Northern Finland). The invitation to participate in the survey and the survey link was emailed to all 21 municipal councillors and 24 deputy councillors. A total of 21 people participated (a response rate of 47 per cent). Ten of these respondents were serving as county councillors and ten as deputy councillors. For one respondent, we were unable to identify whether they were a councillor or deputy councillor.

Funding

The writing of this chapter was supported in part by the Ministry of Social Affairs and Health, Finland (grant VN/10975/2024).

References

af Ursin, P., Kallio, J., Blomberg, H. and Kroll, C. (2023) 'Sosiaalityön pääaineopiskelijoiden ammattiuraan liittyvät preferenssit ja niitä selittävät tekijät' [Career preferences of students majoring in social work and explanatory factors], *Yhteiskuntapolitiikka*, 88 (5–6): 525–38.

Anttonen, A. and Sipilä, J. (1996) 'European social care services: Is it possible to identify models?', *Journal of European Social Policy*, 6(2): 87–100.

Blomberg, H. and Kroll, C. (2017) 'Social work academia and policy in Finland', in J. Gal and I. Weiss-Gal (eds) *Where Academia and Policy Meet: A Cross-National Perspective on the Involvement of Social Work Academics in Social Policy*, Bristol University Press, pp 59–76.

Borchert, J. (2003) 'Professional politicians: Towards a comparative perspective', in J. Borchert and J. Zeiss (eds) *The Political Class in Advanced Democracies*, Oxford University Press, pp 1–25.

Borg, S. (2023) '*Wellbeing Services County Elections Study 2022*': *A Study of Finland's First Wellbeing Services County Elections*, Research Publication No 116, The Foundation for Municipal Development.

Finnish Institute for Health and Welfare (2024) *Municipal Health and Social Services Personnel 2022*, Statistical Report 41/2024, Finnish Institute for Health and Welfare.

Gal, J. and Weiss-Gal, I. (2015) 'The "why" and the "how" of policy practice: An eight-country comparison', *British Journal of Social Work*, 45(4): 1083–101.

Helimäki, T. (2022) 'Uuden alku vai vanhan toisto? Mitä Suomen ensimmäisten aluevaalien äänestäminen osoitti' [A new beginning or a repetition of the old? What voting in Finland's first wellbeing service county elections revealed], *Politiikka*, 64(2): 167–77.

Kallio, J. (2021) 'Political party choice, social policy opinions, and social advocacy among social and diaconal workers', in K. Günther and J. Kallio (eds) *Research-Based Social Work*, Talentia ry, pp 25–39.

Kallio, J.M., Jaakola, A-M., Blomberg, H. and Kroll, C. (2023) 'Wind of change? Social work students' policy engagement and career preferences in Finland', *Social Work Education*, 43(6): 1590–608, doi: 10.1080/02615479.2023.2201262

Karvonen, L. (2011) 'Preferential voting in Finland: How much do candidates matter, and to whom and why?', *SSRN*, Available from: https://ssrn.com/abstract=1908705

Kim, J., Yoon, H. and Oh, S.-H. (2023) 'Social workers' voluntary political participation: Testing a civic engagement model', *Journal of Social Work*, 23(5): 858–75.

Kindler, T. and Ostrander, J. (2022) 'Factors influencing the political activity of social workers: A comparative study among Swiss and United States social workers', *Journal of Sociology & Social Welfare*, XLIX(1): 148–78.

Local Government and County Employers (2022) 'Kunta-alan palkkatilastot' [Local government salary statistics], *KT*, Available from: www.kt.fi/tilastot-ja-julkaisut/palkkatilastot

Lorenz, W.A. (1994) *Social Work in a Changing Europe*, Routledge.

Meeuwisse, A. and Swärd, H. (2006) 'Socialt arbete i ett internationellt perspektiv' [Social work in an international perspective], in A. Meeuwisse, S. Sunesson and H. Swärd (eds) *Socialt arbete: en grundbok*, Natur och kultur, pp 195–224.

Parliament of Finland (2023) 'Mikä on ollut kansanedustajien ikäjakauma eri aikoina?' [What has been the age distribution of Members of Parliament at different times?], *Eduskunta Riksdagen*, Available from: https://www.eduskunta.fi/FI/naineduskuntatoimii/kirjasto/tietopalvelulta-kysyttya/Sivut/mika-on-ollut-kansanedustajien-ikajakauma-eri-aikoina.aspx

Parliament of Finland (nd) 'Naiset kansanedustajina' [Women as Members of Parliament], *Eduskunta Riksdagen*, Available from: www.eduskunta.fi/FI/naineduskuntatoimii/kirjasto/aineistot/yhteiskunta/historia/naisten-aanioikeus-110-vuotta/Sivut/naiset-kansanedustajina.aspx

Ruostetsaari, I. (2003) 'Finland: From political amateurs to political class', in J. Borchert and J. Zeiss (eds) *The Political Class in Advanced Democracies: A Comparative Handbook*, Oxford University Press, pp 107–23.

Schwartz-Tayri, T. (2021) 'The willingness of social work students to engage in policy practice: The role of personality traits and political participation predictors', *British Journal of Social Work*, 51(7): 2381–98.

Statistics Finland (2022a) 'Earnings of full-time wage and salary earners by education level, age and employer sector, 2022', *Statistics Finland*, Available from: https://pxdata.stat.fi/PxWeb/pxweb/en/StatFin/StatFin__pra/statfin_pra_pxt_14ke.px

Statistics Finland (2022b) 'Background analysis of candidates and elected representatives in the 2022 wellbeing service county elections', *Statistics Finland*, Available from: www.stat.fi/til/alvaa/2022/04/alvaa_2022_04_2022-02-16_tie_001_fi.html

Statistics Finland (2023a) 'Employment', *Statistics Finland*, Available from: https://stat.fi/en/statistics/tyokay

Statistics Finland (2023b) 'Background analysis of candidates and elected members of parliament in the 2023 parliamentary elections', *Statistics Finland*, Available from: https://stat.fi/julkaisu/cl8mvm8uq11mr0cvz91n9u1o7

Verba, S., Schlozman, K.L. and Brady, H.E. (1995) *Voice and Equality: Civic Voluntarism in American Politics*, Harvard University Press.

Yle (2024) 'Tässä aluevaltuustojen kulut ja tuet – "Törkeän paljon", sanoo jopa valtuutettu itse' [The costs and allowances of the regional councils – 'an outrageous amount', says even the councillor themself], *Yle*, Available from: https://yle.fi/a/74-20073090

6

Germany: between civic engagement and social advocacy

Eva Maria Löffler

As a federal state, Germany provides numerous opportunities for the policy engagement of social workers. Policy engagement aims to influence policy processes, enabling citizens to exercise their democratic rights to express their opinions and advocate for their interests. This is also relevant for politically engaged social workers, who can participate in decision making through civic engagement. In addition, by holding elected political office, they can represent the interests of their service users and advocate on their behalf in political and policy processes. In doing so, they align with the normative expectations of the profession, which demand assistance in individual cases and addressing of structures and conditions (Fachbereichstag Soziale Arbeit and DBSH, 2016).

Nevertheless, my study of social workers holding political office (SWHPOs)[1] shows that the representation of service users' interests should not be interpreted as the main intention of social workers in their political engagement. However, SWHPOs can transfer their expertise and knowledge to political discourse. Although it is assumed that elected politicians have the best opportunities to apply their professional expertise in political decision-making processes (for example, Lane and Pritzker, 2018; Amann and Kindler, 2022; Binder and Weiss-Gal, 2022), little is known about this form of political engagement in Germany. This chapter aims to change this.

Social work as a profession

In Germany, 'social work' is used as an umbrella term for two lines of development: social work (care for the poor and welfare) and social pedagogy (education and upbringing). The roots of both lines are generally traced back to the late 19th century, emerging in response to the 'social question' that arose during industrialisation in Western Europe. While the narrative of social work history often begins with the Industrial Revolution, measures to combat poverty existed as early as the Middle Ages. These efforts stemmed predominantly from private benefactors, who viewed philanthropy as a means to demonstrate their charitable values through acts of kindness and generosity.

So far, the German professional discourse has had no consensus on the core essence of social work. Various theories define social work's nature, function and role differently (Hammerschmidt and Aner, 2022). Social work is a person-centred social service provided within the social welfare framework. These services aim to support, advise and care for people in various, primarily precarious, situations. In this sense, social work is a service structure of social policy, shaped and implemented at all levels of government, with its origins tracing back to Otto von Bismarck's social legislation at the end of the 19th century.

Providers of these social services are divided into public (municipalities, states, federal government, social insurance providers) and independent or private organisations, which are further categorised into non-profit organisations (welfare and affiliated organisations, associations, churches and so on) and for-profit entities (commercial providers, self-employed individuals and sole proprietors; Bieker, 2011; Falterbaum, 2013). Social services are provided by social workers (and others) who are generally employed either as salaried staff or civil servants by these different service providers, though around 4 per cent work freelance (Meyer, 2024). The largest employers of social workers are non-profit welfare organisations, such as Caritas, Diakonie, AWO (Arbeiterwohlfahrt) and Paritätischer Wohlfahrtsverband. These organisations operate in various fields, including child protection, family support, care for the elderly, services for people with disabilities and refugee assistance. In this sense, the term social work also represents the paid profession that deals with the challenges and problems people experience in society, and it is committed to supporting them.

Formal academic training for social workers originated in 1908 with the establishment of the Soziale Frauenschule Berlin. This institution offered a structured programme that ultimately led to the recognition of social work as an academic discipline. From the 1960s and 1970s onwards, social work became increasingly institutionalised at universities of applied sciences, firmly establishing it as an academic discipline. Nowadays, social work education is offered at various (private) universities and universities of applied sciences, combining theoretical knowledge with practical training. To practise as a social worker, individuals must obtain a degree in social work from an accredited public or private university (of applied sciences). While there is no national licensing system in general, some specific sovereign tasks have been regulated, and to carry these out, state accreditation is required in addition to a degree in social work or social pedagogy. As well, many employers require proof of qualifications and adherence to ethical standards set by professional associations. These regulations ensure that social workers are equipped to handle sensitive issues in areas such as mental health, addiction, domestic violence and child welfare. Additionally, social workers advocate for policy changes and social reforms to address the systemic problems affecting marginalised populations.

In Germany, social workers have no official registration system, making it difficult to determine their exact numbers. Labour market statistics estimate that around 350,000 individuals with a degree in social work were employed in 2023 (Bundesagentur für Arbeit, 2024). This accounts for approximately 1 per cent of the 46.1 million employed individuals (figure for 2024). According to Bundesagentur für Arbeit (2023), as of 2023, women represent a substantial proportion of the workforce in social work, with a share of 75 per cent, and have a notable part-time employment rate of 55 per cent. Overall, women make up 47 per cent of the total workforce. In 2023, full-time social workers' median monthly gross earnings were EUR 4,371, which was higher than the average median monthly gross earnings of EUR 3,796 for all workers (Bundesagentur für Arbeit, 2023).

The German Professional Association for Social Work (DBSH) was established in 1951 to represent the interests of social workers. It has around 6,000 members, meaning only a small proportion of social workers are involved in the professional association. Other important representative bodies include the unions Verdi and GEW, though the number of social workers among their members is unknown. According to estimates, around 15 per cent of the 45,000 GEW members are employed in youth support and social work (Gewerkschaft Erziehung und Wissenschaft, nd).

There is currently no professional law governing social workers. However, since 2002, the professional association DBSH has advocated for legislation 'to define fields of activity for the social work profession and to ensure their quality through training and continuing education requirements' (DBSH, 2002: 1).

Institutional opportunity structures

Germany's political system is characterised by its federal structure, parliamentary democracy and multi-party system (Schüttemeyer, 2019a; 2019b). These elements create institutional opportunities that enable social workers (and others) to engage politically and hold political office. The political system is based on the Basic Law (GG), the German constitution that came into force in 1949. The Basic Law outlines the division of powers between the national government and the governments of the 16 states. Regarding social policy, the Bundestag (federal parliament) and the Bundesrat (federal council) are the central legislative bodies responsible for establishing the fundamental framework of social policy and enacting laws on issues such as pensions, unemployment insurance and health coverage. Social laws are drafted and passed within these bodies. Through the Bundesrat, the states participate in decision making in many areas of social policy. In addition, the state and local administrations are tasked with implementing social policy measures, such as social assistance, youth welfare and housing support measures. The latter bear considerable responsibility in the practical administration of social services and often serve as citizens' primary point of contact.

At all three levels, governments and parliaments exist to fulfil the respective tasks. Therefore, political positions are available at all three levels. Politicians are not required to have 'formal education and thus no entry requirement [is] defined within the education and training system' (Gerster, 2018, p 11). In this respect, the previous professional backgrounds of 'parliamentary representatives, despite the similarities in their political careers, still exhibit a certain degree of diversity' (Edinger, 2018, p 79), and the path to politics is open to social workers at the national, state and local levels.

At the national level, elected representatives serve in either the Bundestag or the Bundesrat, building the legislative body together. The number of seats in parliament has increased from 402 in the 1st legislative period to 736 in the 20th legislative period (see Table 6.1), but there are plans to fix the number at 630. The Bundesrat (parliament of the state governments) has 69 seats and comprises members of the 16 state governments.

The core requirements to run for office in the national parliament are German citizenship, a minimum age of 18 years and the right to vote. The Members of Parliament Act regulates elected representatives' specific rights and duties but also aims to ensure that no one is prevented from running for office due to disability or other factors. The majority of candidates stand on behalf of political parties. Party district associations and state party conventions select these candidates. Typically, only long-standing party members are nominated for candidacy. Within parties, specific support programmes or quota regulations can be designed to promote diversity among candidates. This can be achieved through gender quotas and programmes encouraging young members or those from various ethnic backgrounds to run for office. This could be a significant advantage for social workers, given that the profession is predominantly associated with feminine traits and is often perceived as a female-dominated field. In addition, it is also possible for independent candidates to run for office without party affiliation. They need at least 200 signatures from eligible voters in the respective electoral district to support their candidacy. Independent candidates often receive support from citizen initiatives or other societal groups to increase their chances and visibility.

Elected representatives in the national parliament become full-time politicians and, in this sense, change their occupation. In July 2024, their gross salary was approximately EUR 11,000 per month. Additionally, they receive allowances for expenses (especially to cover staff costs). As elected representatives, they influence national legislation and shape the political discourse. They can introduce legislative proposals, actively contribute to developing existing laws and oversee their implementation.

Turning to the state level, Germany consists of 16 states. Berlin, Bremen and Hamburg are called city-states, while the others are known as territorial states. They all have a parliamentary system with a government (headed by a prime minister or a city mayor) answering to the state parliament. The parliaments in the 13 territorial states are called Landtag. In the city-states, the parliaments are referred to as Abgeordnetenhaus (Berlin) or Bürgerschaft (Hamburg, Bremen). In addition to overseeing the state government, the parliaments are responsible for passing state laws and approving the state budget.

The number of available seats in parliament varies among states; in 2023, there were 1,894 seats at state level. Of these, the state parliament in Saarland, with 51 representatives, was the smallest, and the state parliament in Bavaria, with 203 representatives, was the largest. The requirements for obtaining a mandate differ slightly between the states, but all candidates must have German citizenship and, generally, they must be 18 years old (in the state of Hessen, 21 years) and have the right to vote. Additionally, candidates must have had their primary residence in the state where they run for office for at least three months. As at the national level, candidates can run for election through political parties or as independents. A legislative period lasts four years in Bremen and five years in all other state parliaments.

Members of state parliaments are mostly full-time politicians. Their salary depends on the state and ranges between around EUR 4,000 and EUR 10,000 monthly. Additionally, they receive expense allowances. They can submit motions to initiate or demand specific political actions. Moreover, the representatives work together in parliamentary groups to develop common positions and plan strategies for parliamentary work.

Looking next at the local level, Germany's 16 states are divided into 400 local authorities, comprising 294 counties and 106 cities (Statistisches Bundesamt, 2024), each governed by its own representative body. The number of political offices within these local authorities varies depending on their size and population, ranging from 20 to 100 positions in counties and 8 to 80 in cities. The 294 counties are subdivided into 10,754 municipalities and smaller cities (Statistisches Bundesamt, 2024), offering even more opportunities to hold elected office. Furthermore, the 106 cities and their respective boroughs provide additional avenues for political engagement at the local level. This highlights the extensive opportunities available for taking on a political mandate in Germany, whether as a council member or mayor. In principle, all eligible voters aged 18 and older can run for office, though a higher minimum age applies in some cases for positions such as county administrators. Quantifying the total number of mandates at this level is challenging, but estimates suggest that between 230,000 and 250,000 individuals serve in such roles nationwide.

While, as described, at the state and national levels, holding political office is typically a full-time, paid position, there are three different ways local politicians carry out this role: as a professional full-time job, as a professional part-time activity or as a voluntary activity. These alternatives can be distinguished by the time involved in the political mandate and/or the monetary remuneration for the mandate (Reiser, 2006). There are only a few larger cities where council members are paid for their political work and live off the remuneration for their local political mandate. For example, approximately 3,400 mayors work full time and are paid for their office, while more than 8,000 serve voluntarily. Social workers in such positions usually continue their regular jobs in social work practice alongside their political position (Leitner and Löffler, 2024).

Political recruitment

This section presents findings from my study of SWHPOs.[2] The academic education of social workers in Germany began in the 1970s, and following this, the first academically trained SWHPOs in the national parliament was Margitta Terborg. She completed her study as a social pedagogue in Bremen in 1972. At 39, she won a seat in the 9th Bundestag for the Social Democratic Party (SPD), the largest parliamentary group, with 228 seats at that time. During this legislative period, she was one of three social workers, although the other two had a vocational qualification in social work rather than a degree.

Table 6.1 shows that social workers without a university degree can be traced back even further, starting from the second Bundestag in 1953. Since the establishment of the Bundestag up to the 20th election period, 54 social workers (31 female) won 131 mandates, and 74 per cent of SWHPOs in the Bundestag were members of parties from the Left spectrum (the SPD, Die Grünen [the Green Party] and Die Linke [The Left]). The table shows that since the tenth Bundestag, the proportion of social workers has consistently been at least 1%, ranging between 1.0 and 2.9 per cent. As the third column shows, this higher proportion of social workers is unrelated to a higher proportion of Left-spectrum parties.

I generated more specific data on the current parliaments at national and state levels by scraping the websites of the Bundestag as well as those of all German state parliaments, individual members of parliament and the respective political parties.

At the national level, my data analysis of the 20th Bundestag in June 2022 identified 736 representatives, of whom 11 (1.5 per cent) have a degree in social work. In terms of the gender distribution of those SWHPOs, 9 were female and 2 male – that is, 82 per cent female. This is particularly interesting because for all Bundestag members, only 35 per cent were female. Nearly three quarters (73 per cent, n = 8) of the SWHPOs at the national level belonged to the Green Party. The remaining three were members of the

Table 6.1: Social workers in national parliament, election periods 1–20

Election period		Total number of seats in the Bundestag	Parties from the Left spectrum %	Social workers %	Social workers	Gender (f/m)	
20	2021–25	736	49.3%	1.5%	11	9	2
19	2017–21	709	40.8%	1.8%	13	7	6
18	2013–17	631	50.7%	2.9%	18	11	7
17	2009–13	622	46.6%	2.9%	18	13	5
16	2005–09	614	53.3%	1.1%	7	3	4
15	2002–05	603	51.1%	1.7%	10	7	3
14	1998–2002	669	57.0%	1.3%	9	6	3
13	1994–98	672	49.3%	1.3%	9	4	5
12	1990–94	662	39.9%	1.2%	8	3	5
11	1987–90	497	45.9%	1.0%	5	3	2
10	1983–87	498	44.2%	1.4%	7	2	5
9	1980–83	497	43.9%	0.6%	3	2	1
8	1976–80	496	43.1%	0.8%	4	2	2
7	1972–76	496	46.4%	0.4%	2	1	1
6	1969–72	496	45.2%	0.4%	2	1	1
5	1965–69	496	40.7%	0.4%	2	1	1
4	1961–65	499	38.1%	0.2%	1	1	0
3	1957–61	497	34.0%	0.2%	1	1	0
2	1953–57	487	31.0%	0.2%	1	1	0
1	1949–53	402	32.6%	0.0%	0	0	0

SPD, The Left[3] and the Free Democratic Party (FDP). The average age of social workers in the 20th Bundestag was 48 years (the overall average was 47 years). Of the 11 SWHPOs, 1 won a direct mandate in their constituency, while 10 entered the Bundestag via state lists. Five SWHPOs came from Baden-Württemberg, two from North Rhine-Westphalia and one each from Schleswig-Holstein, Bavaria, Saxony and Berlin.

My Bundesrat data analysis in October 2024 identified 2 SWHPOs among the 69 council members, representing 2.9 per cent. One was female and one male, and both held their mandate for the Green Party.

At the state level, I identified 1,882 politicians in June 2022. Of them, 1,521 held political office in state parliaments and 361 in city-state parliaments. The proportion of SWHPOs was higher at this political level than at the national level, and the highest percentage, 3.6 per cent (n = 13), was held by social workers in the city-states. In the territorial state parliaments, 2.6 per cent (n = 40) were social workers. These 40 SWHPOs were spread across ten state parliaments. In three states, there were no SWHPOs in parliament. Most SWHPOs (a total of 10) sat in the state parliament in North Rhine-Westphalia, while the highest proportion of social workers among all deputies was in Hessen, with 5.8 per cent, and the city-state Bremen, with a much larger share at 9.5 per cent. Of all SWHPOs at the state level, 55 per cent were women (a much lower share than in the Bundestag), and 87 per cent represented a Left-of-centre party. The average age of social workers in the parliaments of the city-states was 55, which is higher than the average age of 50 for all representatives in the state parliaments. This makes them, on average, slightly older than SWHPOs in the Bundestag, where the average age was 48.

My data analysis confirms that social workers hold political office at the national and state levels. However, their share of mandates is rather low compared to other occupational groups (for example, in the Bundestag, social workers make up 1.5 per cent, lawyers make up 20 per cent and economists make up 14 per cent of mandate holders). Nonetheless, it is higher than the share of social workers in the total workforce, which stands at 1 per cent. In addition, there seems to be a correlation between the number of SWHPOs and the political level, with the share of social workers in the Bundestag lower than at the state level. Among the state parliaments, city-states have the highest shares, suggesting that the share of SWHPOs at the local level might be even higher.

Political career patterns

Typically, political engagement begins with a general 'interest in political work, which, upon crossing a threshold, leads to membership in a political party' (Gerster, 2018, p 18). The 72 social workers surveyed in my quantitative study (Löffler, 2023; 2024d) stated that their political interest mostly comes from their parents and other family members. Their parents were politically engaged and often discussed political matters. Another strong influencing factor is education: almost 60 per cent of the survey participants mentioned joining a political party during or after their studies. During their training, they understood that policy engagement is part of social work. Two thirds of the social workers stated that their professional activities included forms of policy engagement. However, from their point of view, social work does not offer the potential to change the reality of people's lives and fundamental changes could 'only be achieved at the political level'.[4] Most participants wanted to make a real difference through involvement in a political party. The decision of social workers to engage politically is also linked to a specific fundamental motivation and the three identified biographical themes:[5] *change*, *participation* and *justice*. These three biographical themes align with the motivation to pursue studies in social work as well. Drawing on both qualitative and quantitative data, my thematic analysis enabled the reconstruction of three ideal-typical pathways for social workers into politics (Löffler, 2024b).

The first is 'an unplanned political career'. Social workers often described this path into politics as 'coincidental' and 'unplanned'. It is characterised by social workers choosing to study social work to act according to their biographical themes. They have worked in practice for many years and have never considered political engagement as an option. They lack the knowledge and awareness of the opportunities that political engagement may offer. They often need 'impulses' to decide on this path. These impulses can come from key people, such as partners, friends or colleagues. They can also stem from critical situations, such as the lack of alternatives during the COVID-19 pandemic or involvement in a specific issue.

The second is 'a political career as an expansion'. This path begins with choosing a degree programme in social work to act according to their biographical theme and contribute to justice and change. Engagement in politics sometimes begins during the period of study and is initiated by teachers or seminars. Furthermore, experiences during internships are a central factor in the decision to engage politically. These initial professional experiences and the start of work in practice are characterised by experiencing the limits of individual- or group-centred casework. It is not enough to 'criticise these grievances, ... we also have to act'. Party political engagement appears as a possible solution and an expansion of the possibilities to advocate for better living conditions for service users.

The third is 'a political career as a starting point'. Typical for this path is the narrative: 'Well, I've always been engaged.' Unlike the first two paths, this one begins with (political) engagement. The SWHPOs grew up with politics, and engagement in a party and other voluntary positions had a special significance in their families. One person described their path into politics as a 'family affliction'. The decision to study social work appears to be a logical consequence. In this group, the choice of study is also linked to individuals' overarching biographical theme and the idea of contributing professionally to justice – something they had done already in the civic sector through engagement. The study of social work also seems to be 'more political' compared with other degree programmes. Their political engagement continues in parallel with their studies and careers.

With some exceptions at the local level, political party membership is described as the 'basic prerequisite for a career in politics in a parliamentary democracy' (Gerster, 2018, p 21). The surveyed social workers joined parties on the Left spectrum primarily, to 'contribute to democracy' and 'change something'. The reasons for joining a party can be summarised as the desire 'to initiate change', 'to achieve improvements' and 'to be able to help shape things'. SWHPOs want to 'be heard' and not just complain. They are willing to exert influence and fight for better living conditions and social justice. Their high approval rates for the political nature of social work in the quantitative study corroborate this finding. SWHPOs seem to attach particular importance to the political side of social work.

To win a political mandate at the state or national level, potential candidates typically must demonstrate their suitability through years of collaboration and extensive political experience (Borchert and Stolz, 2003). The analysis of the SWHPOs in the 20th Bundestag shows that 6 of the 11 individuals had previously held an elected mandate at the local level. Five SWHPOs had been involved at the local and state levels previously but did not hold a mandate. A similarly ambiguous result can be seen for the 17 SWHPOs at the state level who participated in my quantitative survey: 12 of them indicated that they had already held a mandate at the local level before their current mandate. In some cases, they even had several elected mandates before their current position, mainly at local level. The duration of these previous mandates ranged from 1 to 18 years. The duration of their current mandate also covered an extended period, ranging from 1 to 16 years at the national and state levels and even up to 36 years at the local level.

In general, when asked about earlier political activities in my quantitative survey, 30 out of 56 SWHPOs stated they held volunteer positions in a political party before their current mandate. They were members of the party board at the local, district or state levels, members of the youth welfare committee or spokespersons for the party's youth organisation and/or involved in party working groups. One person reported that they had interned in the office of an MP in the national parliament. Volunteering had occurred at all party levels and had lasted between 2 and 38 years. Social workers had been involved most often and for the longest times at the local and district levels of the party. Five politicians had also previously held paid positions at the district and the state levels in the party or its youth organisation.

Six SWHPOs in the 20th Bundestag have held their mandates for 5 to 20 years (two to four legislative periods). For the other five SWHPOs, this is their first mandate at national level. The duration of mandates for all 54 SWHPOs since the establishment of the Bundestag (Table 6.1) ranges from 1 to 29 years; on average, SWHPOs served 9.5 years in the Bundestag. This is in line with the average for all members of parliament: at the end of the 19th legislative period, the average tenure of all Bundestag members was 9.56 years (Deutscher Bundestag, 2024). After the 19th legislative period, seven SWHPOs left the Bundestag: four chose not to run for re-election, while three failed to win a mandate. After their mandate ended, three took board roles and management positions in social service organisations. For four individuals, there is limited information on their post-mandate careers.

It is known that they are all actively engaged in civil society, particularly within various social organisations and across societal and political domains. They contribute to their communities through volunteer activities in local politics and social initiatives, extending their public service work and helping shape the community in meaningful ways.

Social advocacy

Data from my qualitative interviews with SWHPOs at the local level illustrate that social workers, by taking on political office, exercise their civic right to participate in democracy and are not necessarily motivated by social advocacy. One interviewee provided an example:

> that [was] the way to be able to help shape the village [...] yes, to help shape a village that is alive. A village like that needs citizens who don't just say 'something should be done', but also act. And that ... was my idea in 2017 – to get more involved.

Thus, social workers' political engagement is rooted in civic engagement. Moreover, social workers' engagement in local politics takes place in the area where they live, which does not necessarily overlap with their place of work. As a result, the issues they encounter in their professional practice may not be negotiable within the scope of their political involvement, making advocacy for the interests of their clients in the context of their political engagement impossible. In such cases, the knowledge gained from practice could be used indirectly in political decisions or as an additional perspective.

Still, as elected representatives, social workers gain special opportunities to contribute their knowledge to political processes and use their expertise to influence political decisions (Lane and Pritzker, 2018; Binder and Weiss-Gal, 2022; Kindler and Amann, 2022). My interviews with SWHPOs at the state and local levels show that they do use their role as an opportunity for social advocacy: one said: 'my particular interest, of course, is to advocate for people affected by poverty', as they felt 'always a bit like a lobbyist for those in need'. They use their expertise to draw attention to the living conditions of service users and the impact of political decisions on specific population groups. In doing so, they fulfil the normative expectation of their profession to work on structures and conditions.

At the same time, there seems to be a discrepancy between the perceived importance of incorporating profession-specific knowledge into political processes and the actual opportunities available. In my survey, I asked respondents about the extent to which they agreed with the statement: 'Politicians who have studied social work can advocate for the interests of their (former) clients in political decision-making processes.'

SWHPOs across all three political levels only partially agreed with this statement, leaning towards 'somewhat agree'. Similar results were found regarding respondents' perceived ability to integrate knowledge from their (former) professional work into political activities: overall, the SWHPOs indicated that they were only partially successful. A comparison of the mean values by political level shows that social workers at the national and state levels were more likely to feel that they can contribute their professional knowledge. Similarly, when it comes to advocating for the interests of (former) client groups, respondents reported only partial success.

However, they reported that holding political office grants them a wide range of rights to speak and propose motions: 'That counts for something. I can speak up everywhere, participate in discussions, and contribute my opinion.' In their speeches, politicians can comment on motions. One SWHPO used this instrument to demand that with all measures, consideration must always be given to 'how they will be received by the poorer, by those receiving social benefits or lower incomes'. They encouraged other politicians to adopt a different perspective and raise awareness about particular issues. This was also described as 'educational work' that social workers must undertake in the political sphere.

Analysing my survey and interview data allowed me to reconstruct different formats and occasions for the success of knowledge transfer and social advocacy (Löffler, 2024a; 2024c). First, political decisions are prepared in parliamentary committees, among other ways. Analysis of the representation of social workers in committees of the 20th Bundestag shows that 7 of the 11 SWHPOs were full members or alternates in committees addressing topics relevant to social work. Of the 98 members and alternates in the Committee for Labor and Social Affairs, 6 (2 full members and 4 alternates) were SWHPOs. The Green Party held 16 seats in this committee, 4 occupied by social workers. In the Committee for Family Affairs, Senior Citizens, Women and Youth, there were two social workers (one full member, one alternate). The Health Committee included one social worker holding a seat as an alternate. My quantitative survey additionally reveals that most SWHPOs at the local level were members of the social or youth welfare committees. This indicates that they actively seek to be involved in committees where topics related to social work are discussed. In particular, SWHPOs in smaller municipalities emphasised that elected council members are always 'local political generalists'.

In addition, social workers use intra-party processes and positions, the function of the parliamentary group manager or the position of spokesperson for specific fields and topics as formats to transfer their knowledge. Of the 11 SWHPOs in the 20th Bundestag, 4 served as spokespersons for social work-related issues within their factions, including on the topics of disability policy and social assistance, demographics and elderly policy, addiction and drug policy, and labour market and social policy. SWHPOs also participated in working groups on social work subjects within and across parties. While SWHPOs drew on their specific knowledge in the social work-related committees and bodies, in other committees they used their particular perspective to question, criticise and encourage other members to consider the 'human factor' or 'social aspects' in all decisions.

However, neither the direct use of knowledge in the specialist committees nor the expansion of discussions about the human factor automatically contributed to policy changes in the social workers' sense. They expressed that it is always important to 'find majorities' in committees, working groups and within one's party. So, they tried to gain majorities for upcoming decisions by 'networking' and searching for 'alliance partners' across party lines: 'I am trying to create a non-partisan network, which is not bad because you always have to look for allies there.' In the negotiation process, one needs allies and a majority. They emphasised that one also needs to 'stay on it' and 'speak up repeatedly' and not allow oneself to be dismissed with concerns.

Conclusion

In summary, social workers in Germany, like all other citizens, can participate in democracy by holding political office. Elected positions are available to them at all three political levels. At the local level, political office is typically held, as a form of civic engagement, alongside a continued career in social work. In contrast, SWHPOs at the national and state levels tend to shift their occupation, becoming full-time politicians and no longer working (or working only voluntarily) in social work. This transition subjects them to new logic and pressures, differing from their previous experience. Further investigation is needed to explore how they navigate and adapt to this change and its impact on their professional identity as social workers. For example, two SWHPOs in the 20th Bundestag did not list social work as their original profession.

Nevertheless, SWHPOs at all levels are well positioned to advocate for the interests of the social work profession and its clients within political processes. Though various limitations mark this transfer process, they bring their expertise and a unique perspective to politics. In political debates, the challenges are often not about a lack of knowledge or awareness of clients' issues, but rather other aspects and constraints of the political system, such as limited budgets and the absence of legislative authority. Still, my analysis reveals that SWHPOs are actively involved in committees addressing topics relevant to social work. As Velimsky et al (2024) suggest, it can be assumed that their presence increases the likelihood of social work-related issues being raised within these committees. However, further research is needed to explore how they leverage their mandates and the extent to which their social work expertise informs their contributions.

Based on my findings, it is questionable whether the normative expectation that SWHPOs represent the interests of social work users in their political work is fulfilled. The interviews with local politicians reveal different perspectives on local engagement, including the importance of matching place of residence and place of work. In addition, the distinction between the private and professional self was discussed: '[I]t's interesting that people always assume that social workers are social workers in their private lives as well, as if … the professional and private spheres can't be separated.' After all, they are, first and foremost, private individuals who engage in local politics during their free time. Whether it is reasonable to expect that they will represent the interests of the people they work with professionally during their free time is, at the very least, debatable. At the national and state levels, taking on an office is often accompanied by a change in occupation. To what extent the interests of (former) clients can still play a role within the logic of the new position can be debated.

Notes

[1] In the study, I conducted two online surveys, 11 problem-centred interviews and two panel discussions to generate knowledge on SWHPOs in Germany. In the surveys, a total of 69 social workers and 3 social work students with mandates in national (2), state (17) and local (49) councils participated. Four SWHPOs did not indicate in which parliament they were elected. Eleven problem-centred interviews with SWHPOs at the state (1) and local (10) levels were conducted. The participants of the panel discussions held office at the state (3) and at the local level (2). For this chapter, I analysed across materials using thematic analysis and descriptive quantitative analysis.

[2] Since there is no official register of certified social workers in Germany, the first step to identifying social workers in political office was an analysis of the parliaments' websites, the MPs' personal websites and the parties' websites.

[3] In February 2024, the SWHPO from The Left transitioned to the BSW group, which is also a party within the Left-wing spectrum.

[4] Statements in quotation marks are taken from the qualitative data of my study (see also Löffler 2024a; 2020b; 2024c; 2024d).

[5] See Aner (2005, pp 234–7) on the influence of 'biographical themes' on civic action and Löffler (2022, pp 98–9) on professional action.

Funding

This contribution was developed as part of the Welfare State Reform 'from Below' joint project, funded by the Ministry of Culture and Science of the State of North Rhine-Westphalia, Germany, within the framework of the Profilbildung 2020 funding announcement.

References

Amann, K. and Kindler, T. (2022) 'Social workers in politics – a qualitative analysis of factors influencing social workers' decision to run for political office', *European Journal of Social Work*, 25(4): 655–67.

Aner, K. (2005) *'Ich will, dass etwas geschieht'. Wie zivilgesellschaftliches Engagement entsteht – oder auch nicht*, Sigma.

Bieker, R. (2011) 'Trägerstrukturen in der Sozialen Arbeit – ein Überblick', in R. Bieker and P. Floerecke (eds) *Träger, Arbeitsfelder und Zielgruppen der Sozialen Arbeit*, Kohlhammer, pp 12–43.

Binder, N. and Weiss-Gal, I. (2022) 'Social workers as local politicians in Israel', *British Journal of Social Work*, 52(5): 2797–813.

Borchert, J. and Stolz, K. (2003) 'Die Bekämpfung der Unsicherheit: Politikerkarrieren und Karrierepolitik in der Bundesrepublik Deutschland', *PVS Politische Vierteljahresschrift*, 44 (2): 148–73.

Bundesagentur für Arbeit (2023) 'Entgeltatlas, Entgelt für den Beruf: Sozialarbeiter/in / Sozialpädagoge/-pädagogin', *Bundesagentur für Arbeit*, Available from: https://web.arbeitsagentur.de/entgeltatlas/beruf/58775

Bundesagentur für Arbeit (2024) 'Blickpunkt Arbeitsmarkt: Akademikerinnen und Akademiker, Kapitel 2.7 Sozialwesen', *Bundesagentur für Arbeit*, Available from: https://statistik.arbeitsagentur.de/DE/Statischer-Content/Statistiken/Themen-im-Fokus/Berufe/AkademikerInnen/Berufsgruppen/Generische-Publikationen/2-7-Sozialwesen.pdf?__blob=publicationFile&v=2

DBSH (Deutscher Berufsverband für Soziale Arbeit e.V.) (2002) *Erklärung: Initiative Berufsgesetz*, Available from: https://www.dbsh.de/index.php?eID=dumpFile&t=f&f=7991&token=dddb81fa45b21651313e4e955626b4d38efded49

Deutscher Bundestag (2024) 'Das Datenhandbuch zur Geschichte des Deutschen Bundestages', *Deutscher Bundestag*, Available from: www.bundestag.de/datenhandbuch

Edinger, M. (2018) 'Politik als Beruf in der repräsentativen Demokratie', in C. Meißelbach, J. Lempp and S. Dreischer (eds) *Politikwissenschaft als Beruf*, Springer Fachmedien Wiesbaden, pp 75–88.

Fachbereichstag Soziale Arbeit and DBSH (Deutscher Berufsverband für Soziale Arbeit e.V.) (2016) 'Deutschsprachige Definition Sozialer Arbeit des Fachbereichstag Soziale Arbeit und DBSH', *DBSH*, Available from: www.dbsh.de/media/dbsh-www/redaktionell/bilder/Profession/20161114_Dt_Def_Sozialer_Arbeit_FBTS_DBSH_01.pdf

Falterbaum, J. (2013) *Rechtliche Grundlagen Sozialer Arbeit: Eine praxisorientierte Einführung*, Kohlhammer.

Gerster, F. (2018) *Politik als Beruf: Eine motivationspsychologische Analyse*, Nomos.

Gewerkschaft Erziehung und Wissenschaft (nd) 'Die GEW', *Gewerkschaft Erziehung und Wissenschaft*, Available from: https://gew-dill.de/wir-ueber-uns/die-gew

Hammerschmidt, P. and Aner, K. (2022) *Zeitgenössische Theorien der Sozialen Arbeit*, Beltz Juventa.

Kindler, T. and Amann, K. (2022) 'Strategies of social workers' policy engagement – a qualitative analysis among Swiss social workers holding elected office', *Journal of Policy Practice and Research*, 3(4): 302–15.

Lane, S.R. and Pritzker, S. (2018). *Political Social Work*, Springer International.

Leitner, S. and Löffler, E.M. (2024) 'Soziale Arbeit als politische Akteurin in der Kommune', in A. Brettschneider, S. Grohs and N. Jehles (eds) *Handbuch Kommunale Sozialpolitik*, Springer Fachmedien Wiesbaden GmbH, Online first.

Löffler, E.M. (2022) *Haltung und professionelles Handeln in sozialen Berufen. Eine qualitative Untersuchung am Beispiel von Pflegefachkräften in ambulanten Pflegediensten*, Beltz Juventa Verlag GmbH.

Löffler, E.M. (2023) 'Aus der Sozialen Arbeit in die Politik. Der professionelle und politische Werdegang von Sozialarbeiter:innen in der Landes- und Bundespolitik', *Soziale Arbeit*, 72(5): 176–83.

Löffler, E.M. (2024a) '"Da muss ich mir Gehör verschaffen": Das Wissen Sozialer Arbeit in politischen Entscheidungsprozessen', *Soziale Arbeit*, 73(7): 256–63.

Löffler, E.M. (2024b) '"Es ist wichtig, sich mehr mit einzumischen!" Kommunalpolitisches Engagement von Sozialarbeiter:innen', *Blätter der Wohlfahrtspflege*, 3: 90–3.

Löffler, E.M. (2024c) '"I have to make myself heard!" Social workers' knowledge in political decision-making processes', *Czech and Slovak Social Work*, 4: 28–41.

Löffler, E.M. (2024d) 'Social workers as politicians. A quantitative study on social workers holding elected office in Germany/Sozialarbeiter:innen in der Politik. Eine quantitative Studie zu Sozialarbeiter:innen mit gewählten Mandaten in Deutschland', *European Journal of Social Work*, 27(4): 898–910.

Meyer, N. (2024) 'Beschäftigungsstruktur in der Sozialen Arbeit', *Zugriff am*, Available from: https://nbn-resolving.org/urn:nbn:de:0168-ssoar-97776-1

Reiser, M. (2006) *Zwischen Ehrenamt und Berufspolitik: Professionalisierung der Kommunalpolitik in deutschen Großstädten*, VS Verlag für Sozialwissenschaften.

Schüttemeyer, S.S. (2019a) 'Der Deutsche Bundestag und seine Akteure', *Informationen zur politischen Bildung*, 341(3–4): 18–49.

Schüttemeyer, S.S. (2019b) 'Die Logik der parlamentarischen Demokratie', *Informationen zur politischen Bildung*, 341(3–4): 4–7.

Statistisches Bundesamt (2024) 'Verwaltungsgliederung am', Available from: https://www.destatis.de/DE/Themen/Laender-Regionen/Regionales/Gemeindeverzeichnis/_inhalt.html#124808

Velimsky, J.A., Block, S., Gross, M. and Nyhuis, D. (2024) 'The impact of occupational background on issue representation', *West European Politics*, doi: 10.1080/01402382.2023.2294666

7

Israel: a limited presence on the national level

John Gal, Idit Weiss-Gal and Noa Binder-Eilat

Social workers in Israel have sought to influence social policies since the formal establishment of the profession during the pre-state British Mandate of Palestine in the early 1930s. There is very limited research on the policy engagement of social workers and their professional organisations in the pre-state period and in the early decades of the state (which was established in 1948). However, it is clear that throughout much of this period, these efforts focused specifically on the field of social welfare services and were typically led by social workers holding senior positions within the Ministry of Welfare (Deutsch, 1970).

In recent decades, there has been growing evidence of the different civic and professional routes through which social workers and social work academics in Israel seek to influence policies (Gal and Weiss-Gal, 2023). Research has identified engagement in policy practice among social workers (Lavee and Cohen, 2019; Aviv et al, 2021; Gilboa and Weiss-Gal, 2022; Nouman and Azaiza, 2022) and social work academics (Weiss-Gal et al, 2017). It has also shown that social workers engage in policy design on the ground in their role as street-level bureaucrats (Lavee et al, 2018; Serry and Weiss-Gal, 2022). Finally, there is some evidence of the policy change activities of social workers as part of the Israel Union of Social Workers (IUSW) (Kadman, 1988; Gal, forthcoming) and of their voluntary political participation (Cohen, 1987).

In addition to these routes, social workers have also sought elected political office on the national and local levels. Occasionally, some of these social workers were placed in leading policy roles by politicians and political parties. Thus, for example, Yisrael Katz, a social worker, served as the Minister for Labour and Welfare during 1977–81 (Avineri, 2017). However, in most cases, social workers sought political office through election to the Knesset, Israel's parliament, or to local councils at the municipal level. In a previous study that focused on social workers as local politicians in Israel, Binder and Weiss-Gal (2022) identified 34 social workers who ran for office on the municipal level between 1948 and 2018. Of the 20 social workers interviewed for that study, most ran for councillor positions while three ran for authority heads.

Eleven social workers were elected at least one time; ten as councillors and one as mayor. All the social workers elected held positions as heads of committees or deputy mayors. This chapter tells the story of those social workers elected to political office on the national level.

Social work as a profession

The Israeli welfare state and its social services

The Israeli welfare state is best described as a Mediterranean welfare state (Gal, 2010). Though it has certainly been influenced by the market-based liberal welfare state (such as the US) in recent decades and it still maintains key welfare state institutions that are rooted in the Beveridgean tradition and based on a social democratic model, the Israeli welfare state shares with other Mediterranean nations three broad cultural attributes that have had a marked impact on welfare state formulation – these are related to the family, religion and the persistence of clientelistic-particularistic forms of welfare (Fogiel-Bijaoui, 2017; Weinreb, 2020; Gal et al, 2024).

While offering comprehensive social protection and social services, the Israeli welfare state has been only partially effective in dealing with poverty and inequality. Israel has some of the highest levels of poverty and inequality among welfare states, and this reflects low labour market participation rates and high fertility levels among ultra-orthodox Jewish families and Israeli Arabs. This is exacerbated by wide inequality in remuneration for work in the labour market, low social spending levels over time, ungenerous safety net benefits that also suffer from low take-up rates, and an underfunded social welfare sector that is characterised by major gaps between different population groups, particularly between Jews and Arabs (Gal, 2023).

Social work in Israel

Social services in Israel are provided by a mix of state, for-profit and non-profit providers. While local social services are delivered by the local authorities, most of the other social services are outsourced to non-state agencies. Thus, while social workers employed directly by local authorities engage in casework and community work, most of the institutionalised services in the community and out of home are provided by non-profit or for-profit agencies and are funded by the state. Social workers are key actors in the provision of social services in Israel, both in services provided by the state and those provided by non-state agencies. They engage in a wide range of fields of social welfare services, including immigrant absorption, the provision of social services for people suffering from family crises, rehabilitation, community organising, physical and mental health-related social services, child welfare and protection, corrections and long-term care. In terms of problems and populations, social workers in Israel deal with people living in poverty and social exclusion, children, youth and women at risk, older adults, families in distress, adult and juvenile offenders, people with disabilities, victims of war or terror attacks, people suffering from sickness or mental health problems, people with addictions and their families, people who are homeless, immigrants and asylum seekers. They employ a wide range of intervention methods, including therapeutic interventions and emotional support based on diverse theoretical approaches and paradigms, take-up and social rights advocacy, material support, at-risk interventions, counselling, case management, group work, childcare and protection, community work and policy practice.

Following legislation adopted in 1996, social work is a protected profession. Only graduates of social work degree programmes in one of Israel's 13 schools of social work can claim the title of social worker. All social workers must be registered by the Ministry of Welfare and Social Affairs social work registrar office. The Social Workers Act also identifies fields and positions in which only social workers can be employed. These include social services, child welfare, correction services and leadership positions in the social services.

The latest figures, published in 2021, indicate that there are 36,900 registered social workers in Israel, a country with a population of 9.4 million (Ben-Simchon and Lipalevsky, 2021). Of them, 31,500 participate in the labour market out of a total workforce of 4,464,000. The vast majority of social workers (86.8 per cent) are women. The majority (89 per cent) are Jewish and the remainder (11 per cent) are Arabs. Half of them have a second degree, mainly in social work (86 per cent of those with a degree). Most (84 per cent) are employees and the remainder (16 per cent) are self-employed.

While there is large demand for social work training, there is also significant attrition among social workers, and between a fifth and a third of them are not employed as social workers. A quarter of the employed social workers are local authority employees (Ben-Simchon and Lipalevsky, 2021), but these services are significantly understaffed. This is due to low wages, difficult working conditions and high workloads in local social services and harsh criticism of social workers in the public sphere by right-wing politicians.

The IUSW is a part of the Histadrut trade union federation. It has approximately 14,500 members and serves both as a trade union and a professional association. It engages in furthering the labour rights of social workers and protecting their professional status while also advocating for more progressive social policies that reflect social work values. Most, but not all, of the members of the IUSW are employed in the public sector. Although it has used its Facebook page to encourage social workers to vote for social workers seeking local electoral office, the IUSW has not made significant effort to encourage social workers to hold national office.

There is no call to social workers to run for office in IUSW documents or in their social work code of ethics. However, just prior to the 2018 local elections, the IUSW did publish a list of 11 social workers running in local elections on its website, and in 2021 the union offered a training course for social workers seeking political office.

Institutional opportunity structures

Israel is a unitary state with a parliamentary system that is an outlying case of proportional representation. In the elections for its unicameral parliament, the Knesset, nationwide party lists compete for all the 120 seats. Holding office is a full-time and fully paid position. Candidates for election are placed on closed party lists. The electoral threshold is 3.25 per cent of eligible voters. Consequently, the number of party lists in the Knesset is high (at the time of writing, there are ten), and multi-party governing coalitions are the rule. While Knesset terms are elected for four years, in practice terms are often shorter (see Table 7.1). This is due to the fragile governing coalitions in Israel's multi-party system.

There is no written constitution in Israel but there is a traditional division of power between the three branches of government in Israel that is enshrined in basic laws, which are quasi-constitutional legislation. However, this division of power has been the subject of change and conflict in recent years. Indeed, there has been an ongoing process of strengthening the executive branch and undermining that of the legislature and judiciary. This has taken the form of a series of reforms that weakened the capacity of the parliament to oversee the executive branch by limiting the Knesset's ability to adopt effective 'no confidence' motions. In addition, more recently an extreme right-wing government also sought to curtail the power of the judicial branch to intervene in cases of unconstitutional or unreasonable policies. This led to a major constitutional crisis in the country (Gidron, 2023).

While the checks and balances between the executive and legislative branches of the Israeli political system have been weakened and the governing coalition can determine, to a large degree, the legislative agenda of the Knesset, some institutions within the Knesset, particularly parliamentary committees, do enjoy a degree of oversight over government policy and can place issues on the public agenda. There are, in all, 15 permanent parliamentary committees and various ad hoc committees established over time. Members of the Knesset (MKs) can employ these committees and other parliamentary tools to challenge government policies and to raise awareness to various issues. The major political divisions in the country and between politicians within the Knesset concern issues of defence and foreign policy, state and religion, and democratic rights. By contrast, social policy issues are much less salient. The upside of this is that they are also often less divisive, and this offers space for collaboration across the political divide within the Knesset and its committees (Friedberg and Hazan, 2018).

The routes to political recruitment in Israel have changed over time. Uri Ram (2003) notes that in the initial decades following independence, the political class tended to comprise of individuals who rose through the ranks of the traditional political parties. These included the social democratic Mapai (renamed the Labor Party), the right-wing Herut and the centre-right Liberal Party (which united to form the Likud), and the clerical National Religious Party (NRP). The politicians were predominantly Ashkenazi Jews (of European origin), men and often those with a prominent military background.

The decades after saw a decline in the dominance of most of these parties and fragmentation of the political arena with the emergence of new parties, generally in the centre of the political spectrum. There was major growth in the proportion of Mizrahi Jews (African-Asian origin), often from lower socioeconomic roots, and greater representation of minority groups in the parliament, reflecting the mass immigration of Jews from the former Soviet Union and Ethiopia as well as the growing political participation of members of the Arab community. The proportion of women in politics at the national level did not grow dramatically, and on average 85 per cent of the members were men. The share of women remains low and, even in recent years, only a quarter of the MKs have been women. This reflects not only social norms but also recruitment processes within political parties. This is particularly the case for ultra-orthodox Jewish clerical parties (which tend to have 15 seats in the Knesset) that refrain from placing women in their lists.

During recent decades, local political engagement has played a growing role in the national political recruitment process. Similarly, leadership in civil society organisations has led to political careers at national level. Within existing parties, the nomination process of candidates differs across lists: in some parties, primaries are held, while in others, candidates are selected by party leaders.

The structuring of the Israeli political system and the changes that it has undergone over time has shaped the context within which social workers seek elected office. Borchert (2011) offers a useful framework for analysing the impact of the political context on social workers' efforts to attain political office. He identifies three motivations that impact the decisions of individuals regarding embarking on a political career. These are the *availability* of relevant political offices, the degree of *accessibility* of these offices and the *attractiveness* of political office with regard to impact, future options and remuneration. The structure of the state and its political institutions as well as the nature of representation and of political organisations have a major impact on the motivations of individuals, and among them social workers, to embark on a political career.

After offering a quantitative overview of the political recruitment of social workers in Israel at the national level, we explore these issues by looking at the political careers of these social workers. Our analysis is based on diverse sources. These include biographies and documentation, quantitative analyses of data from the Knesset website on the place of social workers in politics and their activities in this arena, and secondary sources relating to the careers of social workers elected to political office.

Political recruitment

Between the establishment of the state of Israel in 1948 and the Knesset starting in 2022, 15 social workers served as MKs. These comprise 1.3 per cent of the 1,095 individuals who have served in the Knesset. As can be seen in Table 7.1, social workers were present in nearly all of the 25 Knessets, with the exceptions of the 6th to the 8th Knesset (1965–77). Between 1988 and 2015, there were between two and three social workers in the parliament. While the social worker MKs elected during the first decades after the establishment of Israel tended to serve lengthy periods in the Knesset, this changed dramatically in the 1990s, after which they tended to serve less time, often a single Knesset term.

A comparison between social workers and other helping professions reveals that teachers played a much greater role in the Israeli parliament than social workers (66 teachers served in the Knesset since its establishment). This may reflect the greater tendency of members of the political elite to engage in teaching (often briefly) prior to the establishment of the state and in the first decades after statehood. Apart from teachers, the social work profession was represented to a much greater degree in the Knesset than other helping professions. Only 11 medical doctors, 2 nurses and 2 psychologists served in the Knesset over all the periods (Knesset website).

The gender, party affiliation, ethnicity and terms of office of the social workers who served as MKs are presented in Table 7.2. As can be seen, the social workers who served as MKs represented diverse political parties. While a third of them (5) were affiliated with the social democratic Labor party (previously Mapai), and another four represented centre or centre-left parties, the remainder (6) were affiliated with parties across the political spectrum. The right-wing Likud party, Jewish clerical parties and parties representing the Arab sector all sent two social workers to the Knesset over the years.

Though the vast majority of social workers in Israel are women, the gender of the social workers elected to the Knesset reflects more the male bias within the Israeli parliament than the gender division within the profession. The share of men among them (8 of the 15) is much larger than the proportion of men in the social work profession. In terms of ethnicity, two findings are interesting: First, three of the social workers were Arabs; this group comprises

Table 7.1: Social workers in the Knesset, terms 1–25

Knesset term	Years of term	Number of social workers in the Knesset
1	1949–51	1
2	1951–55	1
3	1955–59	1
4	1959–61	1
5	1961–65	1
9	1977–81	1
10	1981–84	1
11	1984–88	1
12	1988–92	2
13	1992–96	2
14	1996–99	3
15	1999–2003	2
16	2003–06	2
17	2006–09	3
18	2009–13	3
19	2013–15	2
20	2015–19	1
21	2019–19	1
22	2019–20	1
23	2020–21	2
24	2021–22	1
25	2022–	1

Note: Terms 6 to 8 are not included as there were no social workers in the Knesset.
Source: https://m.knesset.gov.il/

20 per cent of the Israeli population, but is traditionally significantly under-represented in parliament. Arabs comprise a fifth of all social workers in the Knesset but only a tenth of all social work professionals. Second, four social worker MKs were Jews of Ethiopian origin. This is extraordinary given the fact that this community comprises only 1.75 per cent of the population. This can be linked to the fact that social work studies offered Ethiopian Jews who had immigrated to Israel a relatively accessible path to a profession and a social activist career. These individuals were also attractive candidates for parties seeking representatives of the Ethiopian community on their lists. Notably, a half of the MKs of Jewish-Ethiopian origin were social workers (four out of a total of eight).

Three social workers have served as ministers in Israeli governments. Two of these were MKs while a third, Yisrael Katz (Minister of Labour and Welfare, 1977–81), was a leading member of a political party that comprised the governing coalition in the late 1970s, though he preferred not to stand for election to the parliament. Of the three, Katz was the only social worker in government with a social welfare portfolio. Shalom Simchon served as the Minister of Agriculture and the Minister of Industry, Trade and Labour (2006–13), while Shaul Amor was Minister without Portfolio for a short time in 1999 before becoming the Israeli ambassador to Belgium.

Political career patterns

Professional roles before the Knesset

Prior to their election to the Knesset, social workers tended to engage in issues related to social welfare, either in state social services or in civil society. Ten of the MKs served in formal social work jobs in diverse social services, some of them holding managerial positions. For example, Jenia Tversky (who served as MK between 1951 and 1964) established and led the local social services in the city of Haifa between 1932 and 1942. Afterwards, she headed the local social services in Jerusalem, worked with Jewish refugees in Europe after World War II and then returned to head the social services in the city of Haifa in 1948. Sarah Stern-Katan (an MK during 1977–81) was an inspector in the Ministry of Welfare and the Ministry of Education. Nava Arad (an MK during 1981–96) worked as a youth corrections officer until 1964, when she was selected to head the IUSW; she served in that position until 1970. Avi Duan (an MK in 2012) was a social worker for 25 years in local social services and in a psychiatric hospital. Nadia Hilou (an MK during 2006–09) was first employed as a social worker in local social services and afterwards became a youth probation officer. Following that, she was elected as a delegate to the IUSW and established an early childhood centre (Hilou, 2013). Iman Khatib-Yassin (an MK from 2020) worked with young women in distress in local social services for nine years and then headed community centres in two Arab localities.

While the other five social worker MKs were not employed in social work positions prior to their formal political career, they were engaged in the welfare or education fields. Shlomo Molla (an MK during 2006–13) was the head of a centre for immigrants and later became an inspector of centres for immigrants from Ethiopia. Shimon Solomon (an MK during 2013–15) was an educational consultant at a high school for two years before becoming an educational advisor to the Minister of Education between 1994 and 1996. He later served as an advisor to the Association for the Advancement of Education and became executive director of an Ethiopian community centre. Yifat Kariv (an MK during 2013–15) worked in a major non-governmental

Table 7.2: Gender, party affiliation, ethnicity and terms of office of social workers in the Knesset

Name (gender)	Party affiliation	Ethnicity*	Time in the Knesset
Jenia Tversky (F)	Social democratic (Mapai)	Jewish	1951–64
Sarah Stern-Katan (F)	Clerical (NRP)	Jewish	1977–81
Nava Arad (F)	Social democratic (Labor)	Jewish	1981–96
Shaul Amor (M)	Right (Likud)	Jewish (Mizrachi)	1988–99
Shalom Simchon (M)	Social democratic (Labor)	Jewish (Mizrachi)	1996–2013
Adiso Masala (M)	Social democratic (Labor)	Jewish (Ethiopian origin)	1996–99
Yair Peretz (M)	Clerical (Shas)	Jewish (Mizrachi)	1999–2006
Nadia Hilou (F)	Social democratic (Labor)	Arab	2006–9
Shlomo Molla (M)	Centre (Kadima)	Jewish (Ethiopian origin)	2006–13
Avi Duan (M)	Centre (Kadima)	Jewish (Mizrachi)	2012
Shimon Solomon (M)	Centre-left (Yesh Atid)	Jewish (Ethiopian origin)	2013–15
Yifat Kariv (F)	Centre-left (Yesh Atid)	Jewish	2013–15
Avraham Neguise (M)	Right (Likud)	Jewish (Ethiopian origin)	2015–19
Heba Yazbak (F)	Arab (Joint List)	Arab	2019–21
Iman Khatib-Yassin (F)	Arab (Ra'am)	Arab	2020–

Note: * Jewish refers to either Ashkenazi (European) or mixed origin.
Source: https://m.knesset.gov.il/

organisation for youth at risk as a manager and developer of the youth hotline and an initiative for youth who experienced sexual abuse. Later, she worked in diverse jobs in the welfare and educational fields, among them head of the youth department at the Ministry for the Development of the Negev and Galilee.

Political careers

The political careers of the social worker MKs differed over periods of time and reflect the findings in Ram's (2003) study on the formation of the political class in Israel during two distinctive periods in the country's political history.

The social workers elected to the Knesset before the 1990s typically worked their way up, generally over long periods of time, through the ranks of traditional political parties. Jenia Tversky was active in Mapai and was a leader of the women workers' movement, initially in Haifa and then at national level. Nava Arad was active in Mapai from an early age, and this affiliation paved the way for her being appointed head of the IUSW by the Mapai-dominated Histadrut leadership. After her term of office as head of the IUSW, she joined the leadership of Histadrut as a Labor Party representative and in 1977 was elected to head the Histadrut-affiliated women's organisation Naamat. Shaul Amor was a long-time leading activist in Likud and served as the mayor of the town of Migdal HaEmek for two decades. Similarly, Sarah Stern-Katan had been active in the religious youth movement affiliated to the NRP during World War II and continued this in the party following her immigration to Israel.

A more recent example of a social worker working her way up the ranks of the party is that of Heba Yazbak, who became involved with the then newly established party Balad at the age of 15. She joined the party while at university and became chair of the Haifa University branch. She was placed sixth on the party's list for the 2013 Knesset elections, but the party won only three seats. In the April 2019 elections, she was placed high on a joint list (the United Arab List) that Balad formed with other Arab parties and was elected to the Knesset and then re-elected twice for short terms.

By contrast, since the 1990s, many of the social workers spent relatively short periods of time as members of political parties prior to their election to the Knesset. Adisu Massala joined the Labor Party shortly before the 1996 internal elections and managed to attain the place on the party list reserved for immigrants. Shlomo Molla and Shimon Solomon joined parties established just prior to the elections in which they gained seats in the Knesset. Other social workers tended to seek election to the Knesset by moving across party lists or occasionally were recruited directly by party leaders without having any prior ties to the party. Thus, Avraham Neguise established the Atid Ehad party, which contested the 2006 Knesset elections but failed to win a seat. After a number of subsequent efforts to be elected to parliament, he was elected to the Knesset on the Likud list. Shlomo Molla was initially a candidate on the Israel BeAliya list in 1999, but after failing to be elected, he joined Kadima and entered parliament in 2008 after another party MK resigned. In 2012, he ran on the Hatnua list but failed to be elected. Yifat Kariv is an example of social worker recruited directly. She had previously established a local list of candidates to a city council and served in the council. Kariv received a direct invitation to run for office by the head of the Yesh Atid party and was elected to the Knesset in 2013.

Following their terms as MKs, the social workers did not return to serving as street-level social workers, though a few engaged in activities related to social welfare. Sarah Stern-Katan headed the religious women's movement and focused on early childhood education and social welfare institutions. Nadia Hilou served as a consultant to a number of initiatives concerning education and employment in the Arab community. Some of the MKs sought, unsuccessfully, to continue their political career at national or local level. Nava Arad, for example, established a senior citizen's party, but it failed to garner sufficient support to be represented in parliament. Yifat Kariv ran for mayor in her city of residence, but failed. Finally, a number of the former social work MKs developed careers in fields unrelated to social work or politics. Shimon Solomon served as the Israeli Ambassador to Angola. Adisu Massala returned to Ethiopia as a businessman, Shalom Simchon established a winery and Yifat Kariv became an executive director in the legal cannabis industry.

Borchert's (2011) conceptual framework for the analysis of political careers is useful for understanding the political careers of Israeli social workers. The unicameral structure of the 120-seat Israeli parliament and the fact that no intermediate elected institutions exist between the local and the national levels offers relatively limited *availability* of elected positions apart from at local level. This inevitably depresses political options at national level. Similarly, the data on social worker politicians does not offer any strong support for the notion that election to office at the local level, at least in the case of social workers, is a useful step in the ladder to attaining office at national level.

The weak political salience of social welfare issues in the parliament reduces the *attractiveness* of political office to social workers seeking to further a social welfare agenda. It also offers limited motivation on the part of political leaders and party members to include social workers in their Knesset party lists, thus limiting the *accessibility* of political office to social workers (also see other facets of this discussed later). The instability of the political system and the frequent elections to parliament, particularly in recent decades, provide limited job security for MKs and thus further undermines the attractiveness of a national-level political career. Indeed, as we have seen, the political careers of most social workers in the Knesset during recent decades were short, generally lasting a single term. An examination of the careers of the social workers after leaving their posts indicates that serving in the parliament does not appear to be particularly useful for social workers seeking to obtain major positions in the field or for those seeking other elected political positions.

Existing societal obstacles to the political participation of women and the overt refusal of Jewish ultra-orthodox parties, which comprise 12 per cent of the seats in the Knesset, to include women in their lists further limit the *accessibility* to the political system of members of a profession that is predominantly female. It is, thus, not surprising that the majority of social work politicians are men.

Social advocacy

All the social workers in the Knesset were involved, to one degree or another, in social, welfare and human rights issues, and they employed diverse parliamentary tools in support of vulnerable groups, such as immigrants, youth at risk, older adults and women. For example, Avraham Neguise focused on social issues such as helping new immigrants integrate into Israeli society and providing support and education for youth in underprivileged neighbourhoods. The social worker MKs promoted their goals through formal roles in the parliament – as, for example, the head of lobbies or parliamentary committees – by joining relevant parliamentary committees or by tabling laws intended to further social rights.

In order to assess the political activity of social workers in the Knesset, we have employed three indicators, as can be seen in Table 7.3. The first of these relates to the roles held in the parliament. These pertain to leadership roles either in lobbies, which are voluntary cross-party caucuses that MKs can form in order to advance issues of particular importance to them, or in parliamentary committees. A second indicator relates to the parliamentary committees MKs were members of during their entire term of office. The indicator is the proportion of all the parliamentary committees they were members of that dealt with social issues, broadly defined. While membership in the Knesset committees reflects the relative representation of the parties in the Knesset, the decision as to which committees MKs join is indicative of both the individual preferences of the MKs and the demands of the political parties. The final indicator reflects the proportion of all the draft laws that the MKs tabled during their term of office that were devoted to social issues. It should be noted that the use of this parliamentary tool has become more popular over time because of changes in Knesset by-laws and that most of the draft laws are tabled by a number of MKs, often from different parties. Only a very small percentage of these draft laws are actually adopted.

Table 7.3 shows that some of the social workers in the Knesset had leadership roles that reflected their social work background. Jenia Tversky headed the subcommittee that formulated the legislation that led to the establishment of the social security system in Israel in the early 1950s. Others chaired parliamentary committees or ad hoc or subcommittees dealing with social issues such as immigration, foreign workers and drug abuse. Two of the social workers headed the social work lobby in the Knesset.

It is hardly surprising that all the social workers were members of parliamentary committees dealing with social issues. However, our analysis reveals that, apart from three of them, half or more of the committees on which the vast majority of social workers sat dealt with these issues. They ranged from the labour, welfare and health committee to the parliamentary committees on women's rights or children's rights, to the committees on

Table 7.3: Social welfare-related parliamentary activities of social workers in the Knesset

MK	Leadership roles	Social welfare-related parliamentary committees (%)	Social welfare-related draft laws (%)
Jenia Tversky	Chair, Subcommittee, Committee on social insurance	50	100
Nava Arad	–	100	85
Sarah Stern-Katan	–	100	33
Shaul Amour	–	66	45
Avi Duan	Head of social work lobby	100	5
Nadia Hilou	Chair, committee on the rights of children	50	35
Shalom Simchon	Chair, finance committee, economics committee	25	12
Adisu Massala	–	66	23
Yair Peretz	Chair, committee on drug abuse, committee on foreign workers	70	18
Shlomo Molla	–	17	19
Shimon Solomon	Chair, lobby for social workers	50	22
Yifat Kariv	Chair, lobby for holocaust survivors, lobby for the promotion of local services for youth, lobby for young people	25	20
Avraham Neguise	Chair, committee for immigration	60	16
Heba Yazbak	–	100	20
Iman Khatib-Yassin	Head, lobby for early childhood	60	34

Source: https://m.knesset.gov.il/

education or immigration. Alongside this, they also served in committees dealing with other public issues. These included diverse committees such as finance (Shalom Simchon), internal affairs (Yifat Kariv), economic affairs (Iman Khatib-Yassin) and the constitution, law and justice (Jenia Tversky).

Our analysis of the draft laws tabled by the social worker MKs reveals a more varied complex picture. First, it is worth noting that the number of draft laws submitted by social workers ranged from a low of 5 to a high of over 400. This wide divergence reflects the length of the social worker term of office, the difference between being a part of a governing coalition or serving in opposition, and the changes in Knesset by-laws. MKs in governing coalitions tend to table fewer draft laws, while, particularly in recent decades, social workers in opposition have viewed draft laws as a key parliamentary tool despite the fact that the chances of these laws actually being enacted are very slim.

The findings of our analysis reveal that the proportion of draft laws that were on social issues ranged from a low of 5 per cent in the case of Avi Duan to 100 per cent in the case of Jenia Tversky. The daft laws on social issues tabled by six of the social workers comprised more than a third of the laws that they tabled. Thus, one of them, Iman Khatib-Yassin, tabled numerous amendments to the social security legislation and to legislation relating to the social safety net law, and draft laws relating to student rights, to the rights of people with terminal illness and to subsidies for gluten-free products. Four of the social worker MKs devoted between a fifth and a quarter of their daft laws to social issues, while another five devoted less than a fifth of their draft laws to these issues.

Conclusion

In all, 15 social workers served as members of the Israeli parliament from 1948 to the parliament elected in 2022, 1.3 per cent of the total number of individuals that served in the Knesset since its establishment. In some of the Knessets, two or even three social workers served as MKs. The social workers elected in the early decades of Israeli independence tended to have worked their way up the ranks of traditional parties. They were predominantly women from European backgrounds. In recent decades, the social work politicians have reflected more diverse ethnic and class groups and have been more likely to be men. They spent less time as members of political parties prior to their election to office and were often selected by party leaders on the basis of their community leadership. Once in office, all of the social workers devoted much of their efforts to social welfare issues that reflect their social work background.

The structural features of the Israeli political system, the lack of salience of social welfare issues in public debate through much of the country's history and social norms vis-à-vis gender all offer insights into the question as to why relatively few social workers were elected to political office at national level.

Within Israeli social work there is little encouragement for social workers to seek political office. The schools of social work in Israel devote only very limited resources to prepare or to encourage social work students or social workers to run for political office. In other words, social work education does not actively encourage social workers to seek elected office or to nurture political ambition or a sense of qualification to run for office. Similarly, the IUSW has also not encouraged social workers to run for political office. However, there is sign of change in this approach, at least with regard to politics at local level.

The findings of this study indicate that various structural and social constraints have led to relatively few social workers in Israel playing a formal role in national politics. National-level political positions are limited, social welfare issues are not major issues on the agenda and, particularly in recent decades, holding political office does not appear to be an attractive career choice. Nevertheless, our study indicates that social workers have been a nearly constant presence in the Knesset since its establishment. Moreover, despite the diversity in the demographic and social characteristics of the social worker politicians and their diverging political affiliations, those that held elected office did indeed seek to further core social work goals and values during their time in office.

References

Aviv, I., Gal, J. and Weiss-Gal, I. (2021) 'Social workers as street-level policy entrepreneurs', *Public Administration*, 99(3): 454–68.

Avneri, A. (2017) *The Social Pioneer: Dr. Israel Katz, Leader of the Welfare Revolution in Israel*, Maariv.

Ben-Simchon, M. and Lipalevsky, S. (2021) *Registered Social Workers: Administrative and Survey Data*, Ministry of Welfare and Social Affairs.

Binder, N. and Weiss-Gal, I. (2022) 'Social workers as local politicians in Israel', *British Journal of Social Work*, 52(5): 2797–813.

Borchert, J. (2011) 'Individual ambition and institutional opportunity: A conceptual approach to political careers in multi-level systems', *Regional and Federal Studies*, 21(2): 117–40.

Cohen, B.-Z. (1987) 'Political activism of social workers: A cross national replication', *Journal of Social Work and Policy in Israel*, 1: 51–64.

Deutsch, A. (1970) *The Development of Social Work as a Profession in the Jewish Community in the Land of Israel*, unpublished dissertation, Hebrew University (in Hebrew).

Fogiel-Bijaoui, S. (2017) 'Transmitting the nation: Family, individualization and religion in Israel', in M. Gross, S. Nizard and Y. Scioldo-Zurcher (eds) *Gender, Families and Transmission in the Contemporary Jewish Context*, Cambridge Scholars.

Friedberg, C. and Hazan, R. (2018) 'The legislative branch in Israel', in R. Hazan, A. Dowty, M. Hofnung and G. Rahat (eds) *The Oxford Handbook of Israeli Politics and Society*, Oxford University Press, pp 300–16.

Gal, J. (2010) 'Is there an extended family of Mediterranean welfare states?', *Journal of European Social Policy*, 20(4): 283–300.

Gal, J. (2023) 'The Israeli welfare state system: A special focus on poverty and inequality', in C. Aspalter (ed) *The Routledge International Handbook of Welfare State Systems*, Routledge.

Gal, J. (forthcoming) 'Social work professional organizations in Israel', in R. Guidi (ed) *Social Work Professional Organizations*, Policy Press.

Gal, J. and Weiss-Gal, I. (2023) 'The policy engagement of social workers: A research overview', *European Social Work Research*, 1(1): 47–64.

Gal, J., Oberman, O. and Keidar, N. (2024) *Food Insecurity in Israel: Are Food Stamps the Solution?* The Taub Center for Social Policy Studies in Israel.

Gidron, N. (2023) 'Why Israeli democracy is in crisis', *Journal of Democracy*, 34(3): 33–45.

Gilboa, C. and Weiss-Gal, I. (2022) 'Change from within: Community social workers as local policy actors', *British Journal of Social Work*, 52(6): 3540–58.

Hilou, N. (2013) *The Breakthrough from Ajami*, HaKibuutz HaMeohad.

Kadman, Y. (1988) 'Social work and social action: An attempt of professional association to change social policy', in I. Ben-Shahak, R. Berger and Y. Kadman (eds) *Social Work in Israel*, The Israeli Association of Social Workers, pp 31–46.

Lavee, E. and Cohen, N. (2019) 'How street-level bureaucrats become policy entrepreneurs: The case of urban renewal', *Governance*, 32(3): 475–92.

Lavee, E., Cohen, N. and Nouman, H. (2018) 'Reinforcing public responsibility? Influences and practices in street-level bureaucrats' engagement in policy design', *Public Administration*, 96(2): 333–48.

Nouman, H. and Azaiza, F. (2022) 'Personal, professional and political: Minority social workers as policy actors', *European Journal of Social Work*, 25(4): 720–31.

Ram, U. (2003) 'Israel: community, state, and market in the shaping of the political class', in J. Borchert and J. Zeiss (eds) *The Political Class in Advanced Democracies. A Comparative Handbook*, Oxford University Press, pp 203–22.

Serry, A. and Weiss-Gal, I. (2022) 'Social work senior managers as street-level policy-makers', *British Journal of Social Work*, 52(4): 2348–66.

Weinreb, A. (2020) *Population Projections for Israel, 2017–2040*, Taub Center for Social Policy Studies in Israel.

Weiss-Gal, I., Gal, J. and Schwartz-Tayri, T.M. (2017) 'Teacher, researcher and... policy actor? Social work academics involvement in social policy', *Social Policy & Administration*, 51(5): 776–95.

8

Italy: social workers in political office as a municipal phenomenon

Martina Francesconi and Riccardo Guidi

In this chapter,[1] we examine social workers holding elected office (SWHEOs) in Italy, focusing on the national and local levels. Our findings reveal that SWHEOs are predominantly a local phenomenon, with a significant concentration in small and medium-sized municipalities. This local engagement is influenced by the structure of Italy's political system and the specific professional characteristics of social work.

Social work as a profession

Social work in Italy is a legally regulated profession with specific qualifications and certifications required to practice. To become a social worker, one must obtain a degree in social work, pass a national licensure examination and register with the National Council of Social Workers (Consiglio Nazionale Ordine degli Assistenti Sociali). This council acts as the official regulatory body, ensuring that standards of practice and ethics are maintained. It also represents social workers' interests at the national level and works to elevate the profession's status.

Thus, the social work profession in Italy is characterised by a structured system of education, certification and professional oversight. According to recent data, there are approximately 47,000 registered social workers (*assistenti sociali*),[2] about 40,000 of whom work as social workers, constituting approximately 0.2 per cent of the total workforce in Italy. The profession is predominantly female, with women comprising more than 90 per cent of the workforce (National Council of Social Workers, 2025).

Social workers in Italy are primarily employed by local public organisations, such as municipalities and local health agencies, or non-profit organisations, which also mainly operate at the local level. Overall, social work in Italy remains a profession deeply connected to the local community context.

Social workers in Italy serve in various sectors, including child and family services, support for the elderly and disability services. The working conditions for social workers vary strongly depending on whether they are employed in the public or the private sector. In general, public sector social workers tend to have more job security and benefits but might face bureaucratic constraints.

The profession enjoys a moderate level of prestige and is often declared as essential in institutional documents, but it is undervalued in terms of remuneration and negatively biased by public opinion. The relationship between social workers and other social professions – such as psychologists and educators – is generally collaborative, although distinctions in roles and professional boundaries sometimes create tensions. Social workers generally receive less credit than other professions such as physicians or psychologists in public opinion.

Professional associations in Italy, such as the National Council of Social Workers, play a vital role in advocating for the profession. These associations provide resources for professional development, set ethical standards and lobby for social work issues at various government levels. However, the degree of organisation among social workers varies, with a generally low proportion actively engaged in professional or advocacy groups.

Institutional opportunity structures

Italy is a complex southern European country, known for its late transition to democracy and its socio-institutional divide between the North and South (Putnam, 1993). The republic president and prime minister – elected by parliament – are the peak authorities. Comprising the Chamber of Deputies (Camera dei Deputati) and the Senate (Senato), parliament functions under 'equal bicameralism', mainly differing in the electorate's age. Parliament includes 600 elected members and up to five 'life senators' nominated by the president.

Italy is divided into 20 regions, 5 of which have special autonomous status. Sub-national governance has gained importance since the 1970s, especially in health and social policy. Since 2001, municipalities, regions and the national state have had equal institutional standing. Legislative powers are mainly assigned to regions, except for certain national domains (for example, migration) and others that are jointly managed (for example, health). As the core administrative units, municipalities manage most ordinary functions under the principle of subsidiarity. Mayors and region presidents are directly elected by citizens, primarily through double ballot systems.

In Italy, the political system provides various institutional opportunities for social workers interested in holding elected office. While national positions are concentrated in parliament and government, 'the largest part of the political class sits in local institutions' (Recchi and Verzichelli, 2003, p 230). Recchi and Verzichelli (2003) estimate that there are around 120,000 town councillors, 6,500 officials in regional and provincial councils and governments, and approximately 8,000 mayors.

As in other countries, political parties are the primary collective organisations competing for local, regional and national power. According to Russo and

Verzichelli (2015), from 1948 to 1992 (the First Republic), political careers followed a hierarchical, predictable path dominated by mass parties such as the Christian Democrats and the Communist Party. Careers typically started locally and progressed to national positions, with limited flexibility. Since 1992 (the Second Republic), political careers have become more flexible and complex, with territorially defined competition but a diversified pool of candidates and qualifications. The reduced gatekeeping role of political parties broadened elite pathways, leading to a mix of political and technical skills, especially in executive roles where non-professional politicians often enter laterally. The recent rise of populist parties seems to have further highlighted the irregular and volatile nature of Italy's political class, with no clear, structured model for political class selection (Ponzo et al, 2023).

These trends are particularly noticeable at the local level, especially in municipalities. Since 1993, local political competition has become more complex in both regulation and dynamics. Independent lists 'display a remarkably high presence, especially in small-sized municipalities' (Bolgherini and Grimaldi, 2022, p 233). While the rise of the so-called civic lists (*Liste Civiche*) does not indicate depoliticisation or a diminished role for political parties (Bolgherini and Grimaldi, 2022), civic lists are often crucial to the success of mayoral candidates (Freschi and Mete, 2020) and can pose a challenge to political parties (Chiaramonte and Emanuele, 2016). Notably, the identity of council rather than mayoral candidates plays a crucial role in the electoral success of civic lists (Freschi and Mete, 2020).

Considering all of these factors, local-level elected offices – such as mayor, city council member and municipal councillor – seem to be more accessible to social workers, for several reasons. First, local political offices in smaller municipalities often have lower entry barriers than national or regional positions due to less intense competition and the more significant influence of personal networks and community ties in these smaller settings. Social workers who often have deep-rooted connections within their communities and a keen understanding of local social issues might also find these positions more attractive as they allow for direct engagement and impact on social policy at a community level. Moreover, the civic lists might facilitate social workers' access to local elected office. The civic lists often prioritise candidates with strong community ties and local expertise over those with a traditional political background, making them a suitable entry point for social workers whose professional experience closely aligns with the values and needs of local communities.

Political recruitment

Social workers holding elected office at national level

Analysis of the representation and characteristics of SWHEOs in the national government and national parliament from the 1st (1948) to the

19th (2022) legislature shows a significant under-representation of social workers in national political roles. A quantitative analysis of the educational and professional backgrounds of the members of the national parliament (MPs) and government (MGs) was conducted in spring 2024. Official web pages and secondary sources, such as Wikipedia, were consulted to identify social workers among the 605 MPs and 64 MGs at the time, as well as past MPs. This analysis aimed to assess the presence and characteristics of social workers at national level.

Our detailed investigation into the educational and professional backgrounds of current MPs and MGs reveals that social workers were starkly under-represented. The vast majority of MGs (82.0 per cent) hold a bachelor's (BA)/master's (MA) degree, while 16.4 per cent – including Prime Minister Giorgia Meloni and one of her deputies, Matteo Salvini – hold only a secondary school diploma. Among those with a BA/MA, the predominant field of study was law (43.1 per cent), followed by economics (17.6 per cent), arts and philosophy (15.7 per cent), political science and sociology (11.8 per cent) and various other disciplines.

Similarly, most MPs hold a BA/MA (73.3 per cent), while 24.5 per cent hold a secondary school diploma. The distribution of fields of study among MPs with a BA/MA is comparable to that of MGs. The majority hold degrees in law (41.1 per cent), followed by degrees in economics (15.6 per cent), political science and sociology (14.0 per cent), arts and philosophy (10.8 per cent) and other fields.

Out of the 605 MPs and 64 MGs in 2024, only one MP holds a social work qualification. However, he pursued a career in entrepreneurship rather than practising as a social worker. The disparity between the number of practising social workers and their representation in national politics is thus stark. Italy, as noted earlier, has approximately 47,000 social workers, yet they are almost entirely absent from national political roles. By comparison, professions such as law, economics and political science are significantly more represented.

Historical data further reinforce this trend: when examining the historical data across 19 Italian legislative terms from 1948, a persistent lack of social worker representation – in both absolute terms and compared to other professions – is evident.

Since 1948, social workers have rarely appeared in national-level roles. Only four MPs – one man and three women – reported holding a degree in social work, and only two of them – both women – listed 'social worker' as their primary profession.[3] One of them served in the Chamber of Deputies for four legislatures (from 1994 to 2013, with a break from 2001 to 2006), representing the centre-Left parliamentary groups. Her parliamentary work focused on agriculture, economic activities, trade and tourism. Before becoming an MP, she volunteered in Catholic local organisations and held elected office at the municipal level. The other served in the Chamber of

Deputies during the 16th legislature (2008–13) and in the Senate during the 17th legislature (2013–18), also in the centre-Left parliamentary groups. Her parliamentary focus was on labour, childhood and adolescence. Before becoming an MP, she held elected office at municipal level. The other MPs who reported having a degree in social work were affiliated with the Communist (Rifondazione Comunista) and Forza Italia parties.

A diachronic analysis of Senate data[4] shows a clear discrepancy in the prevalence of different professions over time. Since 1948, professions such as lawyer (1,172 entries), university lecturer (645 entries) and manager (543 entries) have dominated Senate membership. By contrast, social workers – together with sports professionals – are at the bottom, with each profession having been declared only twice in the entire history of the Senate.

The findings prompt a consideration of the potential barriers to the political engagement of social workers at the national level. Several structural, cultural and professional factors might contribute to the limited representation of social workers as MPs and MGs. One possible factor is gender dynamics, given that the gender composition of social workers and politicians differs significantly. Social work is a predominantly female profession, whereas the national political arena in Italy remains male dominated. This gender imbalance might present additional challenges for female social workers aspiring to national political roles. Another relevant factor might be related to social workers' professional experience and networks. Social workers might lack the necessary political networks and experience for entry into national politics, partly because their professional activities are often concentrated at the local level. As shown by our local-level analysis (see later), this might limit their appeal or perceived competence for national office. Furthermore, the social workers' occupational roles – often centred on direct service delivery rather than leadership, social advocacy or administrative positions – might not be viewed as suitable preparation for national political roles. Finally, the structure of Italy's political system at the national and regional levels – which favours individuals with substantial party backing and political experience – presents a significant hurdle for social workers, who often come from non-political backgrounds. These barriers might be lower at the local level.

SWHEOs at the municipal level

At the local level, a qualitative methodology with semi-structured interviews was used. A snowball sampling strategy was employed, starting with the presidents of the regional Councils of Social Work, who were asked to identify social workers currently holding elected office at the local (that is, regional and municipal) level. Subsequently, all identified SWHEOs (n = 11) were contacted and interviewed online using Microsoft Teams.

The interviews – conducted between March and July 2024 – were recorded, transcribed and thematically analysed.[5]

Through this process, ten SWHEOs at the municipal level and one mayor with a degree in social work were interviewed to explore their engagement trajectories, drivers of political involvement, career patterns, advocacy efforts, perceived impacts and the relevance of their educational and professional background. Table 8.1 outlines the basic characteristics of our non-representative sample, and the following sections present the findings. The pathways that lead social workers to holding elected office at the local level are shaped by a blend of personal networks, community involvement and professional reputation. Many social workers in the sample were invited to run for office by individuals already active in local politics – mayors or city council members – who were already aware of the social workers' professional and community contributions. As one interviewee stated: 'There was a pressing request from the mayor and the deputy mayor ... they were aware of my professional background and had the desire to employ a figure with those skills' (Interviewee B). These personal connections – often grounded in community-based interactions – were critical in fostering candidacies. Such relationships have been established by belonging to associations, schools, parishes, sports or friends groups or by frequenting the same places or being known as a professional.

Interestingly, none of the interviewees had prior formal political roles, while several had participated in some kind of community engagement (for example, volunteering). Their entry into politics was prompted by their trusted relationships with community leaders, who saw value in their social work expertise. This pattern underscores how political recruitment at the local level can be deeply tied to personal relationships rather than formal political engagement.

Moreover, many social workers joined civic lists, which are independent from national political parties but often align with centre-Left values, as highlighted by one interviewee:

> I never intended to pursue a political career in the sense of joining a party. I have always shunned situations where you have to support a cause as a predetermined way of thinking. The civic list ... is different .... Ours tends to be centre-Left oriented ... but nobody on the list has a party card, so it is more a way of looking at things. (Interviewee E)

These lists provided a politically comfortable space for social workers, allowing them to avoid the rigidity and partisanship of party politics. This independence was a decisive factor for many in accepting the invitation to run for office. Another interviewee described the civic list as something

Table 8.1: Basic characteristics of the interviewed SWHEOs at local level

Code	Age	Political roles	Party	Educational background and profession	Region	Size of municipality
A	50	Mayor (2019–24, 2024–); city council member (2014–19)	Civic list	• BA Social Work • Social worker	Lombardy (North-West)	Small
B	40	City council member (majority; 2020–)	Civic list	• BA Social Work • Social worker	Marche (Centre)	Small
C	47	Municipal councillor (2020–)	Independent	• BA Social Work • Social worker (on leave of absence)	Emilia-Romagna (North-East)	Medium
D	63	City Council Member (minority) and Councillor of the Council of the Union of Municipalities (2021–), Municipal Councillor and Councillor of a Mountain Community (2011–2006, 2006–2001, 1992–1997)	Civic list	• MA and post-graduate training in Social Work • Social worker	Emilia-Romagna (North-East)	Small
E	63	Mayor and chair of the local assembly of mayors (2014–19, 2019–24) Municipal councillor (2008–12); city council member (2004–08)	Civic list	• BA Social Work • Politician (never practised as a social worker)	Lombardy (North-West)	Small
F	66	City council member (majority; 2024–); municipal councillor, deputy mayor (2019–24)	Civic list	• MA Social Work • Freelance social worker	Emilia-Romagna (North-East)	Medium
G	57	Municipal councillor (2024–); city council member (majority), chair of city council (2019–24)	Civic list	• BA Social work • Regional official with a coordinating role in the field of child and family protection • Councillor, Regional Council of Social Work	Emilia-Romagna (North-East)	Medium

Table 8.1: Basic characteristics of the interviewed SWHEOs at local level (continued)

Code	Age	Political roles	Party	Educational background and profession	Region	Size of municipality
H	51	City council member (majority; 2019–24)	Civic list	• MA Social Work • Social worker until 2022 • Public office (in a large city) in the field of protection and health	Emilia-Romagna (North-East)	Medium
I	62	Municipal councillor (2019–24); mayor (2000–05, 2005–10) in a smaller city; municipal councillor in the same small city (1996–2000)	Democratic Party	• PhD in Sociology and Social Work • Social worker (with coordinating/organisational position) and Regional President of the Council of Social Work • Director of the Master in Direction, Coordination and Management of Social Services	Veneto (North-East)	Medium
J	65	Municipal councillor (2019–24)	Independent	• BA Social Work • Retired social worker • University lecturer in social design; social worker supervisor; corporate mediation consultant	Emilia-Romagna (North-East)	Medium
K	56	City council member (opposition) (2024–); municipal councillor, deputy mayor (2019–24)	Civic list	• BA Social Work • Social worker	Sicily (South)	Small

Note: The civic lists mentioned in the table generally lean toward the centre-left, although centre-right civic lists also exist. However, their political positioning is often unclear and open to interpretation. According to the Italian Statistics Institute, small municipalities have 0–5,000 inhabitants and medium-sized ones have 5,001–250,000 inhabitants.

very different from a supposed political party: 'We are basically friends. We have known each other for a long time because the town is small. We had a sports club and we kept in touch from there' (Interviewee H). However, she also added: 'There was this desire to create the list after we had taken action to create a conference on youth disability to bring more knowledge about this reality into local politics, and we did that' (Interviewee H).

Most of the narratives revealed a high level of accessibility to office and support for candidacy. Only in one case was there notably fierce competition, both during the campaign (for example, because there were not many opponents) and during the term in office (due to the opposition group, which never showed a particularly cooperative attitude). However, the majority of the sample talked about a more laid-back climate without heated confrontations, as clearly expressed in the words of one interviewee: 'With the opposition, we were fortunate to have a position that was quite soft, a position that at times was sided with the majority' (Interviewee L).

Drivers of engagement

Several factors facilitate the political engagement of social workers at the local level. One significant driver is their strong sense of civic duty and commitment to community service, which aligns with the core values of the social work profession. According to the interviewees, this strong sense of civic duty and solidarity is typical of small towns, where residents are more likely to know each other and the feeling of being part of a community is stronger.

Among the primary motivating factors within the sample were membership in third sector organisations and a strong willingness to serve the community. Several Catholic associations and parishes were mentioned, highlighting the influence of Christian values – such as helping others – as an additional driver. Many social workers saw entering politics as an extension of their professional mission to promote social justice.

Another key factor was the community's perception of social workers as trustworthy and knowledgeable. Interviewees stated that personal relationships and local visibility significantly enhance social workers' appeal as candidates in small towns. Their professional background in addressing social issues further legitimises their role. As one participant noted: 'When you are a professional in a town with a population of less than 7,000, people can see your skills and how you approach issues' (Interviewee G).

Interviewees also thought that participation in third sector organisations and parishes is vital in political mobilisation. These affiliations provide social workers with platforms to showcase their leadership and advocacy skills. As one interviewee expressed: 'Entering politics seemed to me to be a good opportunity to contribute. Maybe even continuing things I was doing in the voluntary sector' (Interviewee G).

Additionally, interviewed noted that personal experiences such as dealing with social injustices or having a family member with special needs, often inspire social workers to seek political office. These experiences drive their desire to use political power to address systemic issues and advocate for marginalised groups. Finally, some interviewees identified the presence of people on their list or in previous terms of office who were attentive and sensitive to social issues as facilitating factors.

Political career patterns

The political career trajectory of SWHEOs at the local level typically follows a quite simple and reversible path, merging community engagement and formal political roles. Social workers generally viewed political involvement as an extension of their professional commitment to social justice, with many expressing a desire to continue serving their communities. Some indicated they might seek re-election at the municipal level, while others planned to return to their social work roles exclusively, enriched by their political experience.

For a few social workers, the experience of political office strengthened their resolve to pursue public service, although most preferred to remain at the local level, where they felt their impact is more tangible. One respondent reflected a common preference to avoid traditional political careerism, stating: 'At higher [regional or national] levels, no, I can't do it, it doesn't belong to me' (Interviewee A). Another interviewee strongly emphasised this point: 'As an administrator, you care about your community because that's where you were elected. We don't care about our personal power. I don't mind going to Rome. Maybe I could do that, but I want to stay in my area because that's where my vocation is' (Interviewee D).

By contrast, some social workers intended to leverage their political experience to advocate for the profession more effectively, potentially taking on leadership roles within social work organisations. This engagement highlights the strong alignment between their professional ethos and political roles, with political service viewed as a natural extension of their social advocacy.

Social advocacy

Social workers who hold elected office at the local level frequently engage in advocacy efforts that reflect their professional values, focusing on promoting social justice, protecting vulnerable populations and improving local social services. These efforts are deeply rooted in their experience with community challenges, enabling them to push for policies that directly address these issues.

Social workers practise both 'case advocacy' and 'cause advocacy' in their political roles. Case advocacy involves addressing individual cases of injustice, using their influence to secure necessary resources. Cause advocacy focuses on influencing broader policy changes that serve larger groups. For instance, one respondent recounted advocating for 'the reduction of the price of extra municipal transport for elderly people with disabilities' (Interviewee H) and working to establish a fund to assist families struggling with utility bills, reflecting a pressing concern related to geopolitical events. This type of advocacy enables SWHEOs to make a tangible difference in the lives of individuals and families within their communities. Another interviewee described proposing 'a study on drug addiction among young people in order to identify needs, critical aspects, and possible solutions' (Interviewee F). This type of advocacy often requires collaboration with local officials, community organisations and social service agencies, building coalitions to support these initiatives.

Despite their impact at the local level, social workers face challenges in extending their advocacy to higher levels of government. 'It's very difficult to have a voice, especially if you don't join other councillors from other municipalities' (Interviewee F), explained one social worker, underscoring the bureaucratic hurdles and limited reach of local government authority. One interviewee reflected on this, saying: 'I have initiatives in mind, proposals that should be implemented over time. To do advocacy in a supra-municipal context, I am working on it. It is objectively more complex' (Interviewee A). The limitations connected to their office (for example, being city councillor and not mayor) and the lack of significant contacts with supra-municipal party leaders or policy makers – likely exacerbated by the interviewees' affiliation with civic lists – emerged as an obstacle for the respondents.

Perceived impact of action as formal policy actors

SWHEOs perceived their impact on local governance and community wellbeing as very positive. They felt their social work background provides them with a unique perspective, enabling them to address social issues holistically by considering both immediate needs and long-term solutions. One interviewee explained: 'As a politician with social competence, you have power in your hands, or at least you have a recognised role that you can play at the institutional level. The political role gives you the authority to confront and pursue certain projects in institutional places' (Interviewee I).

The impact of social workers on local politics is evident in the policies and programmes that they help to implement. Many social workers have initiated projects that address pressing social issues, such as combating educational and economic poverty and fostering youth engagement. One respondent shared the success of an initiative to prevent school dropouts, stating: 'We did an educational project against school dropouts ... we managed to generate in the community a sharing, a co-responsibility of taking charge. It became an educating community' (Interviewee I). These efforts were thought to not only provide immediate support but also foster a more inclusive and engaged community.

Moreover, social workers reported feeling empowered in their political roles, with greater autonomy and authority to influence decision-making processes. Unlike their roles within social service agencies, where bureaucratic and managerial constraints, heavy workloads and micro-level casework limit their actions, holding office enables them to propose new initiatives and influence budget allocations for social programmes.

Despite this, social workers acknowledged the challenges that they face in politics, such as navigating political dynamics, clashing against budget constraints and securing sufficient support. Several interviewees revealed that their formal political role allowed them to understand the limitations that policy makers have to face, with one stating:

> When you play the political role, you understand that it is not a question of will, but that everything depends on the fact that it is true that these resources are not available. You learn that there are systemic and contextual limits that guide decisions, and that they do not depend on ... there is no personal responsibility or insensitivity. (Interviewee B)

However, they reported that their sense of policy impact is generally stronger in politics than in traditional social work, as they perceived a greater ability to shape policy and advocate for vulnerable populations.

Relevance of educational and professional background

In the interviewees' narratives, social workers' educational and professional backgrounds are highly relevant to their effectiveness as local politicians. Social work education is relevant because it emphasises understanding social systems, advocacy, community engagement and ethical practice, providing a solid foundation for political roles that require addressing social issues and community needs. One interviewee noted that social workers are trained in skills that are essential for political roles, as these require building relationships, collaborating with diverse stakeholders and mediating between conflicting interests.

Social workers bring various skills to their political roles, including conducting needs assessments, planning and implementing social programmes and engaging with community stakeholders. The overlap between social work and political advocacy fosters a sense of continuity for social workers transitioning into politics. For example, one interviewee explained that her skills as a social worker were valuable in understanding the community's needs and using her political position to drive broader systemic change. These skills are also valuable in local governance, where addressing community-specific issues requires a deep understanding of social dynamics and mobilising resources. One participant said: 'The social worker's activity is a work of relationships, and this can also be useful for the political role because it is also based on relationships' (Interviewee C). One of the interviewees viewed social workers' focus on networking as a distinctive characteristic, stating: 'This is our approach. Unlike traditional politicians, by putting ourselves in politics, we have a point in our favour, which is the ability to network and enhance resources' (Interviewee M).

This background allows social workers to focus on the wellbeing of the community or specific groups even when addressing broader issues such as urban planning or tourism. Furthermore, social workers' experience navigating complex social service systems and advocating for clients translates well into political advocacy and policy making. Their focus on social justice often drives their political agenda, ensuring that local governance addresses the needs of vulnerable populations. One respondent recounted a successful initiative in the sports sector, demonstrating how social work skills shape inclusive policies: 'We redid the regulation of gymnasium concessions and … established that they must present a project aimed at the category of minors with socioeconomic fragility' (Interviewee C).

Conclusion

Our research has presented the first evidence on SWHEOs in Italy. Despite some promising findings, the study is subject to several limitations. Although official, the data about the MPs cannot be considered entirely reliable. The sample size of the qualitative interviews is small, and snowball sampling introduces the possibility of bias. However, the findings align with existing research and offer valuable insights into the intersection of social work and politics in Italy, warranting further investigation.

Our analyses show that in Italy SWHEOs are significantly under-represented at national level, while their participation in local politics seems to be more robust, especially in small and medium-sized municipalities. Today, the municipal level serves as the crucial – and perhaps only – arena for SWHEOs in Italy. Social workers are notably absent from national government positions in both branches of parliament. According to key informants – the presidents of the 20 regional Councils of Social Work – there are no SWHEOs at the regional level, although several serve at the municipal level. This suggests that the SWHEO is largely a municipal phenomenon and has significant implications for understanding the intersection of social work and politics in the Italian context.

The interviews conducted with ten social workers and one graduate in social work who hold elected office at the municipal level shed light on the distinctive pathways that lead social workers to engage in local politics. Notably, none of the interviewees were politically active before running for office; rather, they were invited to stand for election by people they knew, typically through friendships or community ties, and were encouraged to join civic lists with centre-Left values. This non-partisan affiliation was a key factor for many in accepting the offer, as they did not wish to be formally aligned with political parties. The electoral environment was described as relatively accessible with substantial support from fellow candidates and minimal electoral competition, partly due to the absence of strong alternatives.

Several drivers were identified as key to the engagement of SWHEOs. Personal drivers include the desire to serve the community, prior involvement in third sector organisations and personal experiences such as caring for a disabled child. Professional drivers are also important, with many interviewees being recognised and valued for their expertise as social workers. Trust and familiarity between the candidates and their communities play a significant role in recruitment, while their prior knowledge of local government mechanisms motivates them by highlighting the potential for substantial impact on citizens' lives if elected.

Regarding their political action, the SWHEOs demonstrate a clear continuity between their professional roles as social workers and their political functions. They remain committed to community wellbeing, and many continue their professional practice even after assuming office. This bi-directional relationship allows them to integrate their professional and political responsibilities, with their political work enhancing their ability to advocate for vulnerable populations. Their political roles afford them greater freedom to implement broader initiatives, such as reducing public transport costs for the elderly and disabled or creating funds to assist families with rising utility bills. However, supra-local advocacy is rare due to the difficulty of accessing higher institutional levels, although regional connections or collaborations between municipalities occasionally enable broader advocacy efforts.

One of the most significant findings is that SWHEOs perceive their political roles as allowing them to make a more significant impact than their professional roles as social workers. Elected office frees them from the bureaucratic constraints of social service organisations, enabling them to make decisions without managerial consent and address issues at a macro level. Most respondents expressed a willingness to stand for re-election if invited, although none were interested in pursuing political office at the regional or national levels.

Uniqueness of social workers as politicians in Italy

These findings largely align with existing literature on SWHEOs at the local level (Binder and Weiss-Gal, 2022), particularly regarding the types of position that social workers occupy (semi-professional roles) and the parties they run for (local non-partisan lists), their function as formal policy actors (evidencing continuities between social work practice and formal policy work in terms of issues and instruments), the recruitment process (highlighting the importance of community-based relations over political party dynamics) and the underlying drivers. Aside from some specific elements, our findings confirm the existence of clear structural differences between national and local-level offices (for example, professional versus non-professional roles; Löffler, 2024).

According to our analysis, social workers in Italy seem to hold a peculiar position when they transition into political roles, largely due to the nature of their professional training and experience. Their background in social work equips them with a deep understanding of social systems, community engagement, and advocacy for vulnerable populations. This expertise allows them to bring a distinctive perspective to local governance, focused on promoting social justice and addressing the needs of marginalised groups. As one interviewee noted, the skills acquired through social work – such as the ability to build relationships, assess community needs and develop social programmes – are directly transferable to the politician role.

Social workers are set apart as politicians by their ability to integrate their professional ethics into their political agendas. SWHEOs at the municipal level are primarily motivated by their commitment to the wellbeing of their communities and show little concern for party loyalty or electoral success. This is reflected in their preference for joining civic lists, which are independent of political parties and allow them to maintain their professional integrity while engaging in politics.

Additionally, the continuity between social work and political advocacy makes social workers uniquely effective in their political roles. Many SWHEOs continue to practise social work while holding office, allowing them to remain connected to the communities they serve and ensuring their political decisions are informed by direct experience with social issues. This dual role enables social workers to significantly influence local governance, as they can draw on their professional expertise to advocate for policies that address the root causes of social inequality.

Localism: Opportunities and problems for SWHEOs in Italy

The study's findings also clearly underscore the importance of localism in Italy for the SWHEO phenomenon. Italy's long history of local governance – particularly in small and medium-sized municipalities – provides a fertile ground for social workers to engage in politics. In regions such as the Centre-North, local municipalities have been central to political and administrative life since the Middle Ages, and their relevance has been reinforced by recent institutional reforms. The electoral laws at the municipal level encourage close relationships between candidates and voters, especially for small municipalities, making it easier for social workers to enter the political arena. Furthermore, the prevalence of civic lists – which are independent from political parties – allows for a recruitment process based on community engagement and expertise, rather than partisan politics. This was a key factor for all SWHEOs interviewed, who did not wish to align themselves with any political party.

While localism provides a unique opportunity for social workers to translate their professional expertise into political action, it also presents some challenges. The political competition in small municipalities is often less intense, and decision making tends to focus on problem-solving rather than ideological debate. While this environment is conducive to the recruitment and sustained engagement of social workers, it also limits the scope of political action. Issues that require engagement at higher levels – such as regional budget allocations for social policies – are difficult to address at the municipal level. The reluctance to face conflict may also prevent social workers from tackling broader structural issues related to social justice, especially when this would imply upscaling their policy action.

Notes

[1] The chapter originates from a strong and ongoing collaboration between the authors. However, as some assessment processes require formal attribution, Riccardo Guidi can be considered as the author of the 'Social work as a profession', 'Institutional opportunity structures' and 'Conclusion' sections, and Martina Francesconi as the author of all the other sections.
[2] In this chapter, the term 'social workers' is used to refer to *assistenti sociali*.
[3] In the history of the Italian Republic, the percentage of women MPs has ranged from 5 per cent in the first legislature (1948) to 33 per cent in the 19th (2022) one (Andreuccioli et al, 2023).
[4] A section of the Senate's official website provides access to the distribution of senators by profession for each legislature, from the 1st to the 19th. Unfortunately, analogous data about the Chamber of Deputies are not available. It should be noted that each senator was allowed to list more than one profession. Additionally, it is important to consider the possibility that the archive might have experienced some loss of information, which could influence the accuracy of the results.
[5] Unfortunately, the snowball sampling strategy does not allow us to determine either the number of SWHEOs at the local level or the possible existence of additional SWHEOs beyond those identified through our key informants.

References

Andreuccioli, C., Borsi, L., Briotti, G., Frati, M. (2023) 'Parità vo cercando. 1948–2022. Le donne italiane in oltre settanta anni di elezioni', Available from: https://www.astrid-online.it/static/upload/da24/da24_parita-_vo_cercando.pdf [Accessed 19 June 2025].

Binder, N. and Weiss-Gal, I. (2022) 'Social workers as local politicians in Israel', *The British Journal of Social Work*, 52(5): 2797–813.

Bolgherini, S. and Grimaldi, S. (2022) 'Italy: Hard-to-decipher local elections and voting', in *The Routledge Handbook of Local Elections and Voting in Europe*, Routledge, pp 233–45.

Chiaramonte, A. and Emanuele, V. (2016) 'Multipolarismo a geometria variabile: il sistema partitico delle città', in V. Emanuele, N. Maggini and A. Paparo (eds) *Cosa succede in città? Le elezioni comunali 2016*, CISE.

Freschi, A.C. and Mete, V. (2020) 'The electoral personalization of Italian mayors: A study of 25 years of direct election', *Italian Political Science Review/Rivista Italiana Di Scienza Politica*, 50(2): 271–90.

Löffler, E.M. (2024) 'Social workers as politicians: A quantitative study on social workers holding elected office in Germany', *European Journal of Social Work*, 27(4): 898–910.

National Council of Social Workers (2025) 'Assistenti sociali iscritti all'Albo professionale – 2023', Available from: https://cnoas.org/numeri-della-professione [Accessed 1 July 2025].

Ponzo, M., Marangoni, F. and Verzichelli, L. (2023) 'Sociologia della classe politica Italiana in tempi di crisi', in S. Martini, L. Verzichelli and P. Isernia (eds) *La classe politica italiana: struttura, atteggiamenti, sfide*, Il Mulino, pp 34–61.

Putnam, R. (1993) *Making Democracy Work: Civic Traditions in Modern Italy*, Princeton University Press.

Recchi, E. and Verzichelli, L. (2003) 'Italy: The homeland of the political class', in J. Borchert and J. Zeiss (eds) *The Political Class in Advanced Democracies: A Comparative Handbook*, Oxford University Press, pp 223–44.

Russo, M.L. and Verzichelli, L. (2015) 'Reshaping political careers in post-transition Italy: A synchronic analysis', in M. Edinger and S. Jahr (eds) *Political Careers in Europe*, Nomos Verlagsgesellschaft mbH & Co. KG, pp 27–54.

9

Portugal: delayed political engagement and short terms of office

Francisco Branco

This chapter analyses the engagement of social workers holding elected office in Portugal, focusing on the 21st century. As background, a historical perspective is adopted, analysing the first participation of social workers as elected politicians in the context of the authoritarian Estado Novo political regime (1933) and the restoration of democracy after the 1974 Carnation Revolution.

Methodologically, analysis of documentary and secondary sources was carried out, and fresh data were gathered through interviews with former and current elected social worker deputies in the national Parliament (Assembleia da República; 3) and the Madeira Regional Parliament (*Assembleia Legislativa Regional*; 1) as well as social workers elected as mayor (2). In the absence of systematic data on social workers elected at the municipal level, an online survey was circulated among members of the National Association of Social Workers (APSS) to provide a census of social workers elected at the municipal level. This covered region, municipality, positions, mandates, political affiliation. Information was gathered from a non-representative sample (n = 43) for the terms from 1990 to 2024.

Social work as a profession

The institutionalisation of social work in Portugal occurred in 1935 under the Francophone strand, which was evident in the early initiatives in training and the campaigns for its professionalisation (Branco, 2017a; 2018). In this context, the profession was termed 'social service' (*serviço social*), with absolute equivalence with the Anglo-Saxon term 'social work'. As Laforest explains, in French-speaking or French-influenced countries where the Catholic religion is dominant, the term 'social work' derives from the decisive role of the Catholic Church in the development and framing of this activity (Laforest 1984, cited in Mayer, 2002).

This chapter is about the social worker (*assistente social*) profession in Portugal, not covering professional disciplines such as specialised educator (social pedagogue) and 'sociocultural animator' that, along with the historical profession of *assistant de service social* compose, according to the Francophone designation, the professions of *travail social* (see Bouquet, 2005, p 35).

In Portugal, social work is a certified profession. Social work education is not regulated by national law, and universities and polytechnic institutes enjoy autonomy in designing their courses. However, these are submitted to a regular accreditation process, a soft regulation contributing to harmonisation of the core education requirements.

Policy engagement is not a core element of social work education in Portugal. Social policy only became a domain of social work education in the context of curricular reforms introduced after the Carnation Revolution in April 1974. Before this, social policy was limited to courses on social legislation. Since the end of the 1970s, social policy has been an established subject in social work curricula. It tends to take the form of standard two-semester courses in social policy or related subjects (Branco, 2009a), characterised by heterogeneity and different syllabi. The main topics covered are an introduction to social policy, the historical development of social policy and the welfare state, the welfare state crisis and its current reconfiguration, and the main areas of social policy in Portugal. The design and implementation of social policy, the relationship between social policy and social work and, specifically, policy practice in social work are often omitted or addressed without great depth (Branco and Amaro, 2018).

Figures regarding the number and sectors of social workers in Portugal are lacking, but Branco (2009b) estimated in 2009 that 14,875 people in Portugal had a degree in social work. Nowadays, the number is estimated to be more than 20,000, representing 0.48 per cent of the active population in the country (4,151,112, according to the 2021 census). It has been estimated that around two thirds of social workers work in the social security and health sectors (Carvalho, 2020). In 2015, 24.4 per cent of social workers operated in the ageing sector, whereas 23.5 per cent did community protection work (Ribeiro, 2015). The non-profit sector constitutes social workers' foremost field of labour since non-profit organisations have been the major social services providers for several years, especially in the fields of older people and children (Branco, 2009b). Non-profit organisations employ 53.6 per cent of social workers, while 33.8 per cent work in the public sector, 5.5 per cent work in the private sector and 7.1 per cent work in more than one sector.

Social workers are a small professional group compared to professionals in education or health, but they can be considered one of the main professional groups in the field of social services. Portuguese social workers' principal activities are direct psychosocial intervention and child protection (child welfare). However, their role is also relevant in the coordination and administration of social services in non-profit organisations, especially in the areas of disability, children, older people and people who are homelessness.

According to Carrilho and Branco (2023), only 9.1 per cent of Portuguese social workers are involved in policy decisions, while 73.9 per cent act on implementing public policies through casework and community work activities.

The expansion of public services observed since the period of democratic restoration (1974) and the development of third sector organisations in the field of social services through agreements with the state has contributed to the consolidation of social work in the system of professions in Portugal, which is shared with professions based in the social sciences (sociology, psychology, anthropology), sociocultural animators, physicians and nurses.

Concerning wages, there is a clear divide between the public, the private social and the for-profit sectors. As public servants, social workers earn salaries similar to those of other social sciences and humanities specialists. In the private social sector, wages are lower than in the public sector, and a collective bargaining agreement regulates labour relations. Also, for social workers, professional careers are less favourable in the private sector than in the public services sector. In the for-profit private sector, except for large companies covered by collective bargaining agreements, a considerable number of entities, particularly in the provision of social services to older adults, have no collective bargaining agreement, and labour relations are marked by precariousness and meagre pay, in some situations at the level of the national minimum wage.

Institutional opportunity structures

According to the Portuguese Constitution, adopted two years after the Carnation Revolution in 1974, the new democratic political system in Portugal is a unitarian three-tiered state structure comprising central, regional and local levels, though administrative regions have only been established in the autonomous regions of Madeira and the Azores.[1] Thus, the primary political structure comprises the central government (and the regional governments of Madeira and the Azores) and municipalities at the local level.[2] Local government has a consolidated and relevant role in public policy administration despite the incomplete, incremental and variable level of decentralisation of competencies from the central government to the local sphere – specifically in relation to the transfer of resources and decision making (Branco, 1997; Magone, 2003; Teles, 2022).

The relationship between the Parliament and government in Portugal can be considered a 'hybrid [form] of semi-presidentialism – a constitutional design that enshrines both presidential and parliamentary powers' (Neto, 2023, p 122). Despite their reduction, presidential powers – namely, to appoint and dismiss the government and dissolve Parliament – remain significant (Neto, 2023, p 125).

The national Parliament is unicameral. It is composed, since 1991, of 230 deputies who are elected for four years by a proportional representation system based exclusively on political party lists. This privileging of political parties serves to prevent the clientelism that was present in the political system in the past (see Goes and Leston-Bandeira, 2022).

At the regional level, the political structure is composed of a regional government and a regional parliament – the regional parliament in Azores has 57 deputies and the regional parliament in Madeira has 47. Portuguese municipalities are governed by an executive council (*Câmara Municipal*) and a municipal assembly (*Assembleia Municipal*), bodies elected for four years[3] by proportional representation and, since 2001, via independent lists. The municipal assembly scrutinises and approves the municipality's main initiatives and governance instruments. The Portuguese political system is completed by the civil parish (*Freguesia*),[4] the lower tier of local government. The elected presidents of these sub-municipal units are inherently members of the municipal assembly (see Oliveira et al, 2014; Teles, 2022).

Parliamentary party groups are central actors in the national Parliament. They are complemented by parliamentary committees, which are organised according to areas of speciality related to legislative activity and public policies. Parliamentary committees, over time, have gained more substantial powers in terms of parliamentary auditing of civil society organisations, academics, cabinet members and other key informants or interests involved in public policy areas, but also in terms of government scrutiny and, on an ad hoc basis, inquiry into critical and controversial issues (Fernandes and Riera, 2019; Goes and Leston-Bandeira, 2022).

At the national Parliament level, proportional representation under the d'Hondt method, closed party lists and the absence of intra-party competition are the characteristics of the electoral system, which 'makes political parties the pivotal actors in the delegation of power' (Fernandes, 2022, p 181). The party statutes provide most of the rules for the candidate selection process, except for the quota system established by law in 2018, which is based on a minimum threshold of 40 per cent for both sexes and prohibits more than two consecutive positions of the same sex on the candidate list. The candidate selection process is characterised by a multilevel negotiation between central bodies and local and regional branches, without affecting the power of the party leaders and the voice of the 'party's people', and with a comparatively low degree of decentralisation (Jalali and Sanches, 2022, pp 329–35 and Table 21.1).

Parliamentary representation has been dominated by four parties since 1974: the Right-wing Democratic and Social Centre (Centro Democrático y Social – CDS); the centre-Right Social Democratic Party (Partido Social Democrata – PSD); the centre-Left Socialist Party (Partido Socialista – PS); and the Portugese Communist Party (Partido Comunista Português).

Another Left-wing party, the Left Bloc (Bloco de Esquerda), was registered in 1999. More recently, four new parties have obtained representation in Parliament: the animal rights party People-Animals-Nature (Pessoas-Animais-Natureza – PAN); the populist radical Right-wing party Enough (Chega); the liberal-libertarian party Liberal Initiative (Iniciativa Liberal); and the green/Left-libertarian party LIVRE.[5]

According to Jalali (2019) and Pratas and Bizzarro (2022), we can characterise the current Portuguese party system as an institutionalised and consolidated party system constructed after the democratisation that followed the Carnation Revolution, with the main parties surviving unchallenged for most of the time since.

From the perspective of a social worker running for elected office, the Portuguese political system can be characterised as an institutional structure that, by its multilevel nature, provides a significant number of political careers opportunities. Analysing the *accessibility* of elected offices in Portugal, we can say that the legal rules for candidates are not restrictive beyond age, citizenship and political rights criteria. The absence of geographical constraints, the electoral rhythm, the order of elections (Borchert, 2011, pp 121–3) and, in particular, the gender quotas can benefit social workers. The quotas are key given the female predominance in the social work profession. Against this formal background, the political career opportunities for social workers in Portugal are similar to those for other professional groups, including professions with a high prevalence of women. Still, it is necessary to put into the equation the profession's social status, political career traditions and the importance of the role of political parties in candidate selection. In Portugal, women have been under-represented in political participation (Barroso et al, 2022; Espírito-Santo and Weeks, 2022), though this has lessened with the introduction of gender quotas in 2006, the activism of women's organisations and the gender equality policy agenda of government agencies (see Espírito-Santo and Weeks, 2022).[6]

The *attractiveness* of a political career is related to the benefits of elected offices. The income varies according to the specific office,[7] making some offices more attractive than others, but attractiveness also depends on the social worker's occupational sector, since wages differ between public, private social and private for-profit workplaces. Career maintenance and advancement are other drivers for pursuing political office, along with other immaterial and material rewards, such as power, prestige, public visibility, political influence and staff support (Borchert, 2011). The erosion of the professional prestige of social workers in the country due to criticism, especially by the media (Payne, 2006; Branco, 2017b), may act as a strong barrier in terms of attractiveness. Still, the evidence does not confirm this assertion given the relatively low number of social workers engaged in elected office, as we observe in the next section.

Political recruitment

The participation of social workers as elected politicians in Portugal started after the establishment of the Estado Novo political regime in 1933, a corporatist and authoritarian system, opposed to public intervention in the social sphere and the welfare state conception. The first social worker was elected in 1949 as deputy of the Assembleia Nacional,[8] the parliamentary body of the political system at the time. In the period up to the Carnation Revolution in 1974, five social workers were deputies in the national Parliament (Table 9.1), all women from the regime's political organisations and Catholic associations, and members of the Parliamentary Committee on Labour, Welfare and Social Assistance and the Committee on Education, Popular Culture and Spiritual and Moral Interest (Vargas, 2000, pp 49–60). As Vargas (2000) notes, in a male-dominated parliament, social workers and teachers were the most represented professional groups among women deputies until 1974, two occupational groups valued by the political regime given its familist and maternalist ideology.

After the fall of the Estado Novo regime and the restoration of democracy, it was almost two decades before there were social worker members of the national or regional parliaments again (Rodrigues, 2014). This meant a long period of distancing of social workers from elected political positions in national and regional legislative bodies, and this is observed also at the level of municipal elected bodies. This study sheds some light on the reasons for this gap. The social workers' biographies (see appendices A and B) reveal that their affiliation to party organisations and participation in local and regional party bodies or local government preceded their prospective candidature for political office. The democratic context of the post-Carnation Revolution can be considered a facilitator in this time-demanding process. However, for a deeper understanding, a comparative analysis of other professional groups is needed.

Table 9.1: Social workers elected to office in the Assembleia Nacional, 1934–74

Legislature	Deputy, age at election	Female deputies in parliament
1949–53 (V)	Maria Leonor Correia Botelho, 34	2/120
1953–57 (VI)	Maria Leonor Correia Botelho, 38	2/120
1969–73 (X)	Maria Raquel Ribeiro, 44	4/130
	Luzia Neves Pernão Pereira Beija, 50	
1973–74 (XI)*	Josefina de Encarnação P. Marvão, 34	9/148
	Maria Ângela Craveiro da Gama, 44	

Note: * Parliament was dissolved in April 1974 in the context of the Carnation Revolution.
Source: Based on Vargas (2000)

Table 9.2: Social workers elected to office in national and regional parliaments, legislative mandate VI to XIV, 1974–2028

Legislative mandate	Deputy, age at election (party)	Female deputies in parliament
NP 1991–95 (VI)	Ema Leite, 47 (PSD)	20/230
NP 1995–99 (VII)	Filomena Bordalo, 48 (PSD) M. Lurdes Farinha, 48 (PS, substitute)	28/230
NP 2005–09 (X)	M Conceição Cruz, 57 (CDS) M José Gamboa, 57 (PS) Paula Nobre Deus, 35 (PS)	49/230
NP 2009–11 (XI)	M José Gamboa, 61 (PS) José P. Marques, 37 (PS, resigned in 2010)	63/230
NP 2022–24 (XV)	Patrícia Faro, 49 (PS) Irene Costa, 49 (PS)	85/230
NP 2024–25* (XVI)	Patrícia Faro, 51 (PS) Irene Costa, 51 (PS)	76/230
RP Azores 1996–2000 (VI)	M Fátima Moniz Sousa (PS)**	5/52
RP Madeira 2015–19 (XI)	Lina Pereira, 32 (JPP; for seven months from 2017 in a replacement regime)	10/47
RP Madeira 2023–24 (XIII)***	Lina Pereira, 36 (JPP) Mónica Freitas, 27 (PAN)	14/47
RP Madeira 2024–28 (XIV)	Lina Pereira, 36 (JPP) Mónica Freitas, 27 (PAN)	21/47

Notes: NP: national Parliament; RP: regional parliament; * the National Parliament was dissolved in March 2025; ** age not available for this RP; *** the Madeira regional Parliament was dissolved in March 2024, five months after the regional elections in October 2023

Source: Based on Rodrigues (2014), Pordata and national and regional parliament websites

As shown in Table 9.2, from 1974 to the most recent legislative mandate (XVI, 2024–28), the elected social workers at national level have all been women, belonging to the 45–60 age cohort, though a younger cohort is found in the Madeira Regional Parliament.

As shown in Table 9.3, social workers represent a low proportion of the parliamentarians at national and regional levels, at most 2 per cent, except for the Madeira Regional Parliament in the most recent election, at 4.25 per cent. Compared with other professional groups, social workers are less well represented than lawyers, magistrates and other legal professions (19.7 per cent and 19.1 per cent in legislative mandates VI and VII, respectively), and teachers at all levels of education (23.2 per cent and 27.3 per cent in legislative mandates VI and VII, respectively), though they compare better with other human sciences and health professions (see Freire et al, 2001).

In legislative mandate XV, according to data from the national Parliament,[9] as of 2024 there were 58 lawyers, magistrates and other legal professionals (25 per cent), 37 teachers at all levels of education (16 per cent) and just 2 social workers (1 per cent).

Analysing the weight of these occupational groups in the Portuguese active population to consider the extent of parliamentary representation, a distorted distribution is observed, with a much higher representation of lawyers (0.88 per cent of the population with 25 per cent of all MPs) and teachers (4.5 per cent of the population with 16 per cent of MPs) compared to social workers (0.48 per cent of the population with 1 per cent of MPs; Table 9.3).

Considering the party affiliation of social workers in national Parliament, they belong primarily to the parties of the parliamentary Left, specifically the Socialist Party, though a minority belong to parties of the centre-Right and Right-wing, such as the Social Democratic Party and the Democratic and Social Centre. This political profile is also observed at the regional level, with some nuance in that in the Madeira Regional Parliament, the elected social workers are affiliated with new political parties: the Together for the People civic movement party (Juntos Pelo Povo – JPP) and the PAN.

According to the data gathered, no social workers from ethnic minorities held political office in the national and regional parliaments. National and regional deputies have degrees in social work, some at postgraduate level (master's and PhD). Their occupational expertise is diverse, covering family and child welfare and protection, equality and women's rights, health, social security and education. Their most common professional activities are

Table 9.3: Occupational groups in national parliament, legislative mandate XV, 2022–24*

	Number of MPs	Percentage of occupational group in national Parliament	Number in the population	Percentage of occupational group in the total population	Percentage of MPs in the occupational group
Teachers	37	16	186,600	4.50	0.02
Lawyers	58	25	36,634	0.88	0.15
Social workers	2	1	20,000	0.48	0.01
Total MPs	230	100			
Active population**			4,151,112		

Notes: * Figures are for 2024; ** the number in the 2021 population census
Source: Based on Pordata, a national Parliament website, Perfil do Docente, 2020–21, Direção-Geral Das Estatísticas da Educação, and Justice Statistics for 2023

coordination of services and victim support, especially for women, followed by teaching, training and, in one case, political consultancy.

The interviews conducted with former and current elected social worker deputies (three from national Parliament and one from a regional parliament) indicate that the motivation to enter politics is related to representation of 'the social realm' and under-represented territories (MP1), the opportunity to 'contribute to a better world' at the political level (MP2), the opportunity 'to be able to change and create public policies adapted to the areas of professional and academic expertise' (MP3) and the opportunity to do politics in a different way by promoting people's participation, listening and giving voice to citizens and enacting political advocacy for people's needs (MP-RP). At the local level, contributing to community development and meeting the human and social needs of peripherical or low-density communities was the primary motivation of social workers elected as mayor (Mayor 1 and Mayor 2). Despite the variation in motivations, these are all associated with the values and purpose of the social work profession.

At the local level, social workers have been elected in municipal political bodies as city councillor and municipal deputy, and less so as mayor (see Table 9.4).

Regarding regional distribution, the sample reveals a higher concentration of elected social workers in the regions of Alentejo, Lisboa e Vale do Tejo, and Central Region. From a longitudinal perspective, the data gathered show increasing numbers of social workers in elected office at the municipal level, the highest figures being observed in Alentejo. This may be explained by greater policy engagement associated with the small scale of these municipalities and political affiliation with Left-wing parties.

Table 9.4: Sample of social workers elected to office at the municipal level, by position, 1990–93 to 2022–25

Municipal body	1990–93	1994–97	1998–2001	2002–05	2006–09	2010–13	2014–17	2018–21	2022–25	Total	Number of office holders*
Mayors		1	1			2	2	1	2	9	4
City councillors	1			2	2	3	2	12	9	26	20
Municipal deputies				3	5	4	3	7	12	33	19
Mandates	1	1	1	5	7	9	7	20	23	68	43

Notes: N = 43, non-representative sample; * one person can be elected several times
Source: Based on the Social Workers Elected Officers in Portugal Survey, 2023

Political career patterns

The interviews with social workers, elected parliamentarians and mayors show that their pathway into politics follows the pattern described in the international political science literature regarding political careers generally. The individuals were recruited based on civic and professional reputation and recognition, previous or current affiliation to party organisations, with prospective candidature for political office preceded by participation in local and regional party bodies or local government offices. These recruitment drivers (see Figure 9.1) are consistent with the thesis that 'individual and group-based resources [are] strongly associated with different forms of activism, in political parties, interest and community groups' (Norris and Lovenduski, 1995, p 143).

According to the evidence gathered from the biographies of four social workers in elected office (see Appendix A), the political career of social workers in Portugal has not been characterised by a typical pattern of professionalisation – which departs from the pattern observed for most professional groups represented in Parliament – or by career maintenance and advancement (Borchert, 2011). Effectively, despite these politicians

Figure 9.1: Recruitment drivers for MPs

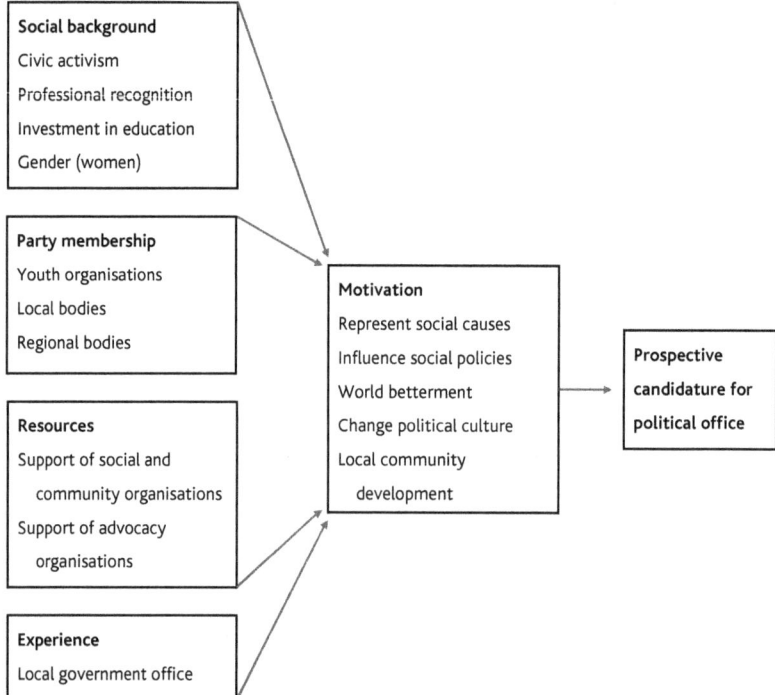

Source: Based on interviews with MPs and mayors, 2024

leaving their former occupations in social work to pursue full-time professional politics, their political biographies do not reflect long-term political careers and advancement opportunities. In the case of MPs, the maximum period in office was two four-year mandates.[10] This may be followed by non-remunerated local government office, returning to a social work post or retirement. In the case of the member of the Madeira Regional Parliament, the parliamentary activity recorded is very recent, but considering that she was elected party leader, this could lead to the advancement of her career as a politician. Despite this, she stated: 'I never stopped to create a strategy of pursuing politics exclusively. It's just that [I wanted] to have a political career or to go into or try public administration. I've never done that because, until today, I've always been mobilised by projects' (MP-RP, Pos 47).

In two cases (MP1 and MP2), it must be emphasised that the social workers were candidates for a new parliamentary mandate in ineligible seats; this was as a direct result of primary elections or the decision of regional political bodies in the face of the occupation of eligible seats by party members who held government posts. As we observe in one case (MP2), after their parliament office mandate, the social worker was appointed to a non-elected political office in the regional administration for two years, which could be seen as a reward for not continuing as an MP. In another case (MP1), retirement was accompanied by a voluntary and honorary position as chair of a local development association, thus following one of the typical stages of the end of a political career, as pointed out in the literature (see Norris and Lovenduski, 1995; Borchert, 2011).

Considering social workers elected to office as mayor, some differences compared to the biographies of MPs are identified. These mayors present a longer political career consisting of several mandates, extending over 20 to 25 years, as city councillors and mayors, covering practically all their working life (see Appendix B). The political career of these social workers took place exclusively in local political bodies. No transition to higher levels of state administration was recorded, in contrast with the general pattern that can be observed of holding local political office as a stepping stone to becoming a member of Parliament (MP) or a member of government. Related to what Norris and Lovenduski (1995, p 174) call 'drive' (or 'the persistence, vigour, and intensity with which applicants try to get selected and elected within a particular opportunity structure'), this can be explained as their choice (M1) or as a lack of opportunities in the recruitment process at local and regional levels (M2).

> A political career, always, in the town hall, yes. I have had several invitations to become a member of [regional] parliament and never accepted. (M1, Pos 31)

I can clearly say that I was not given a chance. […] It did not necessarily have to be as a deputy. Other interesting places were in [city] and around [regional public administration places]. […] I did nothing to stay in politics. I would have liked to, as I said, but I realised that this opportunity could have arisen naturally, and it did not. (M2, Pos 23)

Social advocacy

Analysing elected social workers' commitment to social justice causes, we can consider their involvement in parliamentary committees and their contribution to bills, policy measures and political resolutions related to vulnerable groups and relevant social problems.

The parliamentary participation of Portuguese social worker MPs includes participation in the Labour and Social Security Committee (MP1, MP2), the Health Committee (MP2, MP3, MP-RP), Social Inclusion and Youth (MP-RP), Environment, Climate and Natural Resources (MP-RP), and Rights, Freedoms, and Guarantees Committee – which covers issues of gender equality, domestic violence and migration (MP3), domains that are linked with social workers' professional expertise – or the party's programmatic agenda, as in the case of the PAN regional parliamentarian. The PAN MP-RP is one of the few exceptions, as they were also a member of the Eventual Commission for the Consolidation and Deepening of Autonomy and Reform of the Political System of the Autonomous Region of Madeira, a matter of a highly political nature.

Following this pattern, some of the significant legislative initiatives of these elected officers also show a relationship with their areas of expertise and professional engagement, such as:

- an amendment to the Labour Code to protect the labour rights of victims of domestic violence;
- inclusion of children and young people in the framework of protection for victims of domestic violence;
- an amendment to the Labour Code to promote the reconciliation of professional and personal life;
- early intervention legislation;
- an amendment to the State General Budget to guarantee regular financial support for the National Support Network for Victims of Domestic Violence;
- participation in the Parliamentary Committee on Inquiry of Waiting Lists at Madeira Regional Health Service.

The following comments by MPs emphasise social workers' contribution to parliamentary activity, acting as a liaison and a kind of ombudsman on the ground and in social life, promoting a more effective relationship with citizens and peripheral territories.

> I could tell many stories ... and explain [to the peers] that the country they were talking about was not the country I knew based on my professional experience. Our country was different. It was a country with greater precariousness, weak social protection and fewer rights. (MP1, Labour and Social Security Committee, Pos 21)

> One of the first measures we took when we were elected and had a parliamentary group was to create a mobile support office. We had a van ... we bought a van .... We had a telephone contact publicised on social media and in leaflets people received by post. [...] For example, on Mondays, we would be in [a municipality] and parked there in a well-known place by the town hall. (MP-RP, Pos 51)

This lens of analysis underlines the relationship between social workers' socialisation through education and the professional context. Still, it should also be considered that policy agenda-setting is influenced by several processes and actors and not only by the individual's own agency. Despite the different models of agenda-setting (Garraud, 2014), according to the MPs interviewed, important influences on their parliamentary activity include the specific government programme and the parliamentary group dynamics – namely, peers' perceptions and social representation of their advocacy agenda and vulnerable people, as the following illustrates:

> Intervention in social areas and areas involving minorities are not considered noble policy areas. It will not be politically correct to say this, but it will be honest. Because they are minorities and, therefore, from the electoral point of view, less expressive than drawing up public policies that target citizens in general. (MP2, Pos 29)

This analysis should also consider the social worker MPs' limited parliamentary experience, political careers and skills in terms of political and policy skills, despite their previous participation in local and regional party committees.

A last aspect of reporting is the link that MPs and mayors maintain with their former social work profession through social work organisations. The data gathered reveal low activity and some circumstantial contacts.

Conclusion

In summary, the engagement of social workers holding elected office in Portugal was late historically and numbers at the national and regional parliamentary levels are small. However, a significant increase at the local level is observed, suggesting the relevance of proximity as a recruitment driver.

These social work professionals are recruited based on civic and professional reputation and recognition as well as previous or simultaneous affiliation with party organisations. Prospective candidature for political office is preceded by participation in local and regional party bodies and/or local government office. The political career and professionalisation of social workers in Portugal is not characterised by a typical pattern, as has been observed for most represented professional groups in both career maintenance and advancement.

The engagement of social worker MPs in the social justice agenda is multidetermined, influenced by the specific government programme, the parliamentary group dynamics, the individual's social work experience and political skills and the individual's agency.

Further research is required to incorporate former MPs in national and regional parliaments. Above all, a mixed-methods methodology at the local level is needed; this should combine extensive research to attain a national census of social workers elected at the municipal level and interviews with city councillors and municipal deputies to gather evidence on drivers of recruitment, motivations, prospective careers and advocacy agendas.

Appendix A: Biograms of social workers elected to office in national and regional parliaments

MP1

	Age	Education	Professional career	Political career
1971–72	23	Degree in social work	Social worker Non-governmental organisation for social promotion of women victims of prostitution	
1992–...			Social worker Family and Child Support Project (PAFAC) Ministry of Justice	
1997–98		Postgraduate qualification in child protection	...	
2000			...	PS affiliation PS local and regional committees
2005 (X)	57			**Elected MP, 1st mandate**
2009 (XI)				**Elected MP, 2nd mandate**

	Age	Education	Professional career	Political career
2012 (XII)			Return to Ministry of Justice	MP candidate, not elected
2013–...			Retirement Board Member National Confederation of Social Solidarity Institutions	**Elected President of Parish Council**

MP2

	Age	Education	Professional career	Political career
1995–96	25	Degree in social work	Social worker Child abuse protection non-governmental organisation	
1997–2005			... Social work teacher	
2000			...	PS youth commissioner in municipal elections (2001)
2001			...	PS affiliation (2002) PS local and regional committees
2005 (X)	35			**Elected MP, 1st mandate** Elected Municipal Deputy
2009 (XI)			Returns to child abuse protection non-governmental organisation	MP candidate, not elected Elected Municipal Deputy
2010				**Vice-President CCDR Alentejo (Alentejo Regional Coordination and Development Commission)**
2012			Returns to child abuse protection non-governmental organisation	
2014		Master's degree in social work	...	
2022		PhD in social work	Social work teacher	

MP3

	Age	Education	Professional career	Political career
1988	15			Membership of Socialist Youth

	Age	Education	Professional career	Political career
1992				Socialist Party affiliation
1996	23	Degree in social work	Social worker Social security ministry/ local services	Socialist Youth Oporto Committee (1995–97)
2003	30		…	PS affiliation PS local and regional committees
2003			Social worker Red Cross shelter for victims of domestic violence	
2011		MSc in psychology of justice	…	
2014			…	PS local committee (2014–17)
2017			…	**Elected Municipal Deputy**
2020		Completing a PhD in sociology	…	Chair of the Socialist Women Oporto region (2020–22)
2021			Specialist Office of Secretary of State for Citizenship and Equality	
2022 (XV)	49			President of the Socialist Women Oporto Region and Socialist Women National Council (2022–24) **Elected MP, 1st mandate**
2024 (XVI)				**Elected MP, 2nd mandate**

MP-RP *(Madeira Regional Parliament)*

	Age	Education	Professional career	Political career
2009				Participation in the creation of the Citizens' Movement – JPP
2010	24	Degree in social work		
2012		Master's degree in social work Completing a PhD in social work	Assistant Professor at the University of Madeira	

	Age	Education	Professional career	Political career
2014				Elected member of Parish Council by JPP Movement
2015			JPP Parliamentary Group Advisor	Membership of the JPP (JPP became a political party)
2017			...	MP – Madeira Regional Parliament (replacement regime for seven months)
2018			...	Re-elected member of Parish Council
2024		PhD in social work		Re-elected member of Parish Council MP – Madeira Regional Parliament Elected party leader

Source: Based on interviews with MPs, 2024

Appendix B: Biograms of social workers elected as mayor
M1*

	Age	Education	Professional career	Political career
				Membership of Socialist Youth
1975		Degree in education	Elementary school teacher	
1984		Degree in social work	Social worker Local social security office (1984–94)	
1990				Membership of the Socialist Party Elected as City Councillor (no mandate)
1994				Elected as Mayor
1998				Re-elected as Mayor
2002				Mayor candidate, not re-elected Elected as City Councillor (no mandate)
2010				Elected as Mayor

	Age	Education	Professional career	Political career
2014			Retirement Chair of local development association (2015–23)	**Re-elected as Mayor** Resigns from office in 2015

Note: * Born in Azores

M2*

	Age	Education	Professional career	Political career
1964				
1988	24	Degree in social work	Social worker Local social security office	
1989			Social worker Social solidarity non-profit organisation	
1992		Postgraduate qualification in family and social systems	…	
1994			Social worker at municipality	
1996			Mayoral assistant	Participates in the parliamentary election campaign PS affiliation (1998)
2001				Member of PS national, regional and local committees** Chair of Socialist Women, Coimbra Region (2002–10) **Elected as City Councillor**
2005			Returns to municipality as social worker	Declines invitation to new election as city councillor
2008				**Elected as Mayor**
2012				**Re-elected as Mayor**
2016				**Re-elected as Mayor**
2020			Returns to social security national long-term care network	

Notes: * Born in Coimbra; ** member of regional and local committees, 2002–18; member of National Political Committee, 2002–23

Source: Based on interviews with social workers who were elected mayor, 2024

Notes

1. The implementation of the administrative regions was the subject of ongoing public debate. A referendum in November 1998 resulted in rejection of regionalisation by a two thirds majority (Magone, 2003).
2. Portugal has 308 municipalities, 278 on the mainland, 11 in Madeira and 19 in the Azores.
3. In 2013, a limit of three successive mayoral mandates was introduced. According to Teles (2022: 25), this electoral reform 'had a significant impact on the renewal of local political elites, but ... also produced long-term effects which are yet to be determined'.
4. There are 4,260 civil parishes in Portugal.
5. For more detailed information about Portuguese parties, see Jalali (2019) and Pratas and Bizzarro (2022).
6. The composition of parliament (230 deputies after 1991), evidences the under-representation of women. Before approval of the Parity Law, women made up: 8.7 per cent of deputies in the 1991–95 legislature; 12.2 per cent in 1995–99; 17.4 per cent in 1999–2002; 19.6 per cent in 2002–05; 21.3 per cent in 2005–09. In the first legislature after the Parity Law was implemented, women made up: 27.4 per cent in 2009–11; decreasing to 26.5 per cent of deputies in 2011–15. Ater that, the share was 33 per cent in 2015–19 and 38.7 per cent in 2019. This tendency is observed in all the parties represented, more so in the small and newer political parties (see Pordata at: www.pordata.pt). See also Espírito-Santo and Weeks (2022).
7. In Portugal, the salary for those in elected office is indexed to that of the president of the republic and varies according to the level in the administration hierarchy: central government and parliament, regional government and assembly, executive and municipal assembly, and parish executive. Remuneration at the local level is based on population numbers.
8. Maria Leonor Correia Botelho (legislative mandates 1949–53 and 1953–57) was 34 years old when she was first elected. She was head of the Social Service Department at the Family Assistance Institute; teacher at the School for Social Auxiliary Workers at St Vincent de Paul Homes, the Portuguese Red Cross Nurses' School and the Portuguese Oncology Institute Nurses' Technical School; and national vice-president of the União Noelista Potuguesa, the Red Cross of Benevolence (Vargas, 2000).
9. Data from the Divisão de Informação Legislativa e Parlamentar, February 2024.
10. Some mandates were not completed due to the early dissolution of parliament.

References

Barroso, C., Borges, L.C. and Cabral, M. (2022) *Participação feminina na vida política em Portugal e na Europa*, Assembleia da República.

Borchert, J. (2011) 'Individual ambition and institutional opportunity: A conceptual approach to political careers in multi-level systems', *Regional & Federal Studies*, 21(2): 117–40.

Bouquet, B. (2005) 'Le Service Social Français', in J.-P. Deslauriers and Y. Hurtubise (eds) *Le Travail Social International – Eléments de Comparaison*, Presses Universitaires du Laval, pp 35–65.

Branco, F. (1997) 'Municípios e Políticas Sociais em Portugal: 1977–1989', *Intervenção Social*, 11/12: 67–82.

Branco, F. (2009a) *A Formação de Assistentes Sociais em Portugal: Breve perspectiva histórica e análise curricular da formação superior em Serviço Social pós reforma de Bolonha*, CESSS.

Branco, F. (2009b) 'A Profissão de Assistente Social em Portugal', *Locus Social*, 3: 61–89.

Branco, F. (2017a) 'O Serviço Social como elemento substantivo de efectivação da Política Social', in M.d.C.P. Neves and A.B. Félix (eds) *Ética Aplicada: Protecção Social*, Edições 70, pp 49–72.

Branco, F. (2017b) 'Social work academia and policy in Portugal', in J. Gal and I. Weiss-Gal (eds) *Where Academia and Policy Meet: A Cross-National Perspective on the Involvement of Social Work Academics in Social Policy*, Policy Press, pp 117–32.

Branco, F. (2018) 'Social work education: The Portuguese story in a local and global perspective', *Practice*, 30(4): 271–91.

Branco, F. and Amaro, M.I. (2018) 'Meeting points for social work and social policy: Curricula analysis and pedagogical experiences in the Portuguese context', 8th European Conference of Social Work Research, Edinburgh, 18–20 April.

Carrilho, R. and Branco, F. (2023) 'Social workers' involvement in policy practice in Portugal', *Social Sciences*, 12(2): art 105, doi: 10.3390/socsci12020105

Carvalho, M.I. (2020) *Ser Assistente Social – Retrato(s) da Profissão*, Pactor.

Espírito-Santo, A. and Weeks, A.C. (2022) 'Gender and politics in Portugal', in J.M. Fernandes, P. Magalhães and A.C. Pinto (eds) *The Oxford Handbook of Portuguese Politics*, Oxford University Press, pp 407–22.

Fernandes, J.M. (2022) 'Electoral system', in J.M. Fernandes, P. Magalhães and A C. Pinto (eds) *The Oxford Handbook of Portuguese Politics*, Oxford University Press, pp 181–96.

Fernandes, J.M. and Riera, P. (2019) 'Committee systems in Portugal and Spain', in J.M. Fernandes and C. Leston-Bandeira (eds) *The Iberian Legislatures in Comparative Perspective*, Routledge, pp 71–88.

Freire, A., Matos, T. and Sousa, V.A. (2001) *Recrutamento Parlamentar – Os Deputados Portugueses da Constituinte à VIII Legislatura*, STAPE – Secretariado Técnico dos Assuntos para o Processo Eleitoral.

Garraud, P. (2014) 'Agenda/Émergence', in L. Boussaguet, S. Jacquot and P. Ravinet (eds) *Dictionnaire des politiques publiques. 4e édition précédée d'un nouvel avant-propos*, Presses de Sciences Po, pp 58–67.

Goes, E. and Leston-Bandeira, C. (2022) 'The role of the Portuguese Parliament', in J.M. Fernandes, P. Magalhães and A.C. Pinto (eds) *The Oxford Handbook of Portuguese Politics*, Oxford University Press, pp 136–48.

Jalali, C. (2019) 'The Portuguese party system: Evolution in continuity?', in A.C. Pinto and C.P. Teixeira (eds) *Political Institutions and Democracy in Portugal: Assessing the Impact of the Eurocrisis*, Palgrave Macmillan, pp 77–99.

Jalali, C. and Sanches, E.R. (2022) 'Candidates selection in Portugal', in J.M. Fernandes, P. Magalhães and A.C. Pinto (eds) *The Oxford Handbook of Portuguese Politics*, Oxford University Press, pp 325–38.

Magone, J. (2003) 'The political class in advanced democracies', in J. Borchert and J. Zeiss (eds) *The Political Class in Advanced Democracies*, Oxford University Press, pp 320–35.

Mayer, R. (2002) *Évolution des Pratiques en Service Social*, Gaetan Morin.

Neto, O.A. (2023) 'Semi-presidentialism in Portugal: Academic quarrels amidst institutional stability', in J.M. Fernandes, P. Magalhães and A.C. Pinto (eds) *The Oxford Handbook of Portuguese Politics*, Oxford University Press, pp 121–35.

Norris, P. and Lovenduski, J. (1995) *Political Recruitment: Gender, Race and Class in the British Parliament*, Cambridge University Press.

Oliveira, C.R., Carvalhais, I.E. and Cancela, J. (2014) *Political Parties Openness to Immigrants in Portugal: Between the Opportunity Structure and the Individual Perceptions*, Alto Comissariado para as Migrações.

Payne, M. (2006) *What Is Professional Social Work?* Policy Press.

Pratas, M. and Bizzarro, F. (2022) 'Political parties and party system', in J.M. Fernandes, P. Magalhães and A.C. Pinto (eds) *The Oxford Handbook of Portuguese Politics*, Oxford University Press, pp 353–70.

Ribeiro, S. (2015) *Os assistentes sociais e o burnout em Portugal: Resistência e exaustão do serviço social na contemporaneidade*, Doctoral thesis, Universidade Católica Portuguesa.

Rodrigues, C. (2014) *Deputados Assistentes Sociais_1949–2011*, Master's dissertation, Instituto Superior Miguel Torga, Available at: https://repositorio.ismt.pt/items/30288867-3d48-498d-a9e6-cb0663e7306c

Teles, F. (2022) 'Decentralization and local politics', in J.M. Fernandes, P. Magalhães and A.C. Pinto (eds) *The Oxford Handbook of Portuguese Politics*, Oxford University Press, pp 212–24.

Vargas, A. (2000) 'Mulheres na Assembleia Nacional_1933_1974', *Revista de Estudos Eleitorais*, 6: 43–62.

10

Switzerland: strong representation of social workers in the cantonal and federal parliaments

Tobias Kindler

Social workers in Switzerland have a long and rich tradition of influencing policy and engaging in politics at the local, cantonal, federal and international levels. Some of the early pioneers of social work were actively involved in the political arena. Mentona Moser, one of the forerunners of social work education in Switzerland, was a founding member of the Communist Party in 1921. Emma Steiger, who was a founder of the Conference for Socialist Welfare, was an active member of the Social Democratic Party (Epple and Schär, 2015). In 1923, she published an article in the social democratic magazine in which she elaborated on the connection between the modern economic system and welfare services as follows:

> A socialist system will make a considerable part of welfare unnecessary, because it will eliminate the profit economy as one of the main causes of the need for welfare. Once the right of every person to the necessities of life is established … no old person or cripple will be dependent on charity. (Steiger, 1923, p 229)

Today, social work in Switzerland is still closely linked to political decision-making processes. Taking this into account, the Swiss social work professional organisation, AvenirSocial, defines policy intervention as a core task of social work. In their code of ethics (AvenirSocial, 2010), they even call on social workers to advocate for democracy and social justice in their role as citizens. And, indeed, Swiss social workers do influence policy through lobbying, policy practice, voluntary political participation and other forms of engagement (for example, Ostrander et al, 2021; Kindler, 2024a; Burzlaff et al, 2025). One form of policy engagement by social workers that has received limited attention in the international, but also in the Swiss, discourse is holding political office (Demircali et al, 2024). To address this gap in the literature, this chapter examines the actual number of Swiss social workers in parliament, how their political careers typically unfold and whether they promote social work values once elected.

Social work as a profession

The social sector in Switzerland is growing at an impressive rate. Whereas in 1970 there were around 5,500 professionals working in the social sector, by 2016 this number had risen to 115,000. This growth has been accompanied by the establishment of additional fields of social services, such as school social work or corporate social work. However, AvenirSocial (2018) estimates that half of the workers employed in the social sector do not have a specific degree in social work. This figure is confirmed by the Federal Statistical Office (BFS, 2023a; 2023b), which estimates that the number of social workers in Switzerland in 2021 was 50,000 – 68 per cent of whom were female and 32 per cent male (gender data from the Federal Statistical Office are binary coded). Based on this figure, social workers account for about 1 per cent of Switzerland's working population of 4,420,000. According to AvenirSocial's definition, social workers are professionals with a degree in social work, social pedagogy, sociocultural animation, community animation, child pedagogy or vocational training and workplace integration. These degrees can be obtained at university or university of applied sciences level in the form of a bachelor's or a master's in social work or at higher technical schools in the form of a higher education diploma. While all these institutions offer a general degree in social work, some of them allow students to specialise in one of the three main branches of social work in Switzerland: social work, social pedagogy and sociocultural animation (AvenirSocial, 2018). These qualifications are officially protected, but there is no licensing or registration system for social workers and no legal protection of the title of social worker.

Approximately 4,000 social workers (8 per cent) are currently members of the social work professional organisation. The aims of AvenirSocial are to build a strong network of social workers, to lobby for the interests of both social workers and service users, to fight for a more just society based on human rights, to improve the working conditions of social workers, to promote social work education and to establish the Code of Ethics as a common ethical framework for the profession (Kulke et al, forthcoming).

It was reported in 2018 that 35 per cent of social workers were employed in private organisations. Another 31 per cent worked in associations, 20 per cent in foundations and 14 per cent in public institutions at national, cantonal or local level (AvenirSocial, 2018). The majority of social workers work with people with disabilities or in the fields of early childhood/education, youth work and social welfare (Madörin et al, 2017). While salaries vary considerably between cantons and fields of practice, the average gross salary of a social worker in Switzerland in 2020 was CHF 6,700 per month (CHF 1 is currently worth EUR 1.07), which was exactly the average of all salaries across all professions. To compare, the salaries of some other professions were CHF 5,400 per month for a farmer, CHF 8,000 per month for a lawyer and CHF 9,400 per month for a teacher (BFS, 2022). This mid-position of the social work profession in terms of remuneration reflects in the status of the profession. Using an online questionnaire, Joye et al (2023) asked a representative sample of the Swiss population to rank a number of occupations on a scale from 0 (lowest status) to 100 (highest status). While kitchen assistants were rated lowest (28) and doctors highest (86), social workers received a score of 58, next to photographers (57), priests (57), tax advisors (59) and police officers (61).

Institutional opportunity structures

Previous studies on social workers who run for and hold political office in Switzerland have mainly focused on the individual factors that motivate them to do so. This research shows that social workers' decision to run for office is strongly affected by social work education and social work practice. Additional influencing factors are age, family background, biographical experiences, social networks and membership in professional and political networks (Kindler and Amann, 2022; Demircali et al, 2024). While this body of research certainly enables us to better understand individual experiences, pathways and choices, social workers' opportunities and motivations to hold political office are also influenced by the specific institutional setting of the political system in which they (aspire to) pursue their political careers. Jens Borchert (2011) has shown how, at the institutional level, the perceived *availability*, *accessibility* and *attractiveness* of a particular political office play a crucial role in structuring the ambitions of potential candidates. In the following, these aspects are discussed for the Swiss context.

Availability is defined as the sheer number of existing offices. In Switzerland's multilevel system, which has been described as an archetype of federalism (Vatter, 2018), political offices are available at the local, cantonal and national levels. At the local level, Switzerland consists of more than 2,100 municipalities (BFS, 2023c). They are governed by 15,000 members of the local executive, which consists of 3–21 members of government. In 2011, for 94 per cent of them, this was a part-time post with an average working week of nine hours. The average salary for this part-time position was CHF 11,400 per year, which means that the position is not very attractive from a financial point of view. Only in larger cities do municipal councillors work full time (Geser et al, 2011). Twenty-two per cent of municipalities have not only their own government but also a local parliament, which varies in size from 9 to 124 seats (Strebel, 2023). Taken together, the 461 local parliaments have a total of 17,500 seats, all of which are honorary (Ladner, 2016).

At the cantonal level, each of the 26 cantons has its own executive and legislative bodies. All cantonal governments consist of either five or seven members (156 across all cantons) who are directly elected by the citizens

(Vatter, 2015). With the exception of three small cantons, these are full-time posts. The size of the cantonal parliaments varies from 50 to 180 seats. Taken together, the 26 cantonal parliaments have a total of 2,594 seats. As at the municipal level, these positions are honorary. However, the time spent as a percentage of a full-time job varies considerably from canton to canton: while the average in 2014 was 19 per cent, members of parliament in the canton of Appenzell Innerrhoden devoted 7 per cent and those in the canton of Geneva gave 37 per cent of their time to their parliamentary duties. The salaries of members of parliament are roughly correlated with the amount of time they spend on parliamentary activities. The lowest annual salary in 2014 was CHF 1,500, the highest was CHF 37,500, and the average across all cantonal parliaments was CHF 12,000 per year (Bundi et al, 2017).

Unlike the local and cantonal levels, the national parliament is bicameral. The Council of States, which represents the cantons, has 46 seats. The National Council, which represents the people, has 200 seats. Switzerland's national parliament was originally designed to function according to the militia principle, a typically Swiss political institution based on the 'idea of volunteering one's time to perform political and social tasks communities need' (Ladner, 2019, p 13) in addition to one's main occupation in various professional fields. According to Bütikofer (2013), a politician who spends less than a third of their time on politics is a militia politician, a politician who spends between a third and two thirds of their time can be defined as a semi-professional politician, and a politician who spends more than two thirds of their time is a professional politician. In view of the militia principle, the Swiss national parliament has traditionally been identified as semi-professional. However, the professionalisation of the Council of States and the National Council – both in terms of the time individual politicians devote to politics and the institutional professionalisation, such as the increase in academic staff working in parliament – is progressing (Bütikofer, 2013). In 2014, Council of States members invested 31 hours and National Council members 27 hours per week (Bundi et al, 2018), resulting in an average salary of CHF 115,000–175,000 per year (including all allowances), depending on the number of memberships in specialised committees (Di Capua et al, 2022).

The national government consists of seven members with equal rights. The office is a full-time post and members are elected jointly by the Council of States and the National Council. The federal councillors represent the four largest parties in parliament, the Swiss People's Party (26 per cent), the Social Democrats (17 per cent), the Liberals (15 per cent) and the Centre (14 per cent; Federal Chancellery, 2023). The president changes every year on a rotating basis and chairs the council, but has only a symbolic role (Linder and Iff, 2011). In 2024, the gross annual income of a federal councillor was CHF 450,000 per year, making it the most financially attractive political office in Switzerland (The Federal Council, 2024). Members of parliaments and governments at all federal levels are elected for a fixed term, usually four years. Parliament can't withdraw its confidence from the government, nor can the government dissolve parliament (Freiburghaus et al, 2021).

In summary, there are more than 35,000 political offices at all federal levels, which means that one in every 154 Swiss citizens over the age of 18 is an elected politician (0.65 per cent). Some of these available positions can be very attractive to social workers who want to bring about change not only at an individual level but also at a structural level. As the vast majority of political posts are honorary, especially those in local and cantonal parliaments, members of parliament keep their jobs alongside their political posts. This allows social workers to continue practising their profession and to directly influence policy-making processes in the formal political arena on the basis of their professional knowledge. According to interviews with social workers, they are particularly valued as experts in applied social policy and they are consulted on genuine social work issues, such as addiction, disability, housing, migration and poverty (Amann and Kindler, 2021; 2022). In addition, the structures described provide opportunities for social workers not only to advocate on behalf of service users, but also to engage them directly in policy processes as experts on their own lives – for example, in official hearings, lobbying or public actions to influence parliamentary and governmental decisions, thus opening up opportunities for self-advocacy. Probably the most effective places for social workers to contribute their expertise to parliamentary discussions at all federal levels are the parliamentary committees specialising in social issues. Both chambers of the national parliament have nine standing specialised committees, one of which is the Social Security and Health Committee (SSHC). For social workers in executive positions as members of local, cantonal or national governments, the departments of social services, social welfare or social security would be the most attractive. However, access to parliamentary committees and government departments depends not only on the preferences of individual politicians, but also on several other factors, such as seniority and internal party politics.

Political recruitment

According to the militia principle described earlier, the Swiss political system is designed in a way that offers members of parliament at all federal levels the possibility to remain in their original profession concurrently with their political mandate. The idea behind this principle is that all members of parliament should contribute to political discussion from the perspective of their ongoing professional practice. This approach offers social workers a powerful way to influence policy. This chapter presents original data on the numbers of social workers in the cantonal and national parliaments of

Switzerland. The data was collected in January 2024 through the cantonal state calendars, the official websites of the cantonal and national parliaments, and the personal websites of members of parliament. Further details on data collection and the dataset are available online (see Kindler, 2024b).

At cantonal level, there are a total of 2,594 posts in all 26 cantonal parliaments. In 2024, 65 of these were held by social workers (2.5 per cent). As can be seen in Table 10.1, the vast majority of these social workers belonged to either the Social Democratic Party (51 per cent) or the Green Party (17 per cent). While, as mentioned earlier, 68 per cent of the Swiss social work population is female and 32 per cent male, male social workers were over-represented in political office at the cantonal level with a share of 46 per cent. The average age of cantonal members of parliament was 47.9 years, with the largest age group between 51 and 60. The identified social workers in the cantonal parliaments were in office for an average of 5.6 years, and 78 per cent were currently in their first or second term of office, while three were already in their fifth term of office. Considering that social workers make up 1 per cent of the working population in Switzerland, they were over-represented in the cantonal parliaments, holding 2.5 per cent of all offices. However, representatives of other professions were even more over-represented in 2024, including farmers (9.3 per cent of members of cantonal parliaments; 1.9 per cent of the working population), lawyers (8.2 per cent; 0.8 per cent), teachers (8.2 per cent; 4.2 per cent) and economists (8.1 per cent; 4.2 per cent) (Kindler, 2024b).

At the national level, there were three social workers in the National Council (200 seats) in 2024 – Barbara Gysi (Social Democratic Party), Katharina Prelicz-Huber and Manuela Weichelt (both Green Party) – and two in the Council of States (46 seats) – Maya Graf (Green Party) and Simon Stocker (Social Democratic Party). As can be seen in Table 10.1, only one member of the national parliament identified as male. The mean age of social work members of the national parliament was ten years higher (mean = 57.4) than that of members of the cantonal parliament (mean = 47.9). At the national level, social workers had been members of the parliament for an average of 9.4 years. With five out of 246 members of the national parliament (2 per cent), social workers were slightly over-represented, as was the case in the cantonal parliaments, compared to their 1 per cent share of the total working population. However, in 2024, the over-representation of certain other professions was much more striking – for example, lawyers (21.1 per cent of members of national parliament; 0.8 per cent of the working population), farmers (7.3 per cent; 1.9 per cent) and economists (8.9 per cent; 4.0 per cent) (Kindler, 2024b).

At the national level, members of parliament with a social work background differed from the average member of parliament in a number of ways. First, social workers in the national parliament were predominantly

Table 10.1: Characteristics of social workers in elected political office in the cantonal and national parliaments

Variable	Cantonal parliament (N = 65)	National parliament (N = 5)
Gender		
Female	35 (54%)	4 (80%)
Male	30 (46%)	1 (20%)
Age	M = 47.9 years	M = 57.4 years
21–30	3 (5%)	–
31–40	18 (28%)	–
41–50	15 (23%)	1 (20%)
51–60	19 (29%)	2 (40%)
> 60	10 (15%)	2 (40%)
Party		
Social Democratic Party	33 (51%)	2 (40%)
Green Party	11 (17%)	3 (60%)
Evangelical People's Party	5 (7.5%)	–
The Centre	4 (6%)	–
The Liberals	3 (5%)	–
Alternative List	2 (3%)	–
Swiss People's Party	2 (3%)	–
Other parties	5 (7.5%)	–
Current term	M = 5.6 years	M = 9.4 years
1st (1–4 years)	30 (46%)	1 (20%)
2nd (5–8 years)	21 (32%)	2 (40%)
3rd (9–12 years)	11 (17%)	–
4th (13–16 years)	–	1 (20%)
5th (17–20 years)	3 (5%)	–
6th (21–24 years)	–	1 (20%)

Sources: Kindler (2024b); author's compilation

female (80 per cent), whereas the overall proportion of female members of the national parliament was 38 per cent. In addition, social workers were older (mean = 57.4) than the average member of parliament (mean = 51.4). This difference in age also corresponds to the average number of years in national office, which was higher for social workers (mean = 9.4) than for members of parliament without a social work background (mean = 6.7). Finally, similar to the cantonal level, national social work members of parliament were exclusively affiliated with the Social Democratic Party and the Green Party, which is in stark contrast to the centre-conservative-Right majority in parliament (Kindler, 2024b).

Political career patterns

One of the most prominent and experienced members of parliament with a background in social work is National Councillor Barbara Gysi, born in 1964. She graduated in educational science and later in social work. She worked for almost ten years as a social pedagogue in residential care and as a social worker in a women's shelter. It was during this time, in the early 1990s, that she began her political career in the canton of Sankt Gallen. Her first posts were honorary positions as president of the local Social Democratic Party and as a member of the party's cantonal executive. She stopped working as a social worker in 1997 when she became cantonal secretary general of the Social Democratic Party. At the same time, she was elected to the local parliament, where she served for four years. Between 2000 and 2012, she was a member of the local government, where she was responsible for the department of social welfare, youth and the elderly, and a member of the cantonal parliament. After almost 20 years of political experience at local and cantonal level in various functions, she was elected to the National Council in 2011, where she is serving her fourth term. Since 2016, she has been a member of the important SSHC, which she chaired for the 2024/2025 period. In addition to her formal political career, Barbara Gysi has always been active in trade unions, an additional form of policy engagement. She is an active member of various trade unions, including the Public Service Union (VPOD), the most important union for social workers. She has been a member of the executive committee of the cantonal trade union federation since 2007 and was its president from 2012 to 2024 (Gysi, nd).

Barbara Gysi's political career from local to cantonal to national level provides a vivid illustration of the prototype of the integrated and hierarchical political career of national members of parliament in Switzerland. More than 80 per cent of members of the National Council and the Council of States previously held political office at the local and/or cantonal levels (Pilotti, 2017). In such a political trajectory towards the centre, the cantonal parliaments function as stepping stones for nationally oriented politicians (Stolz, 2003). While local and cantonal parliaments remain non-professional, the national parliament is slowly becoming more professionalised, both institutionally and individually (Di Capua et al, 2022), thus reinforcing unidirectional political career patterns from the local and cantonal levels to the national level (Borchert and Stolz, 2011). While in the 1970s, about 20 per cent of the members of the Council of States were professional politicians (defined as spending more than two thirds of working hours on their political office), by 2007 this proportion had risen to 60 per cent. In the National Council, however, the share of professional politicians remained relatively stable at around 28 per cent over the same period (Bütikofer, 2013).

In her analysis of typical careers of national members of parliament in Switzerland, Sarah Bütikofer (2013) identified three types of parliamentarians. The first type is the experienced politician. These politicians gain extensive experience in previous political offices at the local or cantonal level before being elected to the national parliament. They often hold honorary party posts – for example, as executive members or secretaries of a local party. In addition to their party and political offices, experienced politicians usually have a rich professional background in non-political fields, such as social work. The second type is the young, ambitious politician. These politicians start their political careers at an early age, often with the explicit aim of pursuing a long-term political career at national level. They typically have little professional experience outside the political arena and are elected to national political office when they are under 40. The third type is the career changer. These politicians have little or no political experience when they enter the national parliament and have never held political office at local or cantonal level. According to this typology, in 2013, 8 per cent of national members of parliament were career changers, 28 per cent were young ambitious politicians and 64 were experienced politicians (Bütikofer, 2013).

Based on this categorisation, all five social workers in the national parliament in 2024 clearly resembled the experienced politician type. As can be seen in Table 10.2, they all had extensive experience in political and party offices at local, cantonal and even national level. Manuela Weichelt, for example, was a member of the cantonal parliament from 1994 to 2002 and a member of the cantonal government from 2007 to 2018 before becoming the first woman to represent the canton of Zug in the National Council in 2019. As described earlier, Barbara Gysi combined political positions, such as member of parliament, with (honorary) party service, as, for example, party secretary or executive member, very early in her political career. In addition to their political experience, all social workers in the national parliament had been active in interest groups (such as the social work professional organisation), advocacy organisations or trade unions. Katharina Prelicz-Huber, for example, was president of the Public Service Union from 2010 to 2023. Finally, the five social workers holding national office in Switzerland had strong professional backgrounds in different subfields of social work, including health/ageing population, youth work and residential care.

In summary, the political careers of social workers in the Swiss parliament in 2024 are similar to those of parliamentarians with other professional backgrounds. Like the vast majority in the national parliament, these social workers were seasoned politicians with extensive experience in previous political offices at all federal levels. Most began their political careers at local

Table 10.2: Political and professional background of social workers in elected political office in the cantonal and national parliaments

Variable	Cantonal parliament (N = 65)	National parliament (N = 5)
Previous political offices		
Local	29 (45%)	4 (80%)
Cantonal	–	4 (80%)
National	–	2 (40%)
Previous party/interest group offices held		
Interest group	17 (26%)	5 (100%)
Local party	28 (43%)	3 (60%)
Cantonal party	19 (29%)	4 (80%)
National party	3 (5%)	2 (40%)
Professional social work experience	M = 18.6	M = 15.2
0–5 years	4 (6%)	–
6–10 years	17 (26%)	2 (40%)
11–20 years	17 (26%)	2 (40%)
21–30 years	21 (33%)	–
> 30 years	6 (9%)	1 (20%)
Predominant subfield of social work occupation		
Social welfare	7 (11%)	–
Health sector/ageing population	7 (11%)	3 (60%)
Youth work	7 (11%)	1 (20%)
School social work	5 (8%)	–
People with a disability	4 (6%)	–
Residential care	3 (5%)	1 (20%)
Other fields	32 (48%)	–

Sources: Kindler (2024b); The Federal Assembly (2024); personal websites of politicians

level, continued at cantonal level and were finally elected to the national parliament. While all of them had a profound professional background in social work, at some point they stopped practising social work and became semi-professional or full-time politicians, like more than 80 per cent of national members of parliament (Bütikofer, 2013; Di Capua et al, 2022). This stands in stark contrast to the social workers who were members of cantonal parliaments in 2024. All of them still worked as social workers as their main profession alongside their political mandate, with the largest group in the fields of social welfare, health/ageing, youth work, school social work, disability and residential care (see Table 10.2).

The description of the political careers shows that all five social workers serving in the national parliament possessed a substantial amount of professional expertise and knowledge, acquired through their experience in social work. This background enabled them to bring these insights into the political arena. To revisit the example from the beginning of this section, Barbara Gysi can draw on a mix of profound experience gained from her involvement in social work, trade unions and political offices at all federal levels for her political engagement. It is noteworthy that the areas of social work in which she engaged during her career are closely aligned with her political agenda, which focuses on improving the living and working conditions and the wellbeing of all people (Gysi, nd). Although all five social workers were working full or part time as politicians and were no longer directly involved in the social work sector, they still identified strongly as social workers. It could be argued that by moving from the local and cantonal to the national level, and thus from militia to (semi-)professional politics, social workers change not only the political level but also their profession. With such a transition, their income is dependent on their re-election, and therefore we might also expect their political agenda to shift from social justice and improving conditions for service users to more mainstream policy positions (Borchert, 2011). These issues are explored in more detail in the next section.

Social advocacy

Previous studies on social workers in politics, both internationally (for example, Lane and Humphreys, 2011; McLaughlin et al, 2019; Meehan, 2021; Binder and Weiss-Gal, 2022; Leitner and Stolz, 2023; Löffler, 2024) and in the Swiss context (for example, Amann and Kindler, 2022; Demircali et al, 2024), have assumed, from a normative perspective, that the mere presence of social workers in political offices is desirable. However, we still don't know whether social workers, once elected, use their position to promote social work values and use their insider position in parliaments or governments for social advocacy in favour of social work, service users and the wellbeing of all people. This section addresses this gap by focusing on the following three indicators of a strong link between social work members of parliament and the professional values of social work: involvement in parliamentary committees specialising in social welfare issues, initiation of parliamentary policy papers (*parlamentarische Vorstösse*; these include motions, postulates, interpellations, inquiries and questions) dealing with social work issues, and ongoing contact and identification with social work stakeholders. The information in this section is taken from cantonal and national parliamentary services and personal websites.

Both chambers of the national parliament have nine parallel specialised committees. The most relevant for social work issues are the SSHCs. These committees discuss and prepare parliamentary policy papers on issues such as migration, addiction and social assistance before they are discussed in plenary sessions. The SSHC in the National Council has 25 members (12.5 per cent of the seats in the National Council) and the SSHC in the Council of States has 13 members (28.3 per cent of the seats in the Council of States). In 2024, two out of three social workers in the National Council and one out of two social workers in the Council of States were members of the SSHC. Not all cantonal parliaments have a similar committee at cantonal level. However, in the SSHC of the cantonal parliament of Zurich, for example, 2 of the 15 members in 2024 were social workers. These high numbers clearly show that the professional expertise of social workers is sought after in these particular committees and that social workers are willing to contribute their knowledge.

A second indicator of a continued strong link with the social work profession is the initiation of parliamentary policy papers dealing with social work issues. In 2024, with the exception of Simon Stocker, who was only recently elected to the Council of States, all social work members of the national parliament had initiated and submitted a number of parliamentary policy papers on various topics. Councillor of States Maya Graf had initiated 306 policy papers, 12 per cent of which were directly related to social work issues, including proposals to address domestic violence. While this is still a high percentage, the main focus of her political activity was clearly on environmental, sustainability and animal rights issues. National Councillor Manuela Weichelt had initiated 112 policy papers, 30 of which (27 per cent) focused specifically on the field of social work – for example, measures against discrimination of people with a disability. A second focus of her political activity was clearly the health sector. This was also the case for Barbara Gysi, who often combined health issues with social issues – for example, in her fight for more affordable health insurance. Of her 140 policy papers, 52 (37 per cent) dealt with issues directly related to social work. Finally, Katharina Prelicz-Huber, a politician in the Green Party and president of the public service union for more than ten years, had promoted social work issues in 60 out of 106 of her policy papers (57 per cent). In line with her background, she combined these activities with policy proposals on labour rights and environmental protection. On average, 33 per cent of the 664 parliamentary policy papers submitted by these four national members of parliament focused on social work. This is different from the policy papers by parliamentarians without a social work background as, on average, only 12 per cent of all policy papers in the Council of States directly related to the field of social work (Kindler, 2024b).

The observation that social work members of parliament are considerably more active in proposing parliamentary policy papers in the field of social work is likely to be attributed to their professional knowledge and expertise. This suggests that their contributions are particularly focused on promoting the development of issues specific to the field of social work and advocating for social justice. However, further research is needed to closely investigate the specific content of social workers' contributions to policy development.

Continued contact and identification with social work stakeholders (for example, employers, organisations, associations, radical social work groups) is the third indicator of an ongoing link between elected parliamentarians and the social work profession. While almost all social workers in the cantonal parliaments in 2024 continued to work in the social work sector alongside their political mandate, the five social workers in the national parliament had left social work practice and were full-time or part-time politicians. All of them explicitly and prominently mentioned both their social work training and their practical experience on their websites. However, only one of them referred to their social work background on the parliament's official website. Three out of five were members of the Swiss social work professional organisation AvenirSocial, and all of them were actively involved in social advocacy organisations – for example, as the head of Inclusion Handicap (the umbrella organisation for Swiss disability organisation), alliance f (the federation of Swiss women's organisations) and the Swiss Organisation for Foster and Adoptive Children (PACH), or in leading positions in trade unions at cantonal and national level.

Conclusion

In summary, this chapter provides a snapshot of Swiss social workers in political office by identifying social workers in parliament and examining their political careers and whether they promote social work values once elected. There were 65 social workers in cantonal parliaments and 5 social workers in the national parliament in 2024. Their political careers were similar to those of parliamentarians with other professional backgrounds. Social workers in the national parliament in 2024 were seasoned politicians with extensive experience in previous political and party offices at all federal levels. Although all of them were part-time or full-time politicians and no longer worked directly in the social work sector, they still maintained links with the social work profession – for example, through membership in AvenirSocial or through active involvement in social advocacy organisations. Building on these links and their social work experience, they were the main initiators of social work policy papers and key members of parliamentary committees specialising in social welfare issues. Further research should analyse the political careers and policy initiatives of social workers in political office in earlier periods. This would allow for full political careers to be examined, including biographies after leaving political office. Finally, politicians at local level and in government positions should be included in further analyses to provide a full picture of social workers in political office.

References

Amann, K. and Kindler, T. (2022) 'Social workers in politics – a qualitative analysis of factors influencing social workers' decision to run for political office', *European Journal of Social Work*, 25(4): 655–67.

Amann, K. and Kindler, T. (eds) (2021) *Sozialarbeitende in der Politik*, Frank & Timme.

AvenirSocial (2010) *Code of Ethics*, AvenirSocial.

AvenirSocial (2018) 'Ausbildung und Beschäftigung in der Sozialen Arbeit in der Schweiz', *AvenirSocial*, Available from: https://avenirsocial.ch/wp-content/uploads/2018/12/Ausbildung_und_Beschaeftigung_in_der_Sozialen_Arbeit_in_der_Schweiz_2018.pdf [Accessed 14 June 2024].

BFS (Federal Statistical Office) (2022) 'Monatlicher Bruttolohn nach Berufsgruppen, Lebensalter und Geschlecht – Privater und öffentlicher Sektor zusammen', *BFS*, Available from: www.bfs.admin.ch/asset/de/22988214 [Accessed 14 June 2024].

BFS (Federal Statistical Office) (2023a) 'Ausgeübter Beruf (Nomenklatur CH-ISCO-19) nach Geschlecht und Nationalität', *BFS*, Available from: www.bfs.admin.ch/bfs/de/home/statistiken/kataloge-datenbanken/tabellen.assetdetail.24311552.html [Accessed 14 June 2024].

BFS (Federal Statistical Office) (2023b) Detailed analysis of CH-ISCO-19 codes 13440, 26350, 33530 and 34120 upon request.

BFS (Federal Statistical Office) (2023c) 'Amtliches Gemeindeverzeichnis der Schweiz', *BFS*, Available from: www.bfs.admin.ch/bfs/de/home/grundlagen/agvch.assetdetail.30186257.html [Accessed 14 June 2024].

Binder, N. and Weiss-Gal, I. (2022) 'Social workers as local politicians in Israel', *British Journal of Social Work*, 52(5): 2797–813.

Borchert, J. (2011) 'Individual ambition and institutional opportunity: A conceptual approach to political careers in multi-level systems', *Regional and Federal Studies*, 21(2): 117–40.

Borchert, J. and Stolz, K. (2011) 'Institutional order and career patterns: Some comparative considerations', *Regional and Federal Studies*, 21(2): 271–82.

Bundi, P., Eberli, D. and Bütikofer, S. (2017) 'Between occupation and politics: Professionalization in the Swiss cantons', *Swiss Political Science Review*, 23(1): 1–20.

Bundi, P., Eberli, D. and Bütikofer, S. (2018) 'Zwischen Beruf und Politik', in A. Vatter (ed) *Das Parlament in der Schweiz*, NZZ Libro, pp 315–43.

Burzlaff, M., Kindler, T. and Schwartz-Tayri, T. (2025) 'The engagement in policy practice of social workers in Germany and Switzerland', *The British Journal of Social Work*, 55(4): 1889–906.

Bütikofer, S. (2013) 'Mythos Milizparlament', *Parlament, Parlement, Parlemento*, 16(3): 3–11.

Demircali, S., Kindler, T. and Amann, K. (2024) 'Social workers' intention to hold elected political office: A quantitative study based on the theory of planned behavior', *European Journal of Social Work*, 27(5): 977–87.

Di Capua, R., Pilotti, A., Mach, A. and Lasseb, K. (2022) 'Political professionalization and transformations of political career patterns in multilevel states: The case of Switzerland', *Regional & Federal Studies*, 32(1): 95–114.

Epple, R. and Schär, E. (2015) *Spuren einer anderen Sozialen Arbeit. Kritische und politische Sozialarbeit in der Schweiz 1900–2000*, Seismo.

Federal Chancellery (2023) *The Swiss Confederation*, Swiss Federal Chancellery.

Freiburghaus, R., Arens, A. and Mueller, S. (2021) 'With or against their region? Multiple-mandate holders in the Swiss parliament, 1985–2018', *Local Government Studies*, 47(6): 971–92.

Geser, H., Meuli, U., Ladner, A., Steiner, R. and Horber-Papazian, K. (2011) *Die Exekutivmitglieder in den Schweizer Gemeinden*, Rüegger.

Gysi, B. (nd) 'About me', *Barbara Gysi*, Available from: https://barbara-gysi.ch/fuer-eine-offene-soziale-und-oekologische-schweiz [Accessed 14 June 2024].

Joye, D., Lemel, Y. and Wolf, C. (2023) 'Das Ansehen von Berufen in der Schweiz', *Social Change in Switzerland*, 33, doi: 10.22019/SC-2023-00002

Kindler, T. (2024a) 'Political institutions and social work', *British Journal of Social Work*, 54(1): 437–55.

Kindler, T. (2024b) 'Democratic advocacy', *Zenodo*, doi: 10.5281/zenodo.10413049

Kindler, T. and Amann, K. (2022) 'Strategies of social workers' policy engagement', *Journal of Policy Practice and Research*, 3(4): 302–15.

Kulke, D., Kindler, T. and Kohlfürst, I. (forthcoming) 'Social work professional organisations in Austria, Germany and Switzerland', in R. Guidi (ed) *Social Work Professional Organisations*, Policy Press.

Ladner, A. (2016) *Gemeindeversammlung und Gemeindeparlament*, IDHEAP.

Ladner, A. (2019) 'Society, government, and the political system', in A. Ladner, N. Soguel, Y. Emery, S. Weerts and S. Nahrath (eds) *Swiss Public Administration*, Palgrave Macmillan, pp 3–20.

Lane, S.R. and Humphreys, N.A. (2011) 'Social workers in politics', *Journal of Policy Practice*, 10(3): 225–44.

Leitner, S. and Stolz, K. (2023) 'German social workers as professional politicians', *European Journal of Social Work*, 26(4): 691–704.

Linder, W. and Iff, A. (2011) *Swiss Political System*, Federal Department of Foreign Affairs.

Löffler, E.M. (2024) 'Social workers as politicians', *European Journal of Social Work*, 27(4): 898–910.

Madörin, S., Amstutz, J., Behringer, B. and Zängl, P. (2017) 'Sozialhilfe – eine Arbeitsfeld mit hohen Qualifikationsanforderungen', *Zeitschrift für Sozialhilfe ZESO*, 17(2): 16–17.

McLaughlin, A.M., Rothery, M. and Kuiken, J. (2019) 'Pathways to political engagement', *Canadian Social Work Review*, 36(1): 25–43.

Meehan, P. (2021) 'Water into wine: Using social policy courses to make MSW students interested in politics', *Journal of Social Work Education*, 57(2): 357–71.

Ostrander, J., Kindler, T. and Bryan, J.K. (2021) 'Using the civic voluntarism model to compare the political participation of US and Swiss social workers', *Journal of Policy Practice and Research*, 2(1): 4–19.

Pilotti, A. (2017) *Entre democratization et professionalisation: le Parlement suisse et ses membres de 1910 à 2016*, Seismo.

Steiger, E. (1923) 'Sozialismus und Fürsorge', *Rote Revue*, 2(7): 228–34.

Stolz, K. (2003) 'Moving up, moving down: Political careers across territorial levels', *European Journal of Political Research*, 42(2): 223–48.

Strebel, M. (2023) *Das schweizerische Parlamentslexikon*, Helbing Lichtenhahn.

The Federal Assembly (2024) 'Council members since 1848', *The Federal Assembly*, Available from: www.parlament.ch/en/ratsmitglieder [Accessed 14 June 2024].

The Federal Council (2024) 'How much does a federal councillor earn?', *The Federal Council*, Available from: www.admin.ch/gov/en/start/federal-council/tasks/from-election-to-departure.html [Accessed 14 June 2024].

Vatter, A. (2015) 'Kantonsregierungen', *Historisches Lexikon der Schweiz*, Available from: https://hls-dhs-dss.ch/de/articles/010243/2015-12-18 [Accessed 14 June 2024].

Vatter, A. (2018) *Swiss Federalism*, Routledge.

11

United Kingdom: social workers in Westminster – party or profession?

Christin Reuter and Joanne Warner

In this chapter, we explore the career trajectories and political activities of 32 social workers who became Members of Parliament (MPs) in the United Kingdom. Our findings suggest that the sensibilities we might associate with social work, such as a desire to promote social advocacy through political action, may be more strongly mediated by political party and gender than a professional background in social work. We suggest that there may be an element of *dis*identification with social work and certainly a departure from the profession once on a political career trajectory. Furthermore, the fact that most British MPs are seen as engaging in a form of 'social work' through their representation of constituents with grievances adds another layer of complexity to our understanding of social workers who hold political office in the British context.

Social work as a profession

The increasing trend since the 2000s towards the professionalisation of social work in the United Kingdom resulted in the statutory regulation and registration of social workers from 2001 and the status of 'social worker' becoming a legally protected title from 2005. The regulation of social work is devolved to relevant bodies in England, Wales, Northern Ireland and Scotland. In England, registered social workers must re-register annually with the national regulator, Social Work England, which can also remove them from the register for professional malpractice. The average salaries of social workers range from a starting annual salary of £27,000 to £50,000 for those with experience (see basw.co.uk).

The British Association of Social Workers (BASW) is the independent non-regulatory national membership body for the profession. It acts as a union to its approximately 22,000 members and owns two academic journals, *The British Journal of Social Work* and *Practice*. The BASW runs public campaigns on policy issues such as poverty and lobbies Westminster, acting as 'the voice for social work'. A national College of Social Work was briefly established by government in 2012, but was promptly abandoned in 2015 (Nosowska and Templeton, 2016).

A particular focus politically in the United Kingdom has been the university-based education of social workers. Successive policy makers have regarded the focus on social justice in social work education programmes with – at best – suspicion. Despite this, the level of education required for qualified social worker status has steadily increased from the Certificate of Qualification in Social Work (1975–91) to the undergraduate Diploma in Social Work (1991–2009) to the current bachelor's degree (available since 2003). Postgraduate routes have continued to be available, including a diploma and a master's level qualification. In recent years, controversial 'elite' fast-track postgraduate routes to qualification have reduced the role of universities. The most recent route is the social worker degree apprenticeship, which trains those employed as unqualified care workers.

As of 2022, the total number of registered social workers in the United Kingdom was 115,478, representing 0.35 per cent of the total UK workforce (32,925,000 in 2022; ONS, 2025). By far the largest number of social workers is in England, with 100,654 in 2022 (Social Work England, 2023), followed by Northern Ireland with 6,417 (Department of Health (Northern Ireland), 2022), Scotland with 4,226 (Scottish Social Services Council, 2023) and Wales with 4,181 (Social Care Wales, 2022). In terms of the distribution of social workers by sector, in England, specifically, in services for adults, most are employed in local authorities (18,500), followed by the National Health Service (4,000) and the independent sector (2,200; Skills for Care, 2024). In children's social care, again most are employed in local authorities (33,100) and there are also agency workers (7,200; GOV.UK, 2024). Social work employees constitute the largest subsector of those employed in the voluntary sector, but it is not clear how social work is defined in this context (National Council for Voluntary Organisations, 2021).

In terms of the distribution of social workers across England, there are some striking regional divides. It has been found that London and the South East, taken together, have one social worker per 495 people, a higher rate than in the Midlands (one per 610), the South West (one per 638) and the East (one per 671; Samuel, 2023). There has been a significant increase in applications to register by social workers from overseas, particularly from Africa and India. Social work remains a largely feminised profession as measured by those registered, with 82 per cent of registrants female as at September 2022 (Skills for Care, 2023).

The social work profession has been subject to repeated cycles of crisis and reform resulting from negative media and political reaction to serious events, such as child deaths (Warner, 2015). In a 2023 survey commissioned by Social Work England, only 11 per cent of social workers reported feeling respected, while 44 per cent of the public reported that they respect social workers (Social Work England, 2024). UK social work, at least in the statutory sector, is a profession with low morale that faces increasing demands on services with diminished resources, with retention a significant issue. Of the 5,335 who left the social work register in 2022, almost a quarter had been registered for less than one year (Samuel, 2023).

Institutional opportunity structures

The UK parliamentary system is bicameral, comprising an elected House of Commons and a non-elected revising chamber, the House of Lords, with the Sovereign constituting a third part of the system. In each election, one MP is elected to represent one of around 650 constituencies for the duration of a Parliament through a plurality voting system known as 'first past the post'. Voters cast a vote for a single candidate and the candidate with the most votes is elected. In most elections, this system produces a one-party majority government drawn from one of the two major parties – Conservative and Labour. There are notable exceptions to this rule, one being the 2010 'hung Parliament', which resulted in a Conservative–Liberal Democrat coalition government.

Once elected, MPs have a dual role as legislator and as advocate, both for their constituency as a whole and for individual constituents. MPs have a range of routes into influencing policies and legislation, the most powerful of which is to undertake a ministerial role on the Executive if their party is in government. There is also a wide range of cross-party committees that can influence policies through producing reports and by scrutinising legislation and policies. Parliament and its MPs act as a check on the Executive and can even block government legislation if sufficient numbers of MPs vote against it. For many backbench MPs (those who are not serving as ministers on the government's 'frontbench' in the House of Commons), their main focus is helping their constituents by being a good 'Constituency Member' (Searing, 1994). These constituency activities have long been defined in political circles, often disparagingly, as a form of 'glorified social work' (Crewe, 2015, p 86; see also Warner, 2020).

There are between 800 and 900 Lords, or 'peers', in the House of Lords, making it the largest upper house in the world. Like MPs, they pass laws and scrutinise the work of government. Unlike MPs, peers are not elected, but formally appointed by the reigning monarch and on the advice of the prime minister. For some politicians, an appointment to the Lords is the logical final step in their political career. This particular layer of institutional opportunity structures is therefore closed to all but a tiny minority of UK citizens.

The opportunity structure for would-be politicians in the United Kingdom has expanded significantly since the late 1990s due to the devolution of powers to Northern Ireland, Scotland and Wales, all of which now also have their own unicameral elected parliament or assembly. There have been between 90 and 108 seats available in the Northern Ireland Assembly, 60 in the Senedd Cymru (Welsh Parliament) and 129 in the Scottish Parliament. These distinctive legislatures and executives have a range of devolved powers in policy areas such as health and social care, education, policing and transport. These policy areas in England are retained by the Westminster Parliament, which additionally has reserved powers for policy in areas such as defence, foreign affairs and immigration across the whole United Kingdom.

Local government structures in the United Kingdom are complex and overlapping, with approximately 12,000 local councils, which range in size from small parish councils to large combined authority areas. Like MPs, councillors are generally elected via the first-past-the-post system. There are 16,169 elected local councillors in England (Lawson, 2025), 1,254 and 1,226 in Wales and Scotland, respectively, and 462 in Northern Ireland. Serving on a local council is often a stepping stone to election to Parliament (Cairney, 2007; Allen, 2013), reflecting the growing importance of 'localism', in which voters express a preference for electoral candidates who come from and live in the local area (Campbell et al, 2019). Transition from one of the devolved national legislatures to the UK Parliament appears to be a less well-worn route than that from the local to the national political stage (Stolz, 2024).

In addition to devolution, the United Kingdom's institutional opportunity structures have also been expanded through decentralisation, involving the transfer of powers and budgets to 'metro mayors', who represent combined authorities, including in city deals. Police and crime commissioners, introduced in 2012, make up an additional directly elected tier. They are responsible for ensuring that the police meet the needs of the local community.

For the 2024/25 financial year, the basic annual salary of an MP was £91,346 (Kelly, 2025), which is considerably higher than the national median wage in the United Kingdom of £34,963 in 2024 (Statista, 2025). The prime minister's salary, including their MP salary, was £164,951 in 2022 (GOV. UK, 2022). One attraction for those ambitious to hold political power is the additional earning capacity that can result from a time in front-line politics. It is said that former Prime Minister Boris Johnson earned £5 million during the first six months after leaving office (Thévoz, 2023).

Disincentives to hold political office include high workloads and the proliferation of threats and abuse that MPs receive. Women MPs and those from Black and minority ethnic groups are frequently targeted (Lilly, 2024). As well as there being a high volume of correspondence, constituency surgery work takes an emotional toll (Warner, 2020). The job can involve long periods of time away from family, particularly for those with constituencies far outside London, where Parliament is located.

Political recruitment

Data collection

The research reported in this chapter focuses on social worker MPs (SWMPs) – that is, MPs who had previously been employed and/or qualified as a social worker. The complex range of qualifications and changes to the regulation of the profession were important factors to consider in identifying SWMPs. While some could be identified easily by their qualification, others, particularly older MPs, had practised as social workers in the period before statutory regulation. In those cases, we looked closely at job roles alongside factors such as having a first degree in the social sciences, which was a traditional route into a social work job. A good example is Sylvia Heal, who was elected as a Labour MP four times between 1983 and 2010. Information in the public domain states that she practised as a social worker for several years, including ten years working in drug rehabilitation services, and that she is a graduate, though the degree subject is not specified. Sylvia is included in our group of SWMPs based on her career background even though her social work qualification status is unknown.

We collected data within the 30-year time frame of 1992 to 2022, covering eight elections and 5,215 MPs (most of them re-elected multiple times), to encompass MPs with long experience of Parliament as well as newer incumbents and to include a range of Parliaments in terms of the parties in government. There is no official biographical data available in MPs' parliamentary profiles (UK Parliament, 2023), so it was necessary to consult sources ranging from personal websites to Wikipedia, relevant news articles and *The Almanac of British Politics* (Waller and Criddle, 1995; 1999; 2002; 2007).

We initially identified 78 MPs and then checked these more closely for relevant qualifications and job roles. Six MPs were borderline in that they described themselves as social workers in one or more of the resources we searched but had no identifiably relevant qualification and no clear job role. Only those fitting the definition of 'social worker' in terms of their qualification and/or clear job role were included in the final list of 32 SWMPs that is the basis for all following analyses.

For the purpose of comparison, in addition to the SWMP data, we drew on data available from existing studies on three other groups of professionals – teachers, barristers and solicitors – and created a comparison group for each group. The teacher and solicitor groups were matched to the SWMP group by party; this was not done for the barrister group due to the lack of enough Labour barristers. To deepen our analysis, we created a 'random occupation' group, comprising a group of MPs from random occupations but matched by gender, age, party and region.

Results

During the 30-year period under consideration, there were 32 SWMPs. Seven of them (21.9 per cent) held the Certificate of Qualification in Social Work, while five were awarded a master's in social work (15.6 per cent) and two held a Diploma in Social Work (6.3 per cent). Three SWMPs studied applied social science (9.4 per cent) while two held a degree in social administration (6.3 per cent). One held a degree in sociology with social work, one had a degree in social science, and one completed a social work degree abroad (all 3.1 per cent). For the remainder (n = 10; 31.3 per cent), a qualification in social work was confirmed but not specified. Most of the qualifications of this group predate the United Kingdom's formal social work qualification framework. All of the MPs had relevant working experience as a social worker in addition to their degree.

The vast majority of SWMPs (n = 29; 90.6 per cent) were members of the Labour Party, while only two (6.3 per cent) were Conservatives and one (3.1 per cent) was Plaid Cymru. Accordingly, it comes as no surprise that during years of Labour government, the number of SWMPs was higher (see Figure 11.1).

Of the 32 SWMPs, 18 (56.3 per cent) were female. By comparison, only 23 per cent of *all* MPs elected since 1992 were female. The continuously rising share of female MPs from 9 per cent in 1992 to 34 per cent in 2019 (Cracknell and Tunnicliffe, 2022) was not reflected in rising numbers of SWMPs, however. Furthermore, the gender split in favour of women found in the overall number of social workers in the United Kingdom (as noted earlier, 82 per cent of social workers were female in 2022; Skills for Care, 2023) did not translate to Parliament, which suggests that it tends to be men in the social work profession that feel drawn to more powerful public offices. This would be consistent with a similar split in management positions in social services, where men have tended to predominate despite the otherwise 'feminised' profile of the social work profession (McPhail, 2004).

The average age of first-time-MPs varied between 39 and 43 years between 1979 and 2019 (Cracknell and Tunnicliffe, 2022). The average age of first-time SWMPs (1992–2019) was slightly higher at 44.4 years.

SWMPs are found in almost all regions of the United Kingdom, though most of them represent constituencies in the North of England, the Midlands

Figure 11.1: Number of SWMPs per election, 1992–2019

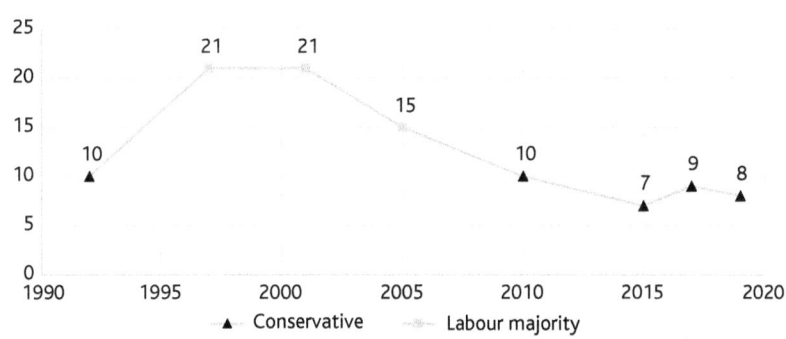

and Wales, those areas where Labour traditionally is most successful. Moreover, SWMPs tend to represent English constituencies with higher rates of deprivation (for deprivation data by constituency for England, see Francis-Devine, 2020). Of the 25 English SWMP constituencies in our sample, 21 were among the most deprived 50 per cent of constituencies. However, in general, we find that the more deprived the region, the higher the percentage of Labour MPs. Labour MPs were vastly over-represented in constituencies in the two most deprived deciles, still over-represented in deciles three and four, and under-represented in all the rest. This suggests that SWMPs do not represent areas that are any more deprived than the areas represented by Labour MPs as a group. On the contrary, our SWMPs tended to represent *less* deprived areas than the average Labour MP (see Table 11.1).

Social work as a politics-facilitating profession

Can social work be seen as a politics-facilitating profession in the United Kingdom? In comparison to their overall share of the UK workforce, SWMPs do indeed appear to be over-represented in the House of Commons. Referring to data for the last 20 years, we find that social workers comprised between 0.26 and 0.41 per cent of the total workforce in the United

Table 11.1: Number and share of English constituencies represented by SWMPs and non-social worker Labour MPs, by constituency deprivation

Deprivation decile	Deprivation index rank	Number of SWMP constituencies (1992–2022) in decile	Percentage of all SWMPs (n = 25) in decile	Number of Labour MP constituencies (2019) in decile	Percentage of all Labour MPs (n = 180) in decile
1st (most deprived)	≤53	3	12.0	44	24.4
2nd	≤107	4	16.0	39	21.7
3rd	≤160	2	8.0	29	16.1
4th	≤213	7	28.0	24	13.3
5th	≤267	5	20.0	14	7.8
6th	≤320	1	4.0	13	7.2
7th	≤373	0	0.0	11	6.1
8th	≤426	0	0.0	5	2.8
9th	≤480	2	8.0	0	0.0
10th (least deprived)	≤533	1	4.0	1	0.6

Source: Based on constituency deprivation data from Francis-Devine (2020)

Kingdom (Office for National Statistics – ONS, 2019). In 1997 and 2001, SWMPs' share of all MPs peaked at 3.2 per cent, with the lowest point being 1.1 per cent in 2015.

However, in comparison to other traditional politics-facilitating professions, such as law and teaching, the share of SWMPs was relatively low (see Figure 11.2). In 2015, 14.2 per cent of MPs had a background as either a barrister or a solicitor, whereas these together made up only 0.64 per cent of the total workforce that year (Cracknell and Tunnicliffe, 2022). Moreover, the share of barristers who went on to be an MP was considerably higher than the share of social workers becoming an MP. As an example, in 2010 there were 120,000 social workers in the United Kingdom and 10 SWMPs (0.008 per cent). In comparison, there were 157,000 legal professionals and 86 barrister or solicitor MPs (0.05 per cent; ONS, 2019).

As Figure 11.2 also shows, barristers appear to have been more closely aligned than solicitors with Conservative rule; we see a steady increase in the number of solicitors across all Parliaments. While schoolteachers were over-represented in the 1990s and early 2000s, numbers have subsequently gone down, and in 2015 there were only 15 former schoolteachers in Westminster, or 2.3 per cent of MPs, compared with their 3 per cent share of the total workforce (ONS, 2019). As such, in that year, they were the only under-represented group out of the ones compared here.

In terms of the time spent in social work prior to entering Parliament, this was 15.5 years on average for SWMPs for whom this information was stated (n = 19). Of those where the field of social work is known, seven worked in child care/protection or fostering (21.9 per cent), four were probation officers (12.5 per cent), three were psychiatric or mental health social workers (9.4 per cent), three were in a managing/director position (9.4 per cent) and one each was a social work tutor, welfare rights officer,

Figure 11.2: Number of SWMPs in comparison to MPs from other occupations, 1992–2015

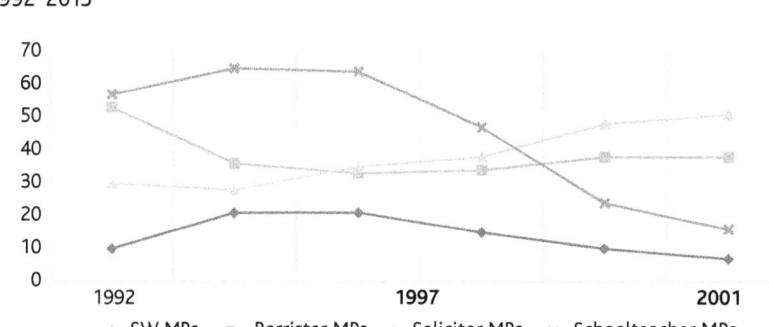

Note: Years in bold indicate a Labour majority.
Source: Based on data from Cracknell and Tunnicliffe (2022)

residential care home inspector, worker in a drug rehabilitation centre and worker with survivors of childhood sexual abuse (3.1 per cent each). Eighteen were still practising social workers when they were elected. The other 14 had worked as social workers in the past but their occupation immediately before being elected was something different (for example, a journalist) or was somewhat unclear.

In conclusion, when considering political recruitment, it is perhaps most accurate to argue that the key factor has been political party, with the complex array of co-occurring factors that this represents. As highlighted in Figure 11.2, the presence of socially oriented professions, such as social work and teaching, increase when Labour is in the electoral ascendancy. Similarly, when the Conservative Party dominates, we see an increased preponderance of law professions, specifically barristers.

Political career patterns

Pathways into Parliament

To understand the different pathways into UK parliamentary politics, a range of factors should be considered. First, a distinction can be made between the 'traditional' route into politics and what has become an increasingly 'professionalised' route. Traditional pathways are characterised by a background of involvement in the relevant political party at a local or regional level, such as by serving as a councillor, or, in the case of the Labour Party, through trade union activism (Durose et al, 2013, p 251). The so-called professionalised route typically involves paid employment in or around Westminster – for example, as a special advisor, known as a 'SPAD'. A university education is a defining feature of the professionalised pathway into politics (Durose et al, 2013).

Turning to our sample of 32 SWMPs, 27 (84.4 per cent) had previous political experience at regional, local or party level, with 23 (71.9 per cent) having served as elected councillors. Judging by this indicator, most SWMPs followed the traditional path into politics, as outlined by Durose et al (2013). This is also supported by their average age at entry into Parliament, which, at 44.4 years, is similar to the average of 43 in 2015 and 42 in 2019. In a 'professionalised' group, we would expect to see a younger average age at entry because politics is their first profession. SWMP Beverley Hughes, a former probation officer, is a good example of someone who became an MP via the 'traditional' route, as she was elected to Parliament in 1997 aged 47 years, having served as a Trafford borough councillor since 1986.

In terms of the 'professionalised' route into politics, only two SWMPs (6.3 per cent) had worked as a case worker for an MP, while three (9.4 per cent) had worked for a union and two (6.3 per cent) had been employed by an executive party committee. The traditional route appears to be more closely associated with Labour-dominated Parliaments, in which SWMPs are more likely to be present. While 62 per cent of the MPs in the 1997 Labour-dominated intake had a background in local elected politics, this proportion fell to 41.6 per cent in the hung Parliament of 2010 (Allen, 2013, p 690). In the random occupation group of MPs, which we created for comparison, only 52 per cent had experience as local councillors, while more of them were parliamentary researchers or personal assistants for other MPs (18.8 per cent), political researchers for councils (6.3 per cent) or involved with a union (18.8 per cent). It seems MPs in random occupations, despite belonging to the same party, age group and region, are somewhat closer to the professionalised route into politics than SWMPs.

Parliamentary careers

Career progression once in Parliament is probably best measured in terms of advances to frontbench positions. Between 1945 and 1974, 28.2 per cent of MPs held ministerial office while between 1974 and 1992 this proportion rose to 45.6 per cent (Rush, 1994). This overall trend reflects the supposed increasing professionalisation of politics plus the expansion of government posts such that the opportunities for MPs to carve out a career within Parliament have grown. Of the 31 SWMPs (excluding the Plaid Cymru MP, who would not have been eligible for a frontbench role), 19 (61.3 per cent) held a frontbench (or shadow) position at some point in their Parliamentary career and 6 (19.4 per cent) of them held cabinet or shadow cabinet roles.

For comparison of SWMPs and non-SWMPs, we focused on Labour and Conservative MPs elected between 2010 and 2023 only. Data collected from UK Parliament (2023) show that 71.9 per cent of this group had held either a ministerial or a shadow ministerial position at some point in their career. This was the case for a higher share of the 16 SWMPs elected during the same period, with 14 (87.5 per cent) having held a frontbench or shadow position at some point. SWMP Tessa Jowell, for example, was a Labour MP for 23 years, between 1992 and 2015, and held a range of major ministerial positions in the cabinets of Tony Blair and Gordon Brown as well as opposition frontbench roles.

In terms of tenure, in 2019 the median time in Parliament of all retiring MPs was 18 years (Cowley, 2022). The median tenure of SWMPs who had left Parliament by 2019 was slightly lower, at 14 years. However, seven SWMPs achieved a tenure of more than 20 years, showing that some of them have served for long periods. Like Tessa Jowell, Hilary Armstrong had a long and distinguished parliamentary career as a Labour MP, sitting, like Jowell, for 23 years, between 1987 and 2010. She held multiple major ministerial portfolios in government under Tony Blair and subsequently was a shadow minister. The relationship between political careers and social work practice was the subject of a social work conference panel event held in 2020 that featured Hilary Armstrong and two other prominent social worker politicians, Mark Drakeford and Julie Morgan (see Scourfield and Warner, 2022).

Careers after Parliament

The professionalisation of politics suggests that more politicians commit the majority of their time to politics, can live off it and have a long-term interest in career maintenance (Borchert, 2003). This means that MPs can leave their pre-politics careers behind. After full-time politics, they might retire but maintain honorary or voluntary positions in charities, while for others their political career can act as a springboard into a further paid position in administrative or other roles.

Of our 32 SWMPs, eight were incumbents, two died in office and no information is known for one. Of the remaining 21, among those who left Parliament, none returned to social work and only two (9.5 per cent) pursued related fields. Cathy Jamieson became chief executive of Care Visions, which provides residential and foster care placements for vulnerable young people in Scotland. Hilton Dawson became chief executive of a care charity and was also chief executive of the BASW.

The low number of only two SWMPs returning to the social work field can be compared with four SWMPs who retired directly from Parliament, five who went to the House of Lords and six who stayed in other politics and related fields (being elected to regional parliaments, returning to local councils, becoming a mayor, founding new parties or becoming a police and crime commissioner). The remaining four SWMPs became consultants or writers. From these figures, we can conclude that the SWMPs largely leave their profession behind for a professional career in politics and do not return to it. This is in stark contrast to barrister MPs, 50 per cent of whom returned to law after leaving Parliament. In this light, it is particularly interesting to have found one case of a non-SWMP, Anne Begg, whose career moved *closer* to social work after leaving the House of Commons. She was appointed a Council member of the Scottish Social Services Council, the regulatory body for social and care workers in Scotland (Begg, nd).

Social advocacy

We define social advocacy as the substantive representation of vulnerable groups and expected this to be reflected in MPs' engagement in different committees or ministries. On policy, MPs with a background in social work might be expected to pursue more socially oriented goals – in other words, to engage in social advocacy more than their colleagues with different backgrounds. To test this, we collected data on SWMPs' government/opposition (frontbench) posts as well as their membership of committees (as found on the House of Commons members career webpage; UK Parliament, 2023). These committees/frontbench posts were coded as social advocacy related if they had a direct connection to a social justice issue, such as immigration, equalities and poverty and/or a direct connection to a social work practice domain, such as mental health, older people, health and education (as this encompasses children and families). Examples of social advocacy committees include those on: Education and Employment, Health and Social Care, and Levelling Up, Housing and Communities. Typical non-social advocacy posts would include those related to: Defence, Energy and Climate Change, Trade and Industry, and Science.

As noted earlier, of the 31 SWMPs who were eligible, 19 (61.3 per cent) held a frontbench position at some point in their career. For 63 per cent of these 19, at least one of the positions was in a social advocacy ministry (see Table 11.2). However, most of them worked in other fields during their time in Westminster as well. Only 32 per cent held a majority of their positions in social advocacy fields. The numbers for committee memberships were fairly similar: 31 of 32 (96.9 per cent) had committee positions listed on their career page; for 26 per cent, the majority were social advocacy committees.

Comparing these numbers to other professions, barristers stand out as the professionals least inclined to be involved in social advocacy-related policy work, particularly at ministry level. The bulk of their ministerial work is in non-social advocacy related arenas. Turning to committee work, the share of MPs across all the groups that had membership of at least one social advocacy committee ranged from 62 per cent to 71 per cent. However, when it comes to having a preponderance of activities on social advocacy committees, the

Table 11.2: Membership in social advocacy ministries and committees, 1992–2022

	SWMPs (%)	Random occupation MPs (%)	Teacher MPs (%)	Solicitor MPs (%)	Barrister MPs (%)
MP was part of **at least 1** social advocacy ministry	63	65	57	63	27
The **majority** of the MP's ministry positions were in social advocacy ministries	32	15	24	4	0
The MP was part of **at least 1** social advocacy committee	71	66	64	70	62
The **majority** of the MP's committee positions were in social advocacy committees	26	24	14	7	10

SWMPs and MPs in the random occupation group appear to be closely matched between 24% and 26%. In contrast, out of all the groups, it was solicitors who seemed to focus almost exclusively on non-social advocacy fields, with barristers – the only group that could not be matched by party and was mainly made up of Conservative MPs – not far behind.

The UK Parliament also houses All-Party Parliamentary Groups (APPGs), which are informal, cross-party groups formed by members of both chambers who share a common interest in a particular policy area (Parallel Parliament, 2024). The APPG on Social Work was linked with the BASW and consisted of ten members, only two of which were former social workers. Notably this means that there were eight other members who shared a strong interest in social work *without* having any professional background in the field. This shows that a background in social work is no requirement for a focus on social advocacy and *may* also suggest a disidentification with their profession on the part of those SWMPs who were not involved.

Similarly, not all SWMPs focus on social work-related issues. Sarah Atherton was an SWMP whose activities in Parliament focused on non-social advocacy themes. A former generic social worker, she previously sat on the Defence Select Committee, leading its inquiry into the experiences of women in the military, and was the Parliamentary Private Secretary to the Wales Office and the Foreign, Commonwealth and Development Office. In contrast, the political activities of Paul Goggins, a former children's social worker, were strongly aligned with social advocacy themes. He was a junior minister for prisons and the probation service, then the voluntary and community sector. He also served on the Social Work and Poverty APPGs.

Conclusion

Our analysis suggests that political party is the key factor in the political recruitment and routes into Parliament of individuals from socially oriented professions such as social work. When Labour is popular electorally, we tend to see more such professionals elected. In future work, it would be interesting to check if this held true in the 2024 general election, particularly given Labour's large majority.

Once in Parliament, while the SWMPs in our study show a slightly stronger focus on social advocacy ministries and committees compared with MPs from other professions, the biggest difference was again along party lines. Furthermore, our analysis shows that a significant proportion of SWMPs are drawn to engage in activities that are firmly outside the social advocacy domain. Rather than using their political position primarily to advocate for social issues that might be considered well-aligned with social work's social justice and human rights agenda, they also use it to stretch their experience in other policy directions, such as defence or foreign policy. Future research might address what motivates these individuals to adopt this approach and, specifically, whether *dis*identification with social work may be a factor. To be taken seriously in politics, perhaps a close affiliation with 'soft' issues as compared with the 'hard' politics of, say, defence is not considered a good strategy. None of the SWMPs in our study returned to social work, suggesting that – like many other MPs, aside from barristers – their political career supplants their original profession. Given that the SWMPs reflect the gender dynamics of the profession in terms of the recruitment of men to more powerful leadership positions, further research should also consider the role that gender plays in this complex picture of politics, power and advocacy.

It is notable that meaningful political activity relating to issues such as defence or foreign policy is only possible in Westminster, whereas advancing social advocacy goals can be effectively pursued at regional or local levels as well as in Westminster. Another avenue for further research would, therefore, usefully focus on the devolved powers and their strong social advocacy focus, as well as these matters for England in Westminster. Similarly, future work should also consider the relationship between social advocacy and social work at local council level.

It is clear from the literature that many British MPs perform 'social advocacy' in their constituency work to the extent that they are seen to become 'like' social workers in certain respects. This may reflect the nature of political representation in a first-past-the-post electoral system, where the connection between an MP and their constituents has a deeply symbolic importance in the public and political imagination. Future research might explore the nature and extent of the constituency work carried out by SWMPs compared with their non-social worker colleagues. Closer analysis of these activities would further deepen our understanding of what characterises social workers holding political office in the UK context.

References

Allen, P. (2013) 'Linking pre-parliamentary political experience and the career trajectories of the 1997 general election cohort', *Parliamentary Affairs*, 66(4): 685–707.

Begg, A. (nd) 'Dame Anne Begg', *Dame Anne Begg*, Available from: https://annebegg.wordpress.com/ [Accessed 7 May 2024].

Borchert, J. (2003) 'Professional politicians: Towards a comparative perspective', in J. Borchert and J. Zeiss (eds) *The Political Class in Advanced Democracies*, Oxford University Press, pp 1–25.

Cairney, P. (2007) 'The professionalisation of MPs: Refining the "politics-facilitating" explanation', *Parliamentary Affairs*, 60(2): 212–33.

Campbell, R., Cowley, P., Vivyan, N. and Wagner, M. (2019) 'Why friends and neighbors? Explaining the electoral appeal of local roots', *The Journal of Politics*, 81(3): 937–51.

Cowley, P. (2022) 'Too much, too young: Are MPs getting younger?', *PoliticsHome*, 13 May, Available from: www.politicshome.com/thehouse/article/too-much-too-young-are-mps-getting-younger [Accessed 7 May 2024].

Cracknell, R. and Tunnicliffe, R. (2022) *Social Background of MPs 1979–2019*, House of Commons Library, 15 February, Available from: https://researchbriefings.files.parliament.uk/documents/CBP-7483/CBP-7483.pdf [Accessed 7 May 2024].

Crewe, E. (2015) *The House of Commons: An Anthropology of MPs at Work*, Bloomsbury Academic.

Department of Health (Northern Ireland) (2022) *Social Work Workforce Review Northern Ireland 2022*, Department of Health, Available from: www.health-ni.gov.uk/sites/default/files/publications/health/doh-social-work-review-ni-2022.pdf [Accessed 7 May 2024].

Durose, C., Richardson, L., Combs, R., Eason, C. and Gains, F. (2013) 'Acceptable difference: Diversity, representation and pathways to UK politics', *Parliamentary Affairs*, 66(2): 246–67.

Francis-Devine, B. (2020) 'Constituency data: Indices of deprivation', *House of Commons Library*, 4 July, Available from: https://commonslibrary.parliament.uk/constituency-data-indices-of-deprivation [Accessed 7 May 2024].

GOV.UK. (2022) 'Salaries of members of His Majesty's Government: April 2022', *Transparency data*, 15 December, Available from: www.gov.uk/government/publications/ministerial-salary-data/salaries-of-members-of-his-majestys-government-april-2022-html#ministers-who-are-members-of-the-house-of-lords [Accessed 14 June 2025].

GOV.UK (2024) 'Reporting year 2023: Children's social work workforce', *Explore Education Statistics*, 29 February, Available from: https://explore-education-statistics.service.gov.uk/find-statistics/children-s-social-work-workforce/2023 [Accessed 7 May 2024].

Kelly, R. (2025) *Members' pay and expenses 2024/25*, Research Briefing, House of Commons Library, 28 March, Available from: https://researchbriefings.files.parliament.uk/documents/CBP-10225/CBP-10225.pdf [Accessed 26 May 2025].

Lawson, J. (2025) 'English Councils 2025', *Open Council Data UK*, Available from: opencouncildata.co.uk/councils.php?model=E&y=0 [Accessed 14 June 2025].

Lilly, A. (2024) 'MPs' security', *Institute for Government*, 1 March, Available from: www.instituteforgovernment.org.uk/explainer/mps-security [Accessed 7 May 2024].

McPhail, B.A. (2004) 'Setting the record straight: Social work is not a female-dominated profession', *Social Work*, 49(2): 323–6.

National Council for Voluntary Organisations (2021) 'UK Civil Society Almanac 2021', *NCVO*, 1 September, Available from: www.ncvo.org.uk/news-and-insights/news-index/uk-civil-society-almanac-2021/workforce [Accessed 7 May 2024].

Nosowska, G. and Templeton, R. (2016) 'One year after college's demise, BASW can give social work its voice', *Community Care*, 22 June, Available from: www.communitycare.co.uk/2016/06/22/one-year-colleges-demise-basw-can-give-social-work-voice [Accessed 7 May 2024].

ONS (Office for National Statistics) (2019) 'Workers by sex in detailed occupation groupings, 2000 to 2018', *ONS*, 12 March, Available from: www.ons.gov.uk/employmentandlabourmarket/peopleinwork/employmentandemployeetypes/adhocs/009745workersbysexindetailedoccupationgroupings2000to2018 [Accessed 7 May 2024].

ONS (2025) 'A01: Summary of labour market statistics', *ONS*, 10 June, Available from: www.ons.gov.uk/employmentandlabourmarket/peopleinwork/employmentandemployeetypes/datasets/summaryoflabourmarketstatistics [Accessed 14 June 2025]

Parallel Parliament (2024) 'Social Work APPG', *Parallel Parliament*, Available from: www.parallelparliament.co.uk/APPG/social-work [Accessed 7 May 2024].

Rush, M. (1994) 'Career patterns in British politics: First choose your party', *Parliamentary Affairs*, 47(4): 566–83.

Samuel, M. (2023) 'Quarter of those who quit register last year had been on it for less than a year, reveals Social Work England', *Community Care*, 16 March, Available from: www.communitycare.co.uk/2023/03/16/quarter-of-those-who-quit-register-last-year-had-been-on-it-for-less-than-a-year-reveals-social-work-england [Accessed 7 May 2024].

Scottish Social Services Council (2023) *Social Worker Filled Posts and Vacancies Six-Monthly Survey: Analysis of the Data Collected as at 30 June 2023*, Scottish Social Services Council, 31 October, Available from: https://data.sssc.uk.com/images/SixMonthSurveyReport/LA_SW_WTE_Vacancy_Report_June_2023.pdf [Accessed 7 May 2024].

Scourfield, J. and Warner, J. (2022) 'Knowing where the shoe pinches: Three Labour ministers reflect on their experiences in social work and politics', *Critical and Radical Social Work*, 10(3): 484–90.

Searing, D. (1994) *Westminster's World: Understanding Political Roles*, Harvard University Press.

Skills for Care (2023) *Headline Social Worker Information: Social Workers Employed by Local Authorities in the Adult Social Care Sector*, Skills for Care, Available from: www.skillsforcare.org.uk/Adult-Social-Care-Workforce-Data/Workforce-intelligence/documents/Social-Worker-headline-Feb2023-FINAL.pdf [Accessed 7 May 2024].

Skills for Care (2024) *Headline Social Worker Information: Social Workers Employed by Local Authorities in the Adult Social Care Sector*, Skills for Care, Available from: www.skillsforcare.org.uk/Adult-Social-Care-Workforce-Data/Workforce-intelligence/documents/Social-Worker-Headline-report-Feb-2024.pdf [Accessed 7 May 2024].

Social Care Wales (2022) *Social Care Workforce Report 2022*, Social Care Wales, Available from: https://socialcare.wales/research-and-data/workforce-reports [Accessed 7 May 2024].

Social Work England (2023) 'Significance of social work in England reflected in major new report', *Social Work England*, 9 March, Available from: www.socialworkengland.org.uk/news/significance-of-social-work-reflected-in-state-of-the-nation-report [Accessed 7 May 2024].

Social Work England (2024) 'New research shows the importance of addressing unhelpful perceptions of social work', *Social Work England*, 18 March, Available from: www.socialworkengland.org.uk/news/new-research-shows-the-importance-of-addressing-unhelpful-perceptions-of-social-work [Accessed 7 May 2024].

Statista (2025) 'Median annual earnings for full-time employees in the United Kingdom from 1999 to 2024 (in nominal GBP)' [Graph], *Statista*, Available from: https://www.statista.com/statistics/1002964/average-full-time-annual-earnings-in-the-uk/ [Accessed 26 May 2025].

Stolz, K. (2024) 'Dual polity, dual careers? The dynamic interaction of political careers and territorial order in the devolved United Kingdom', *Territory, Politics, Governance*, advance online publication, doi: 10.1080/21622671.2023.2294797

Thévoz, S. (2023) 'How Boris Johnson raked in £5m in 6 months after leaving office', *openDemocracy*, 23 March, Available from: www.opendemocracy.net/en/boris-johnson-millions-prime-minister-earnings [Accessed 7 May 2024].

UK Parliament (2023) 'MPs and Lords: Find MPs', *UK Parliament*, Available from: https://members.parliament.uk/members/commons [Accessed 7 May 2024].

Waller, R. and Criddle, B. (1995) *The Almanac of British Politics* (5th edn), Routledge.

Waller, R. and Criddle, B. (1999) *The Almanac of British Politics* (6th edn), Routledge.

Waller, R. and Criddle, B. (2002) *The Almanac of British Politics* (7th edn), Routledge.

Waller, R. and Criddle, B. (2007) *The Almanac of British Politics* (8th edn), Routledge.

Warner, J. (2015) *The Emotional Politics of Social Work and Child Protection*, Policy Press.

Warner, J. (2020) 'Politics as social work: a qualitative study of emplaced empathy and risk work by British Members of Parliament', *The British Journal of Social Work*, 51(8): 3248–64.

12

United States: opportunities and barriers for social work members of Congress

Shannon R. Lane and Allysha Bryant

Although social work has a long history of being involved in the development of social policy, modern US political social work emerged in the 1980s (Powers and Fisher, 2019) with an emphasis on policy within social work practice. In this chapter, we discuss the social work landscape in the United States, highlight the common pathways for social workers to the US Congress and discuss the career patterns of elected social workers. Additionally, we identify unique opportunities and initiatives focused on getting social workers into elected office. Lastly, we determine the continued connections between social workers and the social work values and profession once they are in elected office.

Social work as a profession

In the United States, there are many ways to define a social worker. This includes definition by education, licensure, membership of a professional organisation or employment in human services-related fields. The federal government recognised 751,900 social work positions across the United States in 2023 (Bureau of Labor Statistics, 2024).

Social work education and licensure

Social work education in the United States includes degrees at the undergraduate, master's and doctoral level. The Council on Social Work Education (CSWE) accredits 548 bachelor's and 334 master's degree programmes across the country (CSWE, 2024b). The most common social work degree offered in the United States is the Master of Social Work (MSW), considered a terminal degree for practice, which involves one to two years of coursework and at least 900 hours of practicum. MSW specialisations typically include individuals and families (micro practice), groups (mezzo practice) and community/policy work (macro practice). A Bachelor of Social

Work (BSW) awards a social work degree in four years of coursework and an applied practicum of at least 400 hours (CSWE, 2024a). Although the MSW is generally considered the terminal practice degree, students may pursue a Doctor of Social Work (DSW) or Doctor of Philosophy in Social Work (PhD).

After obtaining a BSW or MSW, social workers may be eligible for licensure. Licensure is regulated at the state level and varies widely across the country. Less than half (352,000) of people doing work classified by the federal government as social work hold a license at one of those levels (National Association of Social Workers – NASW, 2023). Several states legislate title protection as well, requiring social workers to hold a license and/or a social work degree to refer to themselves as a 'social worker'. Although licensure regulations vary, generally applicants for licensure must hold a degree from a programme accredited by the CSWE, sit for the appropriate exam administered by the Association of Social Work Boards and complete any additional steps required by the state in which they wish to practise (Association of Social Work Boards, 2024).

Professional associations

Social workers may hold membership in a social work professional organisation. Examples include the NASW, the National Network for Social Work Managers, the Association for Community Organization and Social Action, the School Social Work Association of America, the Center on Immigration and Child Welfare, the National Association of Black Social Workers, the Latino Social Workers Organization, the Association of Oncology Social Work, the Clinical Social Work Association, the National Association of Forensic Social Workers and state-level associations such as the Minnesota Association of Macro Practice Social Work (Meehan et al, 2021).

The NASW, founded in 1955, is the largest professional social work organisation in the world, serving over 120,000 social workers annually with 55 chapters across the country (NASW, nd-b). The NASW sets the Code of Ethics of the profession, provides training opportunities for social workers, promotes professional growth among its membership and advocates for the advancement of socially just policies.

Practice areas

In 2023, there were 162 million people in the US workforce. Roughly one half of 1 per cent (0.465 per cent) were social workers. Of the 751,900 people doing work classified as social work in 2023 (Bureau of Labor Statistics, 2024), 39 per cent (291,169 people) did not have a degree in social work. In 13 states, more than 50 per cent of the social work workforce is without a social work degree (George Washington University Health Workforce Institute, 2017).

The depth and breadth of the social work profession is vast. Community-based public agencies and non-profits employ high numbers. Social workers can be found in schools, hospitals, older adult centres, prisons and mental health clinics, and some work for elected officials. Social workers serve in administrative and leadership roles (7.5 per cent), but predominantly work in direct or clinical practice (82 per cent) (2019 figures; Fitzhugh Mullan Institute for Health Workforce Equity, 2020). Direct practitioners include those providing clinical mental health services, who outnumber psychiatrists, psychologists and psychiatric nurses by 200,000.

Social workers entering the workforce between 2017 and 2019 were predominantly women (90 per cent) and ethnically diverse (22 per cent were African American and 14 per cent were Hispanic/Latino; Fitzhugh Mullan Institute for Health Workforce Equity, 2020). Responses to a public opinion survey by the NASW (2023) demonstrate that 80 per cent of Americans view social workers in a positive light, with 81 per cent indicating that a social worker had been instrumental in changing a situation for themselves or a loved one and 84 per cent reporting they are in favour of congressional legislation to improve social worker safety. More than half of respondents indicated that social workers should be paid more than the profession's median pay, which was around USD 50,000 at the time of the survey according to the Bureau of Labor Statistics. Many Americans were aware of social work's role in child welfare agencies and social service programmes; however, nearly half (46 per cent) were unaware of the role of social workers in advocacy and community organisation (NASW, 2023).

Institutional opportunity structures

Structure of the US government

The United States has a federalist system of government, sharing power between the federal government and states, with states delegating to the local level. The three branches of the federal government, mirrored in every state, are legislative, executive and judicial (Lane et al, 2019). The legislative branch creates and amends legislation, and at the federal level is the bicameral US Congress, including the House of Representatives (lower chamber) and the Senate (upper chamber). The executive branch, headed by the president and encompassing 15 cabinet-level agencies, implements laws, primarily through regulation and occasionally executive orders, and enforces implementation (White House, nd). The judicial branch is represented by the US Supreme Court and other federal courts (Lane et al, 2019).

The 435 members of Congress (MCs) who serve in the House of Representatives (or 'the House') includes at least one representative from every state, apportioned by population, and is considered the 'People's House' (Lane et al, 2019). The 100 MCs in the Senate include two members from each of the 50 states, and this is designed to serve as a cautionary brake on the actions of the House. While all 50 states have at least three MCs (two senators and at least one House member), US territories and the District of Columbia, where the US government is seated, do not have voting representation in the US Congress (Mamet, 2021). American Samoa, Guam, the Northern Mariana Islands, Puerto Rico, the US Virgin Islands and Washington, DC have non-voting representation which limits the power and voice of those who live in these spaces, including the 700,000 residents of Washington, DC and the 3.5 million people in US territories. Nearly all (98 per cent) of these disenfranchised are members of racial and ethnic minority groups.

The two major parties in the United States today are the Democratic Party (Left/progressive/liberal) and the Republican Party (Right/conservative). The two major parties have significant power to choose congressional candidates, direct campaign funds, determine policy agendas and assign key leadership positions in Congress (United States Senate, nd).

For all elections except presidential, US voters cast votes directly for their preferred candidates. Presidential elections are mediated by the Electoral College (ACE Electoral Knowledge Network, nd). In federal elections and most other kinds of elections, the United States uses a plurality/majority election system: the first-past-the-post (FPTP) electoral system or plurality single-member district system. The candidate with the largest number of votes is elected, even if they do not get more than 50 per cent of the vote (ACE Electoral Knowledge Network, nd). FPTP systems tend to favour the development and maintenance of two major political parties and disadvantage third parties. Voters and candidates who differ from the main two parties and members of minority groups are disadvantaged, particularly in national elections. In this US system, few candidates of colour are elected in majority White districts, and to date the United States has had only one non-White president and no female presidents. FPTP systems can lead to large numbers of wasted votes and feelings of alienation by voters who do not see themselves represented and feel their vote does not matter. This system is heavily influenced by the drawing of district boundaries, a task that is handled at a state level and is often controlled in a partisan manner by the majority party in state legislatures (ACE Electoral Knowledge Network, nd).

Interest groups

In 1929, 500 lobby groups existed in Washington, DC. Today it is estimated there are more than 200,000 interest groups (Schechter, 2021). At the federal level alone, interest groups spent an estimated USD 6 billion to influence political action during the 2022 election cycle, including USD 3.5 billion directly to political candidates and parties and USD 2.7 billion to outside groups (Open Secrets, 2023a).

Social workers are represented in all types of interest groups. The most visible interest group representing social workers is the NASW. In the 2022 election cycle, the NASW raised USD 377,000 and donated USD 29,500 to candidates, all but USD 1,000 to Democrats, including three social workers (Open Secrets, 2023b). The CSWE, which accredits schools of social work nationwide, spends $120,000 per year on lobbying, with no donations to parties or candidates (Open Secrets, 2024a). The School Social Work Association of America spends USD 40,000 per year to lobby the federal Department of Education and Congress about education, including the Student Mental Health Helpline Act and EDUCATORS for America Act (Open Secrets, 2024b).

Accessibility and attractiveness of Congress for social workers

Although there are more than 500,000 elected offices in the United States, the hierarchy of offices generally offers higher status, power and financial reward as one moves up from the local and state levels to the federal level (Copeland and Opheim, 2011). The attractiveness of congressional service includes financial rewards, status and power. Financial benefits include salary, benefits and funds for official expenses. Positions in the US Congress pay a minimum of USD 174,000 (2023 figure; Brudnick, 2023). MCs are eligible for retirement benefits after five years as well as health insurance, life insurance and social security, and they may make more in leadership positions. Social workers in other areas of practice have a median salary of USD 61,330 (Bureau of Labor Statistics, 2025), with no guarantee of retirement benefits or health insurance. Each MC also receives funds to run their office through the House Members' Representational Allowance and the Senators' Official Personnel and Office Expense Account (Brudnick, 2023). Part of the attractiveness is opportunities after leaving office, as MCs often take public policy jobs, including lobbying, which are well-paid. For example, of the 68 MCs who left office in 2021–23, 33 (49 per cent) took up lobbying positions (Open Secrets, nd).

A disincentive for social workers who have been members of Congress (SWMCs) is they can no longer hold social work jobs, either full-time or part-time. MCs are limited by both dollar amounts of outside income (USD 31,815 in 2023) and by ethics rules that preclude them from receiving compensation for professional services other than medical practice (Johnson, 2023). Holding an outside job, even part-time, can bring conflicts of interest. SWMC Kyrsten Sinema taught as an adjunct faculty member. Her students petitioned to remove her from teaching because they believed the way she treated constituents did not align with the NASW Code of Ethics (Priest, 2021).

Others questioned whether a sitting US senator teaching a course on fundraising was appropriate (Klippenstein, 2021).

Other benefits include status and power. This power may be of value to social workers because of their unique position to speak to the ways in which policy can address social problems because of both their training and their experience with populations most directly affected (Haynes and Mickelson, 1991).

Federal offices are available and attractive, but their accessibility is low, particularly for political newcomers. Social workers who have run for office identify useful skills and knowledge developed in social work education/experience, such as communications skills, active listening, conflict management/resolution, bargaining and compromising, forming and maintaining coalitions, political skills, advocating for groups served by social work, social policy and group dynamics (Lane and Humphreys, 2011). Most respondents had learned about the ethical responsibilities of social workers to advocate for clients (91 per cent) and to affect policy (84 per cent), while a majority (64 per cent) had learned about advocacy techniques. However, the power of incumbency makes it difficult for newcomers to enter office unless the incumbent vacates it, and the campaign finance system favours existing office-holders. A significant barrier is the cost of elections in the United States, which gives power to donors, political consultants and, to some extent, political party leaders as key gatekeepers (Copeland and Opheim, 2011).

To address these barriers, several initiatives exist in the United States to make elected office more accessible to social workers. Political Action for Candidate Election (PACE) is the electoral arm of the NASW. PACE is a political action committee that raises money from NASW members or those associated and uses funds to advance a party or candidate (NASW, nd-d). Decisions about which US House and Senate candidates to support are made by the National PACE Board of Trustees (NASW, nd-d), who find candidates to support legislation and policies that are consistent with goals of the social work profession and benefit populations served by social work. PACE not only endorses social workers, but generally has contact with any social worker running for office (personal communication, Dina Kastner, 25 April 2024). Candidates who have not held federal office are asked about their stances on social welfare issues. Those answers and evidence of their positions and values, such as voting records, bill sponsorship and other legislative activities in previous offices, are used to determine endorsement.

To increase the pool of qualified candidates among social workers and decrease barriers to accessibility, the Humphreys Institute for Political Social Work at the University of Connecticut was founded in 1995 by the late Dr Nancy A. Humphreys (UConn School of Social Work, nd). The institute has run the Campaign School for Social Workers since 1996, training more than 3,000 students, social workers and allies to run for office, take leadership roles on campaigns and support social workers and diverse candidates in running for and winning elected office (personal communication, Tanya Rhodes Smith, 28 April 2024). The Institute conducts extensive research on the process and outcomes of the Campaign School, political participation by social workers and voting. The Congressional Research Institute for Social Work and Policy (CRISP) supports the work of social workers in Congress, including by running a political boot camp and media training to help social workers prepare to run for office and serve in leadership positions (CRISP, nd). These efforts are primarily successful in increasing the number of elected social workers at the state and local level (Ostrander et al, 2017; Lane et al, 2018; McClendon et al, 2020). Barriers to accessibility for social workers to serve in Congress remain, however.

Political recruitment

In this section, we present findings about 17 SWMCs since 1917. We used three of the most common definitions of social workers in the United States: education, job title and identification. All MCs with a social work degree from a US school of social work (n = 15) were included. Two individuals who had worked in a social services occupation and identified as a social worker were also included.

The first data source we used was the NASW's compendium of SWMCs, compiled since 2011; this included 13 SWMCs. Second, we carried out a search of the Biographical Directory of the US Congress using the terms 'social work' and 'social welfare'. An additional four SWMCs were identified. An additional search of the NASW Pioneers database and the social work literature did not discover any additional SWMCs. This brought the total sample to 17. While we cannot be sure that all social workers in Congress have been discovered, our process of systematic searches, discussions with experts and reviews of the relevant literature mean we are confident that we have found them all. Although not elected, so not included in this list, two notable appointed social workers at the federal level are Francis Perkins and Harry Hopkins, who served as cabinet secretaries in President Franklin Delano Roosevelt's administration in the 1930s and 1940s. Table 12.1 shows the SWMCs organised by the time they served, the total SWMCs for each session of Congress and the percentage of that Congress that was SWMCs. No social workers served in Congress during 1920–40 or 1943–70.

Results

The 17 SWMCs identified represent just 0.14 per cent of the 12,516 individuals who have served in Congress since 1789 (Manning, 2024), though this share is larger than social work's percentage in the workforce

Table 12.1: Social work members of Congress, 65th to 118th Congress

Congressional term	SWMCs	Total SWMCs	Percentage of Congress that is SWMCs*
118th 2023–24	*Senate* Kyrsten Sinema Debbie Stabenow *House* Sylvia Garcia Barbara Lee Hillary Scholten	5	1
117th 2021–22	*Senate* Kyrsten Sinema Debbie Stabenow *House* Karen Bass Sylvia Garcia Barbara Lee	5	1
116th 2019–20	*Senate* Kyrsten Sinema Debbie Stabenow *House* Karen Bass Susan Davis Sylvia Garcia Barbara Lee	6	1.1
115th 2017–18	*Senate* Debbie Stabenow *House* Karen Bass Susan Davis Luis Gutierrez Barbara Lee Carol Shea-Porter Kyrsten Sinema Niki Tsongas	8	1.5
114th 2015–16	*Senate* Barbara Mikulski Debbie Stabenow *House* Susan Davis Luis Gutierrez Barbara Lee Kyrsten Sinema Niki Tsongas	7	1.3
113th 2013–14	*Senate* Barbara Mikulski Debbie Stabenow	9	1.7

Table 12.1: Social work members of Congress, 65th to 118th Congress (continued)

Congressional term	SWMCs	Total SWMCs	Percentage of Congress that is SWMCs*
	House Susan Davis Luis Gutierrez Barbara Lee Allyson Schwartz Carol Shea-Porter Kyrsten Sinema Niki Tsongas		
112th 2011–12	*Senate* Barbara Mikulski Debbie Stabenow	7	1.5
	House Susan Davis Luis Gutierrez Barbara Lee Allyson Schwartz Edolphus 'Ed' Towns		
111th 2009–10	*Senate* Barbara Mikulski	2	0.4
	House Ciro Rodriguez		
110th 2007–08	*Senate* Barbara Mikulski	2	0.4
	House Ciro Rodriguez		
109th 2005–06	*Senate* Barbara Mikulski	1	0.2
108th 2003–04	*Senate* Barbara Mikulski	2	0.2
	House Ciro Rodriguez		
107th 2001–02	*Senate* Barbara Mikulski	2	0.4
	House Ciro Rodriguez		
106th 1999–2000	*Senate* Barbara Mikulski	2	0.4
	House Ciro Rodriguez		
105th 1997–98	*Senate* Barbara Mikulski	3	0.6

(continued)

Table 12.1: Social work members of Congress, 65th to 118th Congress (continued)

Congressional term	SWMCs	Total SWMCs	Percentage of Congress that is SWMCs*
	House Ron Dellums Ciro Rodriguez		
104th 1995–96	*Senate* Barbara Mikulski	2	0.4
	House Ron Dellums		
103rd 1993–94	*Senate* Barbara Mikulski	2	0.4
	House Ron Dellums		
102nd 1991–92	*Senate* Barbara Mikulski	2	0.4
	House Ron Dellums		
101st 1989–90	*Senate* Barbara Mikulski	2	0.4
	House Ron Dellums		
100th 1987–88	*House* Ron Dellums Barbara Mikulski	2	0.4
99th 1985–86	*House* Ron Dellums Barbara Mikulski	2	0.4
98th 1983–84	*House* Ron Dellums Barbara Mikulski	2	0.4
97th 1981–82	*House* Ron Dellums Barbara Mikulski	2	0.4
96th 1979–80	*House* Ron Dellums Barbara Mikulski	2	0.4
95th 1977–78	*House* Ron Dellums Barbara Mikulski William Francis Walsh	3	0.6
94th 1975–76	*House* Ron Dellums William Francis Walsh	2	0.4

Table 12.1: Social work members of Congress, 65th to 118th Congress (continued)

Congressional term	SWMCs	Total SWMCs	Percentage of Congress that is SWMCs*
93rd 1973–74	*House* Ron Dellums William Francis Walsh	2	0.4
92nd 1971–72	*House* Ron Dellums	1	0.2
77th 1941–42	*House* Jeannette Rankin	1	0.2
65th 1917–19	*House* Jeannette Rankin	1	0.2

Notes: * These percentages are calculated based on the total 541 voting and non-voting members of Congress: 100 Senators and 435 voting Representatives, plus 6 non-voting delegates (from US territories and DC). No social workers served in Congress during 1920–40 or 1943–70.

Source: Based on data gathered from the policy area subject search provided by the Library of Congress at www.congress.gov

(0.465 per cent, as mentioned earlier). It should also be noted that there were no social workers in the first 128 years that Congress existed, because the profession had not been established.

The first SWMC, Jeannette Rankin, was elected in 1916, and she was also the first woman elected to Congress. The 2013–14 session of Congress had the largest number of SWMCs, at nine. The 119th Congress (seated in January 2025) has only two SWMCs, Sylvia Garcia and Hillary Scholten. Both Senate SWMCs retired in 2024, and no social workers were candidates, meaning the 119th Congress now has no Senate SWMCs for the first time in 37 years (personal communication, Charles Lewis, 13 March 2024).

The 17 SWMCs represent 11 of the 50 states, with California (3), Michigan (2), New York (2) and Texas (2) sending more than one each.

All 17 SWMCs (100 per cent) served in the House, and three (18 per cent) also served in the Senate. The average age when elected is 48.24 (with a range from 27 to 69). The average age of MCs serving in the 118th Congress (as of 2024) was 58 (House) and 64 (Senate) with a range from 25 to 89. In comparison, the average age of newly elected House members was 48 and for senators, 50 (Manning, 2024).

In terms of the highest social work degree held for all SWMCs, 11 (65 per cent) held an MSW, 3 (18 per cent) held a BSW degree and 1 (6 per cent) attended the New York School of Philanthropy, a precursor to social work education. Just two (12 per cent) held a degree other than social work. In the 118th Congress, the social workers elected to office were more likely to be Democrats than other members. As of September 2024, Congress had 269 Republicans, 258 Democrats, four independents who caucus with

Democrats and four vacancies (Manning, 2024). All of the SWMCs in this period were Democrats. Taking SWMCs overall, 82 per cent were Democrats (n = 14) and 12 per cent Republicans (n = 2) with 1 an Independent who was formerly a Democrat. The only Republican SWMCs ever to have been elected were the first two SWMCs, elected in 1917 and 1973.

Women made up only 28 per cent of the total 118th Congress (Manning, 2024), while, as of 2024, 50.5 per cent of US adults and 52 per cent of the workforce were female (United States Census Bureau, nd). Of all SWMCs, 71 per cent (n = 12) have been female and 29 per cent (n = 5) male. African Americans made up 12 per cent of the overall 188th Congress (Manning, 2024), 12 per cent of the US population, 13 per cent of the US workforce (United States Census Bureau, nd) and 24 per cent of SWMCs (n = 4). Latinx persons have made up 18 per cent (n = 3) of all SWMCs, 11 per cent of the overall 118th Congress (Manning, 2024), 19 per cent of the population and 18 per cent of the US workforce (United States Census Bureau, nd). The remaining SWMCs have been White (n = 10, 59 per cent). No other ethnic groups, including Asian/Pacific Islanders or Indigenous persons, have been represented among SWMCs. Overall, SWMCs are more diverse than typical members of Congress but do not represent the full diversity of the US population or the social work workforce.

While there is much variety in the career paths of MCs, the typical path includes a college education. In the 118th Congress, 96 per cent held a degree and an additional 34 per cent held a law degree, 23 per cent holding a master's degree (including in social work) and 10 per cent holding a doctorate (Manning, 2024). The most common professions represented were public service/politics, business and law. Half of the US Senate and one third of the House had practised law, 30 per cent of MCs had worked in business and 80 per cent had served as public servants or other elected officials prior to Congress, including 44 per cent of senators who first served in the House. In addition, 18 per cent of MCs had served in the military (Manning, 2024). The number of social workers in the 118th Congress was the same as the number of former professional athletes in this Congress (5). If we take all SWMCs, each of the 17 held undergraduate degrees. Overall, social workers are more likely to have a higher education, with 12 (71 per cent) of all SWMCs holding a master's degree, 4 (24 per cent) a law degree and 1 (6 per cent) a PhD.

As noted earlier, there were five SWMCs in the 118th Congress, and nine is the largest number to have served at the same time. Other professions that social workers are often compared with have been more represented in Congress. For example, 101 members of the 118th Congress (19 per cent) had worked in education and 32 (6 per cent) had been medical professionals (doctors, dentists, an optometrist, pharmacists, nurses and an emergency medical technician). Other social service/mental health professions have been less represented. There was one psychologist in the 118th Congress, and there were no mental health counsellors, marriage and family therapists, or other mental health professionals (Manning, 2024).

Elected social workers had a combination of micro- and macro-focused experiences before they came into their political careers. Nearly all (n = 16, 94 per cent) had professional experience as a social worker before being elected. The exception is Karen Bass, who earned her MSW while serving in Congress. In addition, nearly half (n = 8, 47 per cent) had faculty or academic experience, while around a quarter had legal experience and military experience (both n = 4, 24 per cent).

Political career patterns

Pre-congressional careers

Political careers in the United States typically follow a unidirectional pattern, from the local level to the state level to the federal level (Copeland and Opheim, 2011). Significantly, 80 per cent of MCs in the 118th Congress were elected officials or public servants before arriving in Congress (Manning, 2024). The picture was similar for the 17 elected social workers, with 100 per cent having served as elected officials (71 per cent) and/or appointed officials/staff (35 per cent) before entering Congress. In the 118th term, both Stabenow and Sinema had served in the US House before their election to the Senate, as had 42 other senators, nearly half (Manning, 2024). Many MCs have been state legislators/state senators, mayors or governors prior to running for office, with the largest group (n = 7, 41 per cent) serving as state legislators. No SWMCs in the 118th Congress had served as governor, but one governor at the time, Katie Hobbs of Arizona, was a social worker (Office of the Governor Katie Hobbs, nd).

Congressional tenure

The SWMCs served between 2 and 40 years, with 10 (59 per cent) serving 20 years or longer; the mean was 17.88 years. The two SWMCs in the 118th Congress who were expected to be re-elected, Scholten and Garcia, are relatively junior, serving in their first and third terms respectively. For all MCs in the 118th period, the average length of service was 8.5 years for House members and 11.2 years for senators (Manning, 2024). Thus, even if most of those MCs prolong their time in office for another legislative period or more, social workers seem to have a much longer tenure than non-social workers in Congress.

Post-congressional careers

The post-congressional careers of the 12 SWMCs who have left office show they are more likely than MCs as a whole to turn to 'lower' offices and to leave public life, and less likely to work as lobbyists. None have returned to social work practice.

It is unusual for MCs to move to local or state offices after they serve, but 3 (25 per cent) of the SWMCs looked to those levels after Congress. Karen Bass resigned after 11 years in the House to serve as the Mayor of Los Angeles. Ron Dellums left Congress after 27 years, became a lobbyist (including work for a telecommunications company) and subsequently served as Mayor of Oakland for one term. Allyson Schwartz left Congress after ten years to run for governor of Pennsylvania, but was not elected.

The typical path for members of Congress is to turn to advocacy or lobbying. Of the 12 retired SWMCs, 3 (25 per cent) have formally become lobbyists: Dellums; Ciro Rodriguez, who worked as a lobbyist for technology issues; and Edolphus Towns, who lobbied for business interests and worked in a law firm. Three (25 per cent) served as advocates. Jeannette Rankin advocated for women's rights and peace during the 22 years between her two terms in Congress and after her second term. Schwartz founded the Better Medicare Alliance, a non-profit health advocacy organisation, and then took a position as senior health fellow at the Bipartisan Policy Center. One SWMC had retired but returned to the public eye as an advocate – Luis Gutiérrez retired to Puerto Rico at age 66 after serving 26 years in the House, then returned to Chicago after five years of retirement to advocate for immigration reform, a key priority during his time in Congress.

Four SWMCs (33 per cent) retired from public life. William Francis Walsh retired after six years of service (age 66). Two retired after 12 years of service: Carol Shea-Porter (age 67) and Niki Tsongas (age 73). Susan Davis retired at age 77 after 20 years in the House and has been mostly out of the public eye, although she was appointed by President Biden to sit on the Board of the United States Merchant Marine Academy, a volunteer position that highlights her years of advocating for military veterans and members while in Congress.

The longest-serving SWMC and the oldest at retirement has also been the most active. Barbara Mikulski retired at the age of 81 after 30 years in the Senate and ten years in the House. Mikulski was also the longest-serving woman in Congress. After retirement, she taught public policy at Johns Hopkins University and went on to advise the Dean of Hopkins' Krieger School regarding community engagement. She also serves on the boards of the National Democratic Institute and Baltimore Community Foundation.

To sum up, SWMCs have similar career paths to other MCs. Differences include more education and higher likelihood of holding other elected or appointed offices before being elected to Congress and afterwards. They have longer average tenure than the average for all MCs. After they serve, SWMCs are more likely to turn to office at the state or local levels or to retire from public life, and slightly less likely to serve as lobbyists. They do not return to traditional social work practice.

Social advocacy

The purpose of this section is to determine whether SWMCs act differently from their counterparts legislatively. We examined bills sponsored by SWMCs, their committee assignments and their legislative relationship with the NASW.

Sponsored legislation

The large volume of bills introduced in each Congress and the inconsistencies in coding between Congresses led us to focus on the SWMCs in the 118th Congress. The Library of Congress codes legislation into 31 policy areas, 9 of which we identified as being most relevant to the social work profession, although of course all policy has some relevance to social work. The areas are health, civil rights and liberties; minority issues; education; labour and employment; immigration; social welfare; families; Native Americans; and housing and community development. The 22,036 bills introduced during the 118th Congress are categorised accordingly, and 4,676 bills (21 per cent) were introduced in those nine social work-related categories.

The results of this analysis are shown in Table 12.2. This shows that 37.69 per cent of legislation sponsored by SWMCs related to the social work profession, from a low of 29.22 per cent to a high of 40.67 per cent. In Congress as a whole, only 21.22 per cent of bills introduced were related to the social work profession.

Committee assignments

Congressional committee assignments are made by each party's leadership and are designed to reflect a member's seniority, expertise and ideology and the

Table 12.2: Social welfare-related legislation in the 118th Congress

SWMC	Social work-related bills	Total bills	Percentage of bills related to social work
Sylvia Garcia	190	469	40.51%
Barbara Lee	405	1,008	40.18%
Hillary Scholten	102	319	31.97%
Kyrsten Sinema	109	373	29.22%
Debbie Stabenow	157	386	40.67%
All SWMCs	963	2,555	37.69%
All MCs	4,676	22,036	21.22%

Source: Based on data gathered from the policy area subject search provided by the Library of Congress at www.congress.gov

character of their district. Political factors such as ideology, election margin and support of leadership are also often considered (Schneider, 2008). While less than half of SWMCs (n = 6, 35.3 per cent) served on committees that primarily focus on social welfare-related topics, many used positions on powerful committees such as Appropriations and Budget to advanced social welfare-related causes, including the Affordable Care Act and the Lilly Ledbetter Fair Pay Act.

Relationship with the NASW

Once social workers are elected, the NASW prioritises the linkage with SWMCs, develops strong, long-standing relationships with each of them and works in partnership on issues important to the social work profession. Relationship building happens through individual meetings, connections with chapters and local members, awards and other forms of public recognition, and helping members to connect with social worker constituents (personal communication, Dina Kastner, 25 April 2024).

The NASW worked with SWMCs Stabenow and Lee to sponsor the Improving Access to Mental Health Act in every Congress since the 114th (2015–16). This bill addresses Medicare beneficiaries' (generally those aged 65+ or people with disabilities) need for skilled mental health care by increasing social worker reimbursement and enhancing access to psychosocial services provided by clinical social workers in skilled nursing facilities. It also supports clinical social workers' provision of Health Behavior Assessment and Intervention services (NASW, nd-a). Sinema co-sponsored this bill, and the NASW has encouraged Garcia and Scholten to co-sponsor (personal communication, Dina Kastner, 25 April 2024).

Another piece of important legislation related to the profession is the More Social Workers in Libraries Act. Social workers Lee and Scholten have co-sponsored this legislation, championed by Garcia. This bill has not been introduced in the Senate by Stabenow or Sinema (NASW, nd-a).

The Social Work Caucus, founded in 2011 by SWMC Ed Towns and currently chaired by SWMC Barbara Lee, includes four of the five SWMCs in the 118th Congress. This group, which includes 31 non-social worker MCs, represents the interests of social workers in the United States and spotlights their work (Legistorm, nd). SWMCs have also taken leadership roles in other important caucuses that lead on social welfare issues, including the Congressional Black Caucus, the Congressional Progressive Caucus and the Congressional Hispanic Caucus.

Conclusion

Among SWMCs is the first woman ever elected to Congress and the longest-serving woman in Congress. SWMCs are more educated and more likely to be liberal, female, African American and Latinx than MCs overall. They serve longer tenures. Of particular note in these divided political times in the United States, no Republican SWMCs have been elected since 1973. In many ways, SWMCs continue to keep their social work priorities in mind as elected officials in that they are more likely than other MCs to support legislation that addresses the social welfare of their constituents and they often join the Social Work Caucus and sponsor NASW priority legislation. Social workers in the United States are actively working to address barriers that prevent access for more social workers to be elected to Congress.

References

ACE Electoral Knowledge Network (nd) 'Electoral systems', *ACE*, Available from: https://aceproject.org/ace-en/topics/es/esd/esd01/default

Association of Social Work Boards (2024) 'Licensing requirements by state or province', *ASWB*, Available from: www.aswb.org/licenses/how-to-get-a-license/licensing-requirements-by-state-or-province

Brudnick, I.A. (2023) 'Congressional salaries and allowances: In brief', *Congressional Research Service*, 19 September, Available from: https://crsreports.congress.gov/product/pdf/RL/RL30064

Bureau of Labor Statistics (2025) 'Occupational Outlook Handbook: Social workers', *U.S. Department of Labor*, 18 April, Available from: www.bls.gov/ooh/community-and-social-service/social-workers.htm

Copeland, G. and Opheim, C. (2011) 'Multi-level political careers in the USA: The cases of African Americans and women', *Regional & Federal Studies*, 21(2): 141–64.

CRISP (Congressional Research Institute for Social Work and Policy) (nd) 'Our story', *CRISP*, Available from: https://crispinc.org/our-story

CSWE (Council on Social Work Education) (2024a) 'Prepare for your education: Social work education at a glance', *CSWE*, Available from: www.cswe.org/students/prepare-for-your-education

CSWE (Council on Social Work Education) (2024b) '2020 statistics on social work education in the United States: Summary of the CSWE Annual Survey of Social Work Programs', *CSWE*, Available from: www.cswe.org/getattachment/726b15ce-6e63-4dcd-abd1-35d2ea9d9d40/2020-Annual-Statistics-On-Social-Work-Education-in-the-United-States.pdf?lang=en-US

Fitzhugh Mullan Institute for Health Workforce Equity (2020) 'The social work profession: Findings from three years of surveys of new social workers', *Council on Social Work Education*, August, Available from: www.cswe.org/CSWE/media/Workforce-Study/The-Social-Work-Profession-Findings-from-Three-Years-of-Surveys-of-New-Social-Workers-Dec-2020.pdf

George Washington University Health Workforce Institute (2017) 'Profile of the social work workforce', *National Association of Social Workers*, Available from: www.socialworkers.org/LinkClick.aspx?fileticket=wCttjrHq0gE%3D&portalid=0

Grajeda, A. (2023) 'Democratic social worker to run against Republican incumbent for Northwest Arkansas congressional seat', *Arkansas Advocate*, 24 October, Available from: https://arkansasadvocate.com/briefs/democratic-social-worker-to-run-against-republican-incumbent-for-northwest-arkansas-congressional-seat/

Haynes, K.S. and Mickelson, J.S. (1991) *Affecting Change: Social Workers in the Political Arena* (2nd edn), Longman.

Johnson, C.L. (2023) *Rules of the House of Representatives: One Hundred Eighteenth Congress*, Clerk of the House of Representatives, Available from: https://cha.house.gov/_cache/files/5/3/5361f9f8-24bc-4fbc-ac97-3d79fd689602/1F09ADA16E45C9E7B67F147DCF176D95.118-rules-01102023.pdf

Klippenstein, C. (2021) 'Sen. Kyrsten Sinema is literally teaching a course on fundraising', *The Intercept*, 8 October, Available from: https://theintercept.com/2021/10/08/kyrsten-sinema-fundraising-course-asu

Lane, S.R. and Humphreys, N.A. (2011) 'Social workers in politics: A national survey of social work candidates and elected officials', *Journal of Policy Practice*, 10(3): 225–44.

Lane, S.R., Ostrander, J.A. and Rhodes Smith, T. (2018) 'Politics is social work with power: Training social workers for elected office', *Social Work Education*, 37(1): 1–16.

Lane, S.R., Palley, E. and Shdaimah, C. (2019) *Social Welfare Policy in a Changing World*, Sage.

Legistorm (nd) 'Congressional Social Work Caucus', *Legistorm*, Available from: www.legistorm.com/organization/summary/122507/Congressional_Social_Work_Caucus.html

Library of Congress (nd) 'Federalism and the Constitution', *Congress.gov*, Available from: https://constitution.congress.gov/browse/essay/intro.7-3/ALDE_00000032/

Mamet, E. (2021) 'Representation on the periphery: The past and future of nonvoting members of Congress', *American Political Thought*, 10(3): 390–418, Available from: www.journals.uchicago.edu/doi/full/10.1086/715010

Manning, J.E. (2024) 'Membership of the 118th Congress: A profile', *Congressional Research Service*, 12 September, Available from: https://crsreports.congress.gov/product/pdf/R/R47470

McClendon, J., Lane, S.R., Ostrander, J. and Rhodes Smith, T. (2020) 'Training social workers for political engagement: Exploring regional differences in the United States', *Journal of Teaching in Social Work*, 40(2): 147–68.

Meehan, P., Ostrander, J. and Lane, S.R. (2021) 'Who is a social worker? Lessons on sampling from political participation research', *Advances in Social Work*, 21(4): 1–13.

NASW (National Association of Social Workers) (2023) 'National social work public opinion survey', *NASW*, Available from: www.socialworkers.org/News/News-Releases/ID/2618/National-Survey-from-Ipsos-finds-80-percent-of-Americans-have-a-favorable-opinion-of-Social-Workers

NASW (National Association of Social Workers) (nd-a) 'Action Center', *NASW*, Available from: www.socialworkers.org/Advocacy/Action-Center

NASW (National Association of Social Workers) (nd-b) 'Facts about NASW', *NASW*, Available from: www.socialworkers.org/News/Facts/Facts-About-NASW

NASW (National Association of Social Workers) (nd-c) 'Social workers in elected office', *NASW*, Available from: www.socialworkers.org/Advocacy/Political-Action-for-Candidate-Election-PACE/Social-Workers-in-State-and-Local-Office

NASW (National Association of Social Workers) (nd-d) 'Political Action for Candidate Election (PACE)', *NASW*, Available from: www.socialworkers.org/advocacy/political-action-for-candidate-election-pace

Office of the Governor Katie Hobbs (nd) 'Meet Governor Katie Hobbs', *Office of the Governor Katie Hobbs*, Available from: https://azgovernor.gov/governor/meet-governor-katie-hobbs

Open Secrets (2023a) 'Interest groups', *Open Secrets*, Available from: www.opensecrets.org/industries?cycle=2022

Open Secrets (2023b) 'PAC profile: National Assn of Social Workers', *Open Secrets*, Available from: www.opensecrets.org/political-action-committees-pacs/national-assn-of-social-workers/C00060707/summary/2022

Open Secrets (2024a) 'Client profile: Council on Social Work Education', *Open Secrets*, Available from: www.opensecrets.org/federal-lobbying/clients/summary?cycle=2025&id=D000049802

Open Secrets (2024b) 'Client profile: School Social Work Assn of America', *Open Secrets*, Available from: www.opensecrets.org/federal-lobbying/clients/summary?id=D000114129

Open Secrets (nd) 'Former members of Congress: 117th Congress', *Open Secrets*, Available from: www.opensecrets.org/revolving-door/former-members-of-congress?cong=117

Ostrander, J., Lane, S.R., McClendon, J., Hayes, C. and Rhodes Smith, T. (2017) 'Collective power to create political change: Increasing the political efficacy and engagement of social workers', *Journal of Policy Practice*, 16(3): 261–75.

Powers, J. and Fisher, R. (2019) 'Political social work in the United States', *Oxford Bibliographies Online in Social Work*, doi: 10.1093/OBO/9780195389678-0275

Priest, R. (2021) 'Sinema gets thumbs down from students in petition to terminate her ASU contract', *The State Press*, 18 November, Available from: www.statepress.com/article/2021/11/social-work-students-start-petition-to-fire-kyrsten-sinema

Schechter, S. (2021) 'Interest groups in the federal system', *Center for the Study of Federalism*, Available from: https://encyclopedia.federalism.org/index.php/Interest_Groups_in_the_Federal_System

Schneider, J. (2008) 'House committees: Assignment process', *Congressional Research Service*, 25 February, Available from: https://crsreports.congress.gov/product/details?prodcode=98-367

UConn School of Social Work (nd) 'Nancy A. Humphreys Institute for Political Social Work', *UConn*, Available from: https://socialwork.uconn.edu/humphreys-institute

United States Census Bureau (nd) 'Quick facts: United States', *United States Census Bureau*, Available from: www.census.gov/quickfacts/fact/table/US/RHI725222

United States Senate (nd) 'About parties and leadership: Historical overview', *United States Senate*, Available from: www.senate.gov/about/origins-foundations/parties-leadership/overview.htm

White House (nd) 'The cabinet', *The White House*, Available from: www.whitehouse.gov/administration/cabinet

13

Comparative considerations on social workers in political office

Klaus Stolz, Sigrid Leitner and Tobias Kindler

Even a cursory glance at the chapters compiled for this volume reveals that the impact social workers have on social policy in liberal democracies via holding elected political office is far from uniform. In fact, what we observe is a striking variation in motivations and pathways that lead social workers into and out of elected politics as well as variations in their political careers and with regard to their personal ambition to advance social policy aims once they are elected and their success in doing so.

One of the most prominent social workers in political office identified in this volume is Johannes Rauch, who served as the Austrian Federal Minister for Social Affairs, Health, Care and Consumer Protection from 2022 until 2025 (see Chapter 2). Concurrent to working as a social worker and social work manager between 1986 and 2004, he started his political career at the local and state level, where he was the spokesperson for the Green Party in one of the nine Austrian states (Vorarlberg) between 1997 and 2021. He was a member of the state parliament for more than ten years and served in the state government for eight years before being nominated as a federal minister. In this prestigious and powerful position, he continued to strongly identify with the social work profession, illustrated by his continued membership of the obds, the Austrian social work professional organisation. He used his political position to advocate for the interests of social work and service users. Among other projects, he was involved in the implementation of the Social Work Designation Act and policy initiatives aiming to reduce poverty. This is the career of a *social work politician*.

Rauch's strongly social work- and social policy-oriented political career finds its antipode in the career of the Israeli Labour Knesset member Shalom Simchon. Before first entering parliament in 1996, Simchon completed a BA in social work and was heavily involved in the Moshavim movement, a cooperative settlement movement of villages that maintains a range of collective (social) services, where he chaired the youth and social department before becoming its secretary general. As a member of the Knesset, he left his former occupation to concentrate on his rather long and successful parliamentary career (1996–2013), focusing on mainstream politics. Between

1999 and 2013, he not only chaired the finance and the economic committee of the Knesset, but also served in the cabinet as Minister for Agriculture (twice), Minister for the Environment, Minister for Industry, Trade and Labour and finally as Minister for the Minorities. In 2013, he did not stand again for the Knesset. Drawing on his strong economic and political expertise gathered in parliament and government, he launched a consultancy company providing advice and expertise to public bodies in the field of economics and rural development. He also served on the board of directors for a number of private companies. His career could best be summarised as the career of a *social worker turned politician*.

A third type of political career, completely different from the two identified, was pursed by the Canadian Louise Hardy. A social work graduate, she entered the Canadian federal parliament for the New Democratic Party in 1997. During her short stint in Ottawa, she concentrated heavily on key social work issues such as human rights, housing, citizenship and immigration as well as aboriginal affairs. Losing her seat at the Canadian general election of 2000, she returned to front-line social work, pursuing a clinical practice career as counsellor and art therapist. This is the career of a social worker who temporarily engaged in front-line politics and is, thus, a *political social worker*.

The fundamental differences apparent in these almost ideal-typical pathways of social workers in politics reflect the diversity we have found in terms of the social work profession in each country (its institutionalisation, its social status and so on) and with regard to the opportunity structure provided for social workers by the political institutions in these countries. However, as we cannot easily attribute these ideal-types to country cases, any explanation of the empirical variation of career pathways has to complement country-specific factors with a whole range of individual properties of social workers (gender, party, social work experience and so on) that may impact their career choices.

This final chapter provides a comparative perspective on social workers holding political office. Using the analytical frame set out in our introduction, we attempt to identify common features across countries and to unravel some of the more intriguing differences between them. In this endeavour, we follow the template of the country chapters, discussing issues of political recruitment, political career patterns and social advocacy in turn. Country-specific characteristics of the social work profession and the political opportunity structure are drawn on in our explorative deliberations on potential causal relationships.

Political recruitment

Social workers are represented in national parliaments in all the countries examined in this volume. Confirming previous research in this field (for example, Amann and Kindler, 2022; Löffler, 2024), the chapters show that social workers run for elected political office because they believe that certain social problems cannot be effectively addressed at the individual level alone and need to be tackled at the structural level as well. Several of the chapters in this volume highlight that professional experience and social work methods, such as conflict management or communication skills, equip social workers well for a political career.

Aggregating the data collected in the chapters, Table 13.1 provides a comparative overview of the basic characteristics of social work members of national parliaments (SWMPs). At the time of data collection in 2023/24, all 11 countries had at least one SWMP, with Canada, the United Kingdom and Germany having 7, 8 and 13, respectively.

Comparing this representation of social workers in parliament with the proportion of the total workforce, which was between 0.2 and 1.0 per cent in all the countries analysed, we see that social workers have been slightly over-represented in most of the parliaments. The clearest over-representation was found in Canada, where the 70,000 social workers represented 0.4 per cent of the workforce, while the seven SWMPs represent 2.1 per cent of all MPs.

However, these figures should be interpreted with caution as they vary not only between countries but also over time. In Israel, for example, there have been between 0 and 3 social workers serving simultaneously in the Knesset since 1948. Comparable variations are to be found in other countries: In Finland, Italy and Portugal, there have been between 1 and 3 SWMPs in recent legislatures; in Czechia, between 1 and 4; in Switzerland, between 1 and 5; in Austria, between 1 and 6; in the United States, between 1 and 9; in Germany, between 0 and 18; and in the United Kingdom, a rather exceptional case, between 7 and 21 SWMPs have simultaneously held political office in the national parliament. The strongest representation to date was in the late 1990s and 2000s, when in the United Kingdom, notably in a legislative period with a strong Labour majority, 21 out of 650 MPs (3.2 per cent) were SWMPs. Similarly, in the 17th and 18th German Bundestag between 2009 and 2017, 18 out of 622/631 MPs (2.9 per cent) were SWMPS. Furthermore, in the 14th, 17th and 18th Knessets in Israel, three out of 120 MPs (2.5 per cent) were SWMPs. Finally, the most recent parliament in Canada saw an all-time high in the numbers of SWMPs, with 7 out of 338 MPs (2.1 per cent). In all other countries, the proportion of SWMPs in parliament has never exceeded 2 per cent.

Reflecting on the possible correlation between welfare regimes and the *long-term* share of social workers in national parliament,[1] no clear-cut conclusions can be drawn. The data show that the Mediterranean welfare regimes (Italy and Portugal) have exhibited the lowest shares of SWMPs over time. This may be seen as a simple reflection of the smaller pool of

Table 13.1: Comparison of main characteristics of social work members of national parliaments

Country	Seats In parliament	Representation of social workers		Representation of women			SWMPs' party affiliation		
		In parliament	In workforce	Social workers	SWMPs	MPs	Left	Centre	Right
Austria	243	1 (0.4%)	42,883 (1.0%)	78.2%	86.0%	40.0%	83.0%	17.0%	0.0%
Canada	338	7 (2.1%)	70,000 (0.4%)	77.0%	55.0%	30.0%	75.0%	0.0%	25.0%
Czechia	281	4 (1.4%)	22,415 (0.4%)	90.0%	25.0%	25.0%	25.0%	50.0%	25.0%
Finland	200	1 (0.5%)	8,200 (0.3%)	93.2%	100.0%	46.0%	75.0%	25.0%	0.0%
Germany	805	13 (1.6%)	350,000 (1.0%)	75.0%	76.9%	35.0%	92.3%	7.7%	0.0%
Israel	120	1 (0.8%)	31,500 (0.8%)	86.8%	46.7%	25.0%	46.0%	27.0%	27.0%
Italy	605	1 (0.2%)	40,000 (0.2%)	90.0%	75.0%	33.0%	75.0%	0.0%	25.0%
Portugal	230	2 (0.9%)	20,000 (0.5%)	92.0%	87.5%	38.7%	87.5%	12.5%	0.0%
Switzerland	246	5 (2.0%)	50,000 (1.0%)	68.0%	87.5%	38.0%	87.5%	12.5%	0.0%
United Kingdom	650	8 (1.2%)	115,478 (0.4%)	82.0%	56.3%	23.0%	93.8%	0.0%	6.2%
United States	535	5 (0.9%)	751,900 (0.5%)	90.0%	71.0%	28.0%	82.0%	6.0%	12.0%

Notes: The percentages in columns 5–10 are based not only on the most recent representation of social workers, SWMPs and MPs, but also on historical data, including previous legislatures. In Israel, the Arab parties were included on the Left and the Jewish religious parties on the Right. The social worker holding elected office in Italy has studied social work, but is currently not registered with the National Council of Social Workers.

social workers, at least in Italy (0.2 per cent of the labour force), but it might also indicate that the late-runner clientelistic welfare states hamper social workers' motivation to run for political office. For Israel, a relatively high share of social workers in the labour force might explain the higher long-term share of SWMPs *despite* the characteristics of a Mediterranean welfare state. Czechia, as a post-communist welfare regime, resembles the Mediterranean type, with low long-term shares of SWMPs going hand in hand with a late-runner (but market-driven) social security system. Similar to Portugal, a belated process of political democratisation might also explain the historically low political engagement of social workers in Czechia. Surprisingly, Finland, though one of the generous social democratic welfare states, has also featured a low share of SWMPs over the long term. This might be explained by the multiple opportunities for social workers to influence policy outside parliament (see Kroll et al, Chapter 5). On the other hand, the conservative-corporatist welfare regimes (Austria, Germany, Switzerland) and the liberal welfare regimes (the United Kingdom and the United States) have had rather high shares of SWMPs in a long-term perspective. In the more generous conservative-corporatist welfare states, the corporatist nature of policy making might draw more social workers into politics than elsewhere. Alternatively, this high long-term share of SWMPs might again be explained simply by a high share of social workers in the labour force (1 per cent). We might further speculate that rudimentary developed, market-driven welfare states are a trigger for pursuing social advocacy and motivate social workers to run for elected office. The lobbying of the social work professional organisation in the United States supports this argument (see Lane and Bryant, Chapter 12). Canada, though, does not fit the picture since the long-term share of SWMPs was only 0.5 per cent (see McLaughlin, Chapter 3).

As shown in Table 13.1, social work is strongly influenced by women in the profession, with between 68 and 93 per cent of the social worker populations being female. The high proportions of female social workers is also reflected in high proportions of female SWMPs. Compared to MPs in general, MPs with a social work background are much more likely to be female. In the United Kingdom, for example, 56 per cent of SWMPs but only 23 per cent of all MPs are women. However, compared to their proportion in the social work population, female SWMPs are still considerably under-represented in seven national parliaments: Canada (with 77 per cent of social workers but only 55 per cent of SWMPs being women), Czechia (90 per cent versus 25 per cent), Israel (87 per cent versus 47 per cent), Italy (90 per cent versus 75 per cent), Portugal (92 per cent versus 88 per cent), the United Kingdom (82 per cent versus 56 per cent) and the United States (90 per cent versus 71 per cent). And they are only over-represented in four national parliaments: Austria (78 per cent versus 86 per cent), Finland (93 per cent versus 100 per cent), Germany (75 per cent versus 77 per cent) and Switzerland (68 per cent versus 88 per cent). This tendency for female social workers to be under-represented in parliaments is consistent with Meehan's (2018) finding that female social workers feel significantly less qualified to run for political office than their male counterparts.

In line with expectations stated in the introductory chapter, a common feature of SWMPs in most of the countries analysed is their affiliation with political parties on the Left or liberal part of the political spectrum. A clear majority of the SWMPs in the 11 cases were members of Left-of-centre or liberal parties. This finding is not entirely surprising, as there are crucial overlaps between the goals of Left parties and the goals of the social work profession, such as social justice, solidarity and social cohesion (International Federation of Social Workers and International Association of Schools of Social Work, 2014). In Switzerland, for example, eight SWMPs have sat in the national parliament since 1987. Four of them belonged to the Green Party, three to the Social Democratic Party and one to the Christian Democratic People's Party. In the United States, 14 out of 17 SWMPs were Democrats, two were Republicans and one was an Independent. Only in Czechia is the situation slightly different: four of the eight SWMPs were affiliated with political parties of the centre, two with Left-of-centre parties and two with a Right-of-centre party. These findings apparently support the hypothesis that the number of SWMPs increases when Left-of-centre parties win more seats. Indeed, Reuter and Warner (Chapter 11) show for the United Kingdom that the average number of SWMPs was 19 during Labour years and 9 during Conservative years. However, Löffler (Chapter 6) did not find such a correlation between a Left-of-centre majority and the share of SWMPs in parliament for Germany.

Political career patterns

The political careers of social workers, just like those of politicians from any other occupational group, generally start and mostly remain on the local level. While this is hardly surprising given the much higher number of political positions at this level (*availability*), some of our case studies (Czech Republic, Finland, Germany, Italy, Portugal) show that in addition to absolute numbers, the local level – and in some cases also the regional level – exhibits higher shares of social workers than the national level. The reason for this disparity is generally seen in the prevalent allocation of decision-making competencies across territorial levels of government in most countries, which usually assigns large parts of social policy issues to the local and regional levels. This makes not only for a higher *attractiveness*, providing a stimulus for social workers to engage in local rather than national politics, but also for an elevated *accessibility*, as political parties gladly recruit their local and regional representatives from the realm of the social work profession.

The most obvious case in point is Finland. According to Kroll et al (Chapter 5), the establishment of wellbeing services county councils – which are responsible for the organisation of health care, social and emergency services – provided an almost ideal opportunity for social workers to contribute their professional expertise to the field of elected politics. As a result, the first-ever elections in 2022 saw a total of 111 social workers standing for one of the 1,379 seats on the wellbeing services county councils, of which 21 were elected. The proportion of social workers in these county councils (1.5 per cent) is thus three times higher than the proportion of Finnish social workers in the national parliament (0.5 per cent).

The case studies of Italy (see Francesconi and Guidi, Chapter 8) and Portugal (see Branco, Chapter 9) show that social worker politicians are often strongly committed to their municipalities and do not want to move up to regional- or national-level offices. Especially in Italy, the civil lists (*Liste Civiche*) provide an opportunity for political engagement outside of the traditional party system that seems to be attractive for social workers. In addition, the political climate at the local level seems to be less stressful and more consensus oriented than in national politics. Kohlfürst (Chapter 2) makes the argument that in Austria, national politics is less attractive for social workers because they fear being exposed to fierce conflicts.

The political careers of those social workers who do enter the national level, though, closely resemble the predominant career pattern of professional politicians in each country. In most countries, this means a long pre-parliamentary political career with a high number of prior offices held in political parties and/or interest groups as well as in local and regional government. If SWMPs' career patterns do deviate from the conventional career pathway, they seem to enter national politics with more rather than less previous political experience than their colleagues (see, for example, Canada, Czechia, Switzerland and the United States). Social workers seem to be both willing and capable to undergo a long and time-demanding political apprenticeship that is a necessary condition (but far from a guarantee) for entry into the realm of professional politics.

In a similar vein, the parliamentary tenure of social workers in national parliaments does not deviate much from that of non-social workers. In countries that feature a rather long average parliamentary tenure (like Finland, Germany, the United Kingdom and the United States), individual SWMPs might serve for more than 20 years with averages of 10 years and more (15 years in the United Kingdom and 18 years in the United States). By contrast, their colleagues in the Czech Republic, Israel and Portugal will typically leave the national legislature after one stint, serving less than five years on average. However, if SWMPs deviate from their non-social work colleagues, they tend to serve longer rather than shorter periods, suggesting that their social work skills and qualifications make them well-equipped for political office. The extremely long tenure in the United Kingdom and the United States can be partly explained by the incumbency bonus of majoritarian electoral systems. The years social workers have in the US Congress in excess of their colleagues from a non-social work background, though, might perhaps best be attributed to the strong support they get in their legislative duties as well as in their electoral campaigns from their national social work association, a feature exclusive to the United States.

In terms of advancing to executive office or a leadership position in parliament, SWMP careers are quite diverse. Some reflect high levels of political ambition, shown in cumulations and sequences of various different offices with a mainstream policy portfolio. An example from Finland is Anneli Taina, who served as Minister for the Environment and later as Defence Minister; another example, from the United Kingdom, is long-term (23 years) Labour MP and government minister Tessa Jowell, who served in the Cabinet Office and in Culture, Media and Sport. Others, however, do focus on social policy issues and offices with social policy responsibility and may eventually even reach the position of minister for social affairs. Correspondingly, some of our case studies show SWMPs retaining their self-perception as social workers and advocates for social justice well into their political career (see Chapter 7, on Israel), while others report a trend towards the opposite – that is, social workers distancing themselves from their former occupation in order to fully immerse themselves into their new professional career (see Chapter 11, on the United Kingdom). Despite these variations, for all but a few exceptional cases, assuming a full-time, fully paid mandate in a national parliament is tantamount to leaving the social work profession for good.

This is reflected not only in the sometimes rather long parliamentary tenure of SWMPs, but also in their post-parliamentary careers. In line with their non-social work colleagues, most SWMPs leaving parliament either retire or continue their career in another political or administrative position. Others use their parliamentary reputation to enter elevated positions in public or private boardrooms. Only very few return to the occupational field of social work at all. Those who do so, though, usually do not return to their former job or any front-line social work position, but serve in leadership or managerial positions of social service agencies and welfare organisations (see, for example, Finland, Germany and the United Kingdom). In addition, SWMPs (just like their non-social worker colleagues) tend to retain links to or even re-engage in voluntary work for political and social causes, in some cases in continuation of their parliamentary advocacy for disadvantaged and socially excluded groups (as illustrated especially in Chapter 3, on Canada).

All in all, the political careers of social workers seem to be moulded by the same institutional opportunity structures that shape their colleagues' careers. While social work-specific features are rather rare in their careers, social workers appear to be well-equipped to pursue long and successful political careers, some of them with a clear focus on social policy issues.

Social advocacy

Previous research on social workers in politics has assumed that social workers use their political office to promote social justice and other social work values (for example, Lane and Humphreys, 2011; McLaughlin et al, 2019; Meehan, 2021; Amann and Kindler, 2022; Binder and Weiss-Gal, 2022; Leitner and Stolz, 2023; Löffler, 2024). From such a perspective, the mere presence of social workers in political offices would be desirable. However, it remains an empirical question whether social workers, once elected, really do engage in social advocacy on behalf of social work and service users.

Commitment to social advocacy might depend on continued proximity to the social work profession. One indicator of the closeness of a social work politician to their profession is the simultaneous practice of social work. For several countries, it has been shown that at local (Czechia, Germany, Italy, Portugal) or even regional (Finland) and national (Switzerland) levels, the linkages between SWMPs and the social work profession remain strong because SWMPs continue to work as social workers during their political mandate. Their motivation to run for political office is closely linked to the desire to improve social justice for the benefit of social work and its clients. However, data from Germany show that social workers also get involved in local politics as citizens who want to influence politics in general and refuse to be reduced to their professional background.

Given the process of political professionalisation concomitant with entry into the national parliament (see earlier discussion) we might expect a notable shift in SWMPs' political agenda from social justice issues to more mainstream and reputable policy fields. However, while some SWMP careers exhibit such a shift, the empirical data of our country studies also clearly shows social advocacy at work. This may be best explored along the indicators specified in the introductory chapter: involvement in parliamentary committees, holding executive positions, contributions to parliamentary debates, and continuous connections to social work practice.

In most countries there was at least some evidence that SWMPs were members of parliamentary committees dealing with social issues. In six countries, it was possible to collect concrete data: in Austria, 43 per cent (3 out of 7) were spokespersons on social affairs; in Israel, 60 per cent (9 out of 15 SWMPs) had a leading role in parliamentary committees on social welfare issues and all were members of such committees; in Switzerland,

60 per cent (3 out of 5) were members of the Social Security and Health Committee; in the United Kingdom, 26 per cent (8 out of 31) spent the majority of their time in social advocacy committees; and in both Germany, with 36 per cent (4 out of 11), and the United States, with 37 per cent (6 out of 16), time was served in committees related to social work issues.

Some social workers even held government positions in social affairs. In Austria, as noted earlier, a social worker, was Minister for Social Affairs, Health, Care and Consumer Protection (Johannes Rauch, 2022–25); in Finland, a social worker was minister of social and health affairs (Terttu Huttu-Juntunen, 1995–99); and in Israel, a social worker served as minister for labour and welfare (Yisrael Katz, 1977–81). Holding such ministerial positions obviously offers strong opportunities for social advocacy. In the United Kingdom, 19 per cent of SWMPs (6 out of 31) had a majority of their frontbench positions in social advocacy fields.

Concrete data were gathered for five countries regarding SWMPs' initiation of social work-related legislation. In Austria, 71 per cent of SWMPs' parliamentary activities in the most recent parliamentary period were related to social work issues, and two SWMPs from opposition parties were particularly active in raising social issues. In contrast and rather surprisingly, Canadian SWMPs did not initiate any social welfare bills in the federal parliament. In Israel, 40 per cent of SWMPs devoted more than a third of their bills to social issues, 27 per cent of SWMPs devoted 20 to 25 per cent to social issues and 30 per cent of SWMPs devoted less than 20 per cent to social issues. In Switzerland, a third of all policy papers by SWMPs dealt with social work issues, contrasting with only 12 per cent for all policy papers. In the United States, 37 per cent of bills sponsored by SWMPs were related to social work, in contrast to 21 per cent of bills sponsored by non-social workers in Congress. This indicates that SWMPs in Switzerland and the United States are more active in promoting social work issues than MPs as a whole.

During the time of their national mandate, many SWMPs remain in contact with their former profession. In some countries, such as Germany, they even expand their social work network as a result of their mandate. However, the intensity of these contacts seems to vary from country to country. While in Switzerland, all SWMPs are actively involved in social advocacy organisations, and in the United States, the National Association of Social Workers promotes strong links between social work practice and SWMPs, Portuguese SWMPs are reported to have only occasional contacts with social work practice.

Taken together, the data show that many SWMPs do fulfil a social advocacy function: they take part in parliamentary committees and debates on social issues, they initiate social policy legislation and some of them even hold executive positions related to social affairs. During their mandate, they often stay in touch with social work practice. Having said that, SWMPs are not the only advocates for social issues and not even for social work issues in parliament. In the United Kingdom, the All-Party Parliamentary Group on Social Work had ten members, of whom only two were SWMPs, and in the United States, the Social Work Caucus had 35 members, of whom only four were SWMPs. Thus, social advocacy might be understood as resulting from personal commitment and ideological positions rather than as the property of one particular occupational group.

Final observations and research perspectives

The global definition of social work clearly identifies social work as a profession that not only intervenes at an individual or group level, but also addresses the structural inequalities that underlie social problems. To this end, social workers are encouraged to engage in policy making alongside individual casework (International Federation of Social Workers and International Association of Schools of Social Work, 2014). While their political activities can take a variety of forms and occur in different routes, our edited volume focuses on one particular type of policy engagement – namely, holding political office (Gal and Weiss-Gal, 2023). For most of the countries included here, this is the first time this route of policy engagement has been studied. Our sample of 11 case studies, thus, does not – and is not meant to – provide a comprehensive image of social workers in political office and a full set of explanatory variables to account for the variations across liberal democracies. Having said that, our comparative view reveals some tentative trends and patterns that allow at least for some provisional generalisations.

With regard to the numbers and types of social workers drawn into politics, our data suggests some connections with the welfare regime type of the country and the more general features of the profession of social work. Thus, the liberal and conservative-corporatist welfare regimes seem to motivate more social workers to actively engage in the formal political process. And the high share of female social workers and their mostly Left-of-centre political orientation are directly reflected in their parliamentary representation. A comparative look at social workers' political careers and how they pursue them, though, should make us cautious with regard to any notion of social worker exceptionalism. Once social workers enter professional politics, they leave the occupational field of social work, and most leave it for good. In their new professional career, they are subjected to a new opportunity structure, a complex system of incentives and limitations that condition the pursuit of political careers in each country. This results in SWMP careers being very similar to overall political career patterns in each country. To what extent these structures leave room for the pursuit of specific social workers' interests or for social advocacy, and to what extent this room is actually exploited, varies considerably not only across countries but also across individual SWMPs.

There is no clear result with regard to the individual properties needed and the institutional features that facilitate a specific social work-oriented interpretation of an electoral mandate. However, as the illustrative examples in almost all the country cases show, dedicated individual SWMPs do find a way to actively make an impact on the social policy process.

The manifold variations found, the difficulties in making sense of the complexities of each individual case and, above all, the many questions left open in them clearly point to the need for further investigation in this field. Following this first exploratory project, meaningful advancements may be made in different directions. More detailed case studies on single aspects of social worker politicians, their careers and parliamentary behaviour (for example, more detailed accounts of the role of SWMPs in concrete social policy processes) could not only improve our empirical knowledge of individual cases but also help to further specify and fine-tune our conceptual lenses (for example, the indicators for social advocacy). Diachronic studies and process tracing efforts might help us to reveal potential critical junctures in the interrelation between social work, social workers and social policy making. These might be found in the regulation or organisation of the social work profession as well as in institutional reforms (or even regime changes) at the political level. Finally, theory-driven small-n comparisons as well as quantitative studies may be used to test more systematically the tentative hypotheses emerging from our preliminary initiative (for example, the interrelation between social work background and policy initiatives related to social issues).

With regard to adequate methodological approaches, the limitations encountered in the studies of this volume show the need for more elaborate and comprehensive forms of data collection, which of course are usually time-consuming and expensive. This encompasses not only cutting-edge quantitative methods (for example, data crawling to excavate more exhaustive biographical data) but also traditional qualitative approaches. One finding from our case studies is the insight that the variations detected in SWMPs careers can be attributed neither to single isolated variables nor to specific configurations of formal institutional structures. Instead, interviews with SWMPs suggest that it is the perception and interpretation of these structural conditions that have to be revealed in order to understand the rationale behind their career decisions. Future research on the conditions and motives of social workers' policy engagement should thus not forget that if we want to explore the reasons for individual choices, we may as well start by asking those who make these personal decisions.

Note

[1] The long-term share of SWMPs is not given in Table 13.1. It refers to the number of SWMPs in relation to the overall number of seats in the parliament across the last decades. The exact time span under investigation depends on data availability.

References

Amann, K. and Kindler, T. (2022) 'Social workers in politics – a qualitative analysis of factors influencing social workers' decision to run for political office', *European Journal of Social Work*, 25(4): 655–67.

Binder, N. and Weiss-Gal, I. (2022) 'Social workers as local politicians in Israel', *British Journal of Social Work*, 52(5): 2797–813.

Gal, J. and Weiss-Gal, I. (2023) *When Social Workers Impact Policy and Don't Just Implement It*, Policy Press.

International Federation of Social Workers and International Association of Schools of Social Work (2014) 'Global definition of social work', *IFSW*, Available from: www.ifsw.org/what-is-social-work/global-definition-of-social-work [Accessed 4 November 2024].

Lane, S.R. and Humphreys, N.A. (2011) 'Social workers in politics', *Journal of Policy Practice*, 10(3): 225–44.

Leitner, S. and Stolz, K. (2023) 'German social workers as professional politicians', *European Journal of Social Work*, 26(4): 691–704.

Löffler, E.M. (2024) 'Social workers as politicians: A quantitative study on social workers holding elected office in Germany', *European Journal of Social Work*, 27(4): 898–910.

McLaughlin, A.M., Rothery, M. and Kuiken, J. (2019) 'Pathways to political engagement', *Canadian Social Work Review*, 36(1): 25–43.

Meehan, P. (2018) '"I think I can … Maybe I can … I can't": Social work women and local elected office', *Social Work*, 63(2): 145–52.

Meehan, P. (2021) 'Water into wine: Using social policy courses to make MSW students interested in politics', *Journal of Social Work Education*, 57(2): 357–71.

Index

References to figures appear in *italic* type; those in **bold** type refer to tables. References to endnotes show both the page number and the note number (95n1).

A

accessibility (Borchert) 3–4, 17, 32, 100, 209
Alberta 31
alliance F (organisation) 162
Amor, Shaul 103, 105
Arad, Nava 103, 105, 106
Arlt, Ilse 12
Armstrong, Hilary 175–176
Atherton, Sarah 178
Attlee, Clement 1
attractiveness (Borchert) 3–4, 17, 32, 100, 208–209
Austria 12–25
  accessibility, attractiveness and availability 17
  Austrian People's Party (ÖVP) 16, 19
  career patterns 23
  characteristics of social workers 19, **22**
  education and qualifications 13–14
  Federal Council (Bundesrat) 15–16, 25
  gender 14, 23
  influence of professional identity 25
  National Council (Nationalrat) 15, 18–19, 24, 25
  national government 16, 25
  parliamentary activities 212
  political career patterns 19–23
  political offices 12–13, 16–17
  political recruitment 18–19
  political system 15–16
  population 15
  professional organisations 14
  social advocacy 23–25
  Social Democratic Party (SPÖ) 16, 19, 25
  Social Economy Austria (SWÖ) 14
  Social Work Designation Act 2024 13, 14
  social workers in parliament 19, **20–21**, **22**, **206**, 207
  Sozialarbeit (social work) 13
  Soziale Arbeit (social work) 13
  Sozialpädagogik (social pedagogy) 13–14
Austrian Professional Association of Social Work (obds) 12, 14, 21, 23
Austrian Society for Social Work (ogsa) 12, 14
availability (Borchert) 3–4, 17, 32, 100, 208
AvenirSocial 150–151, 162
AWO (Arbeiterwohlfahrt, NGO) 81

B

Barrett, Dave 38
Barrie, D. 39
Bass, Karen 195, 196
Begg, Anne 176
Berlin 84
Bernard, J. 56
Binder, N. 96
Bizzarro, F. 133
Bolgherini, S. 114
Borchert, J. 3, 17, 32, 49, 56, 100, 106
Botelho, Maria Leonor Correia 134, 147n8
Branco, F. 130, 131
Bremen 84
British Association of Social Workers (BASW) 166
British Columbia 31
The British Journal of Social Work 166
Brown, Bonnie 40
Bütikofer, S. 153, 158

C

Canada 30–42
  accessibility, attractiveness and availability 32–34
  Conservative Party of Canada 34
  education and qualifications 30
  federal parliament and government 32–34, 37, 39
  First Nations communities 33
  House of Commons 34, 35–36, 37, 41, 42
  initiating legislation 42, 212
  institutional opportunity structures 32–35
  liberal welfare state 33
  municipal governments 32–33
  New Democratic Party (NDP) 34
  nursing profession 35
  parliamentary activities 212
  parliamentary careers 36–40
  political experience 38–39, **38**
  political parties 34–35
  political recruitment 35–36
  political system 33–34
  post-parliamentary careers 40–41
  pre-parliamentary careers 36
  provincial and national politics 37–38
  provincial governments 31
  provincial regulatory bodies 30–31

Index

public service 40
regional cultures and identities 38
regulation 31
representation in parliaments 205, **206**, 207
Senate 34
social advocacy 41–42
social work parliamentarians (SWPs) 35–36
social work practices 36, **37**
social work profession 30–32
territorial governments 31
women 35
Canadian Association for Social Work Education (CASWE) 30
career pathways 3
Caritas (NGO) 81
Carrilho, R. 131
case studies 214
CASW 30, 31–32
Čermák, D. 56
Civic Voluntarism Model (Verba) 71–72
Congressional Research Institute for Social Work and Policy (CRISP) 189
conservative-corporatist welfare regimes 213
conservative regimes 4
conventional opportunity structures 4
Czechia (Czech Republic) 47–60
  accessibility 51
  attractiveness 51–52
  availability 49–50
  bills proposed 59–60
  Chamber of Deputies 49, 50, 55–58
  education and qualifications 47–48
  female social workers 48
  helping professions in parliament 55–56, **56**
  institutional opportunity structures 49–52
  mandate accumulation 57–58
  Ministry of Education 48
  Ministry of Labour and Social Affairs 48
  MPs with degrees 56, **56**
  multilevel political system 56
  municipal councillors 56–57
  political career patterns 56–58
  political parties/groupings 51
  political recruitment 52–56
  political system 49–50
  proportional electoral system 51
  representation in parliament **206**, 207
  Senate 49–50, 56–57
  social advocacy 58–60
  Social Policy Committee 50
  Social Services Act 47
  social work members of parliament (SWMPs) 49
  social work profession 47–49
  societal challenges 48–49
  sociodemographic characteristics 52–56, **53–54**
  teachers 55
  unitary parliamentary republic 49–50
  women 57

D

Davis, Susan 196
Dawson, Hilton 176
Dellums, Ron 196
diachronic studies 214
Diakonie (NGO) 81
Docherty, D. 39, 41
Dodeigne, J. 38
Dönmez, Efgani 19
Duan, Avi 103, 109
Durose, C. 174

E

Elsässer, L. 23
England 166, 167, 172–173
Esping-Andersen, G. 4
Ethical Principles of Social Work (obds and ogsa) 12
Ethiopian Jews 102
Europe 5
executive offices of governments 4, 210

F

female social workers **206**, 207–208
see also women
Fernandes, J.M. 132
Finland 64–77
  Act on Wellbeing Services Counties 2021/611 68
  career paths at county level 73–74
  career paths at national level 72–73
  education and qualifications 64, 65
  electoral system 66, 76
  government ministers 73, 210
  institutional opportunity structures 65–68
  JulkiSuosikki register 70
  MPs 69–70, **70**
  national level political recruitment 69–70
  policy advocacy 77
  political advocacy 66–67
  political career patterns 72–74
  political participation 71–72, **72**
  political parties 66
  political recruitment 68–72
  psychological engagement 72, **72**
  recruitment networks 72
  representation in parliament **206**, 207
  'six-pack' government 73
  social advocacy 74–76, **75**
  Social Welfare Act 1301/2014 65

social work profession 64–65
survey data 71, 72
Valvira register 70
welfare system 64–65
wellbeing services counties 64, 67–69, 70–72, 76, 209
women 69
First Nations communities, Canada 33

G

Gal, J. 4
Garcia, Sylvia 193, 198
German Professional Association for Social Work (DBSH) 82
Germany 4, 80–93
  Basic Law (GG) 82
  Bundesrat (federal council) 82, 83
  Bundestag (federal parliament) 82, 83, 86, **86**, 89
  city- and territorial states 84, 86–87
  civic engagement 90
  education and qualifications 81
  gender distribution 85, **86**
  history of social work 80
  institutional opportunity structures 82–85
  intra-party processes 91–92
  Members of Parliament Act 83
  parliamentary committees 91–92, 212
  political career patterns 87–90
  political party membership 88–89
  political recruitment 85–87
  political system 82–83
  politicians 83–85
  professional knowledge and political processes 90–91
  registration system 82
  social advocacy 90–92
  social services providers 81
  social work and social pedagogy 80
  social workers holding political office (SWHPOs) 80, 85–86
  social workers in national parliament 85–86, **86**, **206**, 207
  social work profession 80–82
  state and local administrations 82–83, 84
  unplanned political careers 88
Gerster, F. 83
Gibbins, R. 39
Golasowská, Pavla 52, 59–60
Graf, Maya 161
Grimaldi, S. 114
Gutiérrez, Luis 196
Gysi, Barbara 155, 157–158, 160, 161

H

Hamburg 84
Hardy, Louise 40, 204
Heal, Sylvia 170
Helimäki, T. 69
Hilou, Nadia 103, 106
Histadrut trade union federation 98
Hopkins, Harry 189
Hughes, Beverley 174
Humphreys Institute for Political Social Work (University of Connecticut) 188–189
Huttu-Juntunen, Terttu 73

I

ideal-typical pathways 204
Inclusion Handicap (Switzerland) 162
institutional opportunity structures 3–4
Israel 96–110
  accessibility, attractiveness and availability 106
  draft laws **108**, 109
  education and qualifications 98
  Ethiopian Jews 102
  gender, party affiliation, ethnicity 101–102, **104**
  institutional opportunity structures 99–101
  Knesset 99
  Mapai (Labor Party) 100, 101, 105
  Mediterranean welfare state 97
  Mizrahi Jews 100
  numbers of social workers 98
  parliamentary activities 103–104, 107, **108**, 212
  parliamentary committees 107–108, **108**
  parliamentary system 99
  political careers 103–106
  political parties 100, 101
  political recruitment 101–103
  poverty and inequality 97
  representation in the Knesset 101, **102**, **206**, 207
  social advocacy 107–109
  social policy issues 99–100
  Social Workers Act 98
  social work profession 97–99
  teachers 101
  training 98
  ultra-orthodox parties 106
  women in politics 100, 106
Israeli Arabs 97, 100, 101–102
Israel Union of Social Workers (IUSW) 96, 98–99, 105, 109–110
Italy 112–127
  bi-directional relationships 125
  'case advocacy' and 'cause advocacy' 122
  civic lists (*Liste Civiche*) 114, 209
  Councils of Social Work 116
  education and qualifications 112, 115–116

First Republic 114–115
gender dynamics 116
impact on local governance 122–123
institutional opportunity
  structures 113–114
interviews 116–117, 122, 125
local political engagement 120–121
municipalities 112, 113–114, 116–120,
  118–119, 124–127, 209
National Council of Social
  Workers 112, 113
national government and
  parliament 114–116, 124
non-partisan affiliations 125
personal and professional drivers 125
political career patterns 121
political parties 113–114
political recruitment 114–121
political system 113–114
professional ethics and political
  agendas 126
representation in parliament **206**, 207
Senate 116
social advocacy 121–124
social work and political
  advocacy 123–124
social workers (*assistenti sociali*)
  112–113
social workers holding elected office
  (SWHEOs) 112
social work profession 112–113
SWHEOs 114–116
third sector organisations and
  parishes 120–121
uniqueness as politicians 126
wellbeing of the community 124, 126

J

Jalali, C. 133
Jamieson, Cathy 176
Jowell, Tessa 175, 210

K

Kariv, Yifat 103–104, 106
Karvonen, L. 66
Katz, Yisrael 96, 103
Khatib-Yassin, Iman 103, 109
Kubjátová, Yvona 58

L

Laforest, [initials required] 129
Lebouthillier, Diane 41
Lee, Barbara 198
left-of-centre political orientation 213
liberal democracies 5–6, 213
liberal welfare regimes 4, 213
Lipponen, Paavo 73
Lovenduski, J. 138

M

Massala, Adisu 105, 106
McDonough, Alexa 38, 41
McLaughlin, Audrey 40
medical doctors, Czechia 55
Mediterranean welfare states 97
Meloni, Giorgia 115
Mikulski, Barbara 196
Mitchell, Margaret 41
Mizrahi Jews 100
Molla, Shlomo 103, 105
Moser, Mentona 150

N

Neguise, Avraham 105, 107
neo-institutional perspectives 3
Neto, O.A. 131
Nordic welfare model 64, 76
Norris, P. 138
Northern Ireland 166, 167
Northern Ireland Assembly 168–169
Northwest Territories 31

O

opportunity structures 3–4, 4
'ox tours' 19–21

P

Paritätischer Wohlfahrtsverband
  (NGO) 81
parliamentary committees 211–212
parliamentary tenures 209–210
Parlinfo Canadian parliamentary
  database 35
Perkins, Francis 189
Petitpas Taylor, Ginette 41, 42
policy interventions 150
political career patterns 5–6, 208–211
political institutions 3
political majorities 17
political opportunity structures 4
political parties 208
political recruitment 5, 204–208
political social workers 204
politics-facilitating profession 172–174
Portugal 129–147
  accessibility and attractiveness 133
  assistant de service social 130
  Azores regional government 131,
    132, **135**
  biograms of social workers as
    mayors **145–146**
  biograms of social workers in national
    and regional parliaments **142–145**
  Carnation Revolution 130, 131,
    133, 134
  education and qualifications 130
  Estado Novo political regime 134

ethnic minorities 136
'hybrid semi-presidentialism' 131
institutionalisation of social work 129
institutional opportunity structures 131–133
Madeira Regional Parliament 129, 131, 132, 135, **135**, 139, **144–145**
mayors 137, **137**, 139, **145–146**
municipalities/local government 131, 209
National Association of Social Workers (APSS) 129
non-profit organisations 130
occupational groups in parliament 135–136, **136**
parliamentary committees 140
Parliament (*Assembleia da República*) 129
political career patterns 138–140
political parties 132–133, 136
political recruitment 134–137
political system 131–132
recruitment drivers 138, *138*
regional governments 131–132
representation at Assembleia Nacional 134, **134**
representation at municipal level 137, **137**
representation in national parliament 135, **135**, **206**, 207
representation in regional parliaments 135, **135**
salaries 131
social advocacy 140–141
'social service' (serviço social) 129
social worker (*assistente social*) profession 129–131
women 133, 135, **135**
Pow, J.T. 39
Pratas, M. 133
Prelicz-Huber, Katharina 155, 158, 161
Prince Edward Island 33
professional political careers 6

R

Ram, Uri 100
Rankin, Jeannette 193, 196
Rauch, Johannes 12, 18, 21–22, 23–24, 203
Recchi, E. 113
Rhéaume, Eugène 40–41
Robillard, Lucienne 39–40
Rodriguez, Ciro 196
Russo, M.L. 113–114

S

Salvini, Matteo 115
Schäfer, A. 23
Schennach, Stefan 18
Schlesinger, J.A. 3
Scholten, Hillary 193, 198
Schwartz, Allyson 196
Scotland 166, 167
Scottish Parliament 168–169
Senedd Cymru (Welsh Parliament) 168–169
Shea-Porter, Carol 196
Simchon, Shalom 103, 106, 203–204
Sinema, Kyrsten 187, 198
social advocacy 6–7, 176, 211–213
Social Democratic Party of Austria (SPÖ) 16, 19, 25
social democratic regimes 4
Social Economy Austria (Sozialwirtschaft Österreich, SWÖ) 14
social inequality 4
social policies 1
social work 6–7, 213
Social Work England 166, 167
social workers
 defining 3, 151
 political office 1–2
 representation in parliaments 205–207, **206**
 and social pedagogues 13
social work members of national parliaments (SWMPs) 205, **206**
social work-related legislation 212
sociodemographics of political representation 23
Solomon, Shimon 103, 105
Soziale Frauenschule Berlin 81
Stabenow, Debbie 198
Steiger, Emma 150
Stern-Katan, Sarah 103, 105, 106
Stocker, Simon 155, 161
Stolz, K. 38, 56
Swiss Organisation for Foster and Adoptive Children (PACH) 162
Switzerland 150–163
 accessibility, attractiveness and availability 152–154
 applied social policy 154
 Council of States 153, 161
 education and qualifications 151
 Federal Statistical Office 151
 gender 155, **156**
 institutional opportunity structures 152–154
 national and cantonal parliaments 154–155, **156**, 159–160, **159**, **206**, 207
 National Council 153, 155, 161
 national government 153–154
 parliamentary activities 150, 212
 parliamentary committees 154, 161, 211–212
 parliamentary policy papers 160–161
 political career patterns 157–160

political parties 155, 157, 208
political recruitment 154–157
salaries 151–152
social advocacy 160–162
Social Security and Health Committee (SSHC) 154, 157, 161
social workers' backgrounds 158, **159**
social work profession 151–152
social work stakeholders 162

T

Taina, Anneli 73, 210
teachers 55, 101, 173
Terborg, Margitta 85
Tsongas, Niki 196
Tversky, Jenia 103, 105, 109

U

United Kingdom 166–179
  All-Party Parliamentary Groups (APPGs) 178, 213
  College of Social Work 166
  councillors 169, 174
  decentralisation and devolution 168–169
  disincentives to holding political office 169
  education and qualifications 167, 170–171
  gender 171
  House of Commons 168, 172–173
  House of Lords 168
  institutional opportunity structures 168–169
  local government 169, 174
  MPs' salaries 169
  parliamentary careers 175–176
  parliamentary committees 176–178, **177**, 212–213
  parliamentary system 168
  parliamentary tenures 175, 210
  political career patterns 174–176
  political parties 171, 174, 178
  political recruitment 169–174
  'professionalised' route into politics 172–175, *173*
  regulation and registrations 166–167
  representation in parliaments **206**, 207
  social advocacy 176–178, 179
  social advocacy ministries and committees 177–178, **177**
  socially oriented professions *173*, 174
  social worker MPs (SWMPs) 169–175, *171*
  social work profession 166–168
  special advisors (SPADs) 174
  university education 174
  welfare state 1
United States 183–199
  accessibility and attractiveness 187–189
  committee assignments 197–198
  conflicts of interest 187–188
  Congress 185–186
  congressional committees 197–198, 212
  congressional tenure 195
  Council on Social Work Education (CSWE) 183
  defining social workers 183
  education and qualifications 183–184
  electoral system 186
  executive branch 185
  federal government 185–186
  gender 194
  House of Representatives 185–186
  Improving Access to Mental Health Act 198
  institutional opportunity structures 185–189
  interest groups 186–187
  More Social Workers in Libraries Act 198
  National Association of Social Workers 212
  National Network for Social Work Managers (NASW) 184, 188, 189, 198
  parliamentary tenures 210
  Political Action for Candidate Election (PACE) 188
  political career patterns 194–196
  political parties 186
  political recruitment 189–195
  practice areas 184–185
  professional associations 184
  the Senate 185–186
  social advocacy 197–198
  social welfare-related legislation 197, **197**, 212
  Social Work Caucus 198, 213
  social work members of Congress (SWMCs) 189–195, **190–193**, 198–199, **206**, 207
  Supreme Court 185
  University of Connecticut 188–189
  unplanned political careers 88

V

Vandal, Dan 41
Vargas, A. 134
Velimsky, J.A. 92
Verba, S. 71
Verzichelli, L. 113–114

W

Wales 166, 167
  Senedd Cymru 168–169
Walsh, William Francis 196
Weichelt, Manuela 155, 158, 161
Weiss-Gal, I. 4, 96

women **206**, 207–208
  Austria 14, 23
  Canada 35
  Czechia 57
  Finland 69
  Germany 85, **86**
  Israel 100, 106
  Italy 116
  Portugal 133, 135, **135**
  Switzerland 155, **156**
  United Kingdom 171
  United States 194

Y

Yazbak, Heba 105
Yle (Finnish Broadcasting Company) 70

www.ingramcontent.com/pod-product-compliance
Lightning Source LLC
Chambersburg PA
CBHW051539020426
42333CB00016B/2009